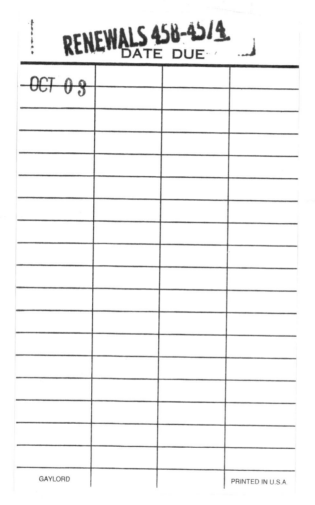

RENEWALS 458-4574

DATE DUE

OCT 0 3			
GAYLORD			PRINTED IN U.S.A.

HORTON FOOTE

NUMBER NINE
THE JACK AND DORIS SMOTHERS SERIES
IN TEXAS HISTORY, LIFE, AND CULTURE

HORTON

FOOTE

A

LITERARY BIOGRAPHY

CHARLES S. WATSON

UNIVERSITY OF TEXAS PRESS, AUSTIN

Requests for permission to reproduce material from
this work should be sent to Permissions, University
of Texas Press, P.O. Box 7819, Austin,
TX 78713-7819.

⊗ The paper used in this book meets the minimum
requirements of ANSI/NISO Z39.48-1992
(R1997) (Permanence of Paper).

Library of Congress Cataloging-in-Publication Data
Watson, Charles S., 1931–
Horton Foote : a literary biography /
by Charles S. Watson.
p.   cm. — (The Jack and Doris Smothers series
in Texas history, life and culture ; no. 9)
Includes bibliographical references (p.   )
and index.
ISBN 0-292-79160-7 (alk. paper)
1. Foote, Horton.   2. Dramatists, American—
20th century—Biography.   3. Screenwriters—
United States—Biography.   4. Texas—
Biography.   I. Title.   II. Series.
PS3511.0344 Z94   2003
812'.54—dc21   2002011206

To my sister, Dorothy Hale Watson, devotee of the theatre,
and my son-in-law, Kevon Shane Watson

CONTENTS

In the year 2002, Horton Foote can look back on a remarkable career of more than sixty years in the American theatre beginning in 1938. In 1995 he won the Pulitzer Prize for Drama with *The Young Man from Atlanta,* the climax to a series of his many works for the theatre. Although other media have their appeal and he would not willingly give them up, Foote is happiest when writing for the stage, which is his most enduring love.

Foote's work has been awarded many prizes. In addition to the Pulitzer Prize and others, this productive writer has won the following awards: the Academy Award for the adaptation of *To Kill a Mockingbird* (1962), the Academy Award for the original screenplay of *Tender Mercies* (1982), the Academy Award nomination for the screenplay adaptation of *The Trip to Bountiful* (1985), and the William Inge Lifetime Achievement Award (1989).

This playwright has consistently shown his unflagging compassion for others. Describing the Southeast Texas setting of an early play, he said it was true to the towns he had known: "It has its tragedies and comedies, its rich and poor, its great virtues and its terrible injustices. It has my heart." [1]

Although many people have written about the work of Horton Foote, I believe that a systematic examination is urgently needed; his life and plays should be better understood. The resources available are abundant—the Horton Foote Collection, the previous scholarship, his published plays, my teaching of them and attendance at performances, and my interviews with Foote, including a memorable visit to Wharton, on March 12, 1994. Two superior dissertations have appeared, by Terry Barr (1986) and Marion Castleberry (1993). Thematic studies have been published by Rebecca Briley (1993) and by Gerald Wood (*Horton Foote and the Theatre of Intimacy,* 1999).

Foote's papers, a massive trove of manuscripts and correspondence, have been placed in the DeGolyer Library at Southern Methodist University. My book is the first to make extensive use of the correspondence in this collection, which is abbreviated in this text as "HFC" (Horton Foote Collection).

A literary biography is a life in the context of literary works.[2] This book uses letters and works of a well-known playwright. There is no closure to a literary biography if the subject is still alive. A balance exists—

between friendship and a professional spirit. When I said I would need to be "objective," Foote remarked, "Of course." Leon Edel in "Literature and Biography" says that the literary biography that deals with externals is incomplete: "The biography which looks also to the writings for its truth is more useful."[3]

This literary biography examines Foote's life, career, and best plays in a single volume. I begin with chapters on Foote's early life, then move to plays written for the New York theatre. Next I examine his teleplays composed during the Golden Age of Television in the early 1950s. A biographical chapter based on his letters follows. After noting his screenwritings in original works and adaptations for the movies and television, I recount his triumphant return to the theatre from the 1970s to the 1990s. Foote's life provides the framework for analyzing the development of his art and thought in the leading plays.

For their assistance, I wish to thank Philip D. Beidler, Ralph Voss, and Sally Desaussure Davis, all of the University of Alabama; Kay Bost, curator, Horton Foote Collection, Southern Methodist University, Dallas, Texas; Jackson Bryer, University of Maryland; Robert L. Phillips, Mississippi State University; and Charles Samuel Haun of Covenant Presbyterian Church, William C. Lary, and William A. Hill, all of Tuscaloosa, Alabama. Most especially I am grateful to Ellen Currie Watson, my daughter; Whitten Sullivan Watson, my son; and my dear wife, Juanita Goodman Watson.

1

FOOTE AND WHARTON, TEXAS

W HAT distinguishes Horton Foote from other playwrights of his time? It is the deep compassion that shapes his many plays. He is not a social protester like Arthur Miller, a constant experimenter with dramatic techniques like Eugene O'Neill, nor a psychological investigator like Tennessee Williams. Rather it is his sensitivity to the troubled men and women who live in Southeast Texas that gives his work unity. Foote's most precious resource comes from his personal experience in Wharton, where he absorbed into art the sensibility of his kindred. He has said that more than one-half of his plays have begun with tales told by his father, Albert Horton Foote, Jr.[1]

While working at the haberdashery run by his father, Foote observed his father's compassion. On Saturday evenings over fried oysters, the elder Foote would recount to his son the hardships of his customers and would be moved to tears.[2] The memory of his admired father marked the son indelibly. It permeates his playwriting, develops his art, and shapes his writing.

Wharton is still a small town in Southeast Texas, as it was when Horton Foote was born there in 1916. The future playwright assimilated its life before leaving at age sixteen to begin his work in the theatre, first as an actor and later as a playwright. Foote saw and heard all about this place. He absorbed its history, beginning before the Civil War when his great-great-grandfather Albert Clinton Horton arrived to claim many acres of rich farmland.

Few American dramatists have recorded the changing life of their hometown with such single-minded devotion as Horton Foote. Marion

Castleberry has aptly spoken of Foote's "compassionate depiction" of a small town in the series of plays about Wharton.[3] Born and reared there, this loyal son has never long been physically absent and, more importantly, never spiritually absent.

Even during his professional career in New York City, Foote's thoughts returned to the people of this community, which, though small, was dense in dramatic life. Like Faulkner, Eudora Welty, and Katherine Anne Porter as well as other writers of the Southern Literary Renascence, Foote moves surely from the local to the universal human topics familiar to all.

Since Foote is a playwright of Texas, it is instructive to specify just what part of the gigantic state he derives from. Though the region is sometimes called Gulf Coast Texas, this designation is misleading for Wharton and its mythic equivalent, "Harrison." All descriptions of it by Foote resemble the southern plantation society of cotton. It is more accurate, at least for the time covered by Foote—that is, from 1900 to 1950—to call it Southeast Texas, as Foote does in "Wharton—Then and Now," a biographical lecture (1989).[4] Foote's home country is not the port cities of the Gulf Coast, like Houston and Galveston. As in East Texas, Foote's are farming people, with their gaze on land, practicing the social customs of the Lower South.

Foote's ancestors, led by the Hortons, came from Alabama and Georgia. Foote is a typical Texan in that his home region bleeds into others and is hard to locate. His Texas does not embrace West Texas (the cowboy country) or the border, next to Mexico.

T. R. Fehrenbach concludes that the planter society made the strongest mark on Texas life by its customs, social codes, and way of life. The main immigrant streams coming into Texas, he says, were from Tennessee and Alabama. He sees the Mexico-Texas conflict as essentially a culture clash; the two peoples were incompatible. Texans conquered; they did not just settle the land.[5]

By 1850 in Texas the Lower South planters were challenging the Upper South hegemony. Significantly, upper southerners were localized in one part of Texas, and lower southerners in another. They were separated by a line running roughly from Texarkana in the northeastern corner to San Antonio.

By 1860, blacks formed a majority in eighteen counties of East and Southeast Texas. They even exceeded "80 percent in plantation dominated Wharton County."[6] This is another reason to compare Wharton

County's society to that of the eastern South of Faulkner and O'Connor, who write of Mississippians and Georgians.

Often Foote speaks of himself as a chronicler or historian. Answering one questionnaire, he said that if he could choose any other profession besides a dramatist's, it would be a historian's.[7] Not surprisingly, Wharton is also quite conscious of its own history, having erected and stocked the Wharton County Historical Museum. Foote states that he is writing "a moral and social history" of Wharton.[8] More specifically, he says that in writing the *Orphans' Home Cycle,* he is trying "to arrive at a social and moral history of a town and a place and an era."[9] In all his plays, he is careful to name the time of a particular play, thus placing it clearly in history.

Foote concentrates on change and loss, which he considers inevitable. He recounts the transition from the Old South to the New South. Wharton began as an agricultural community, dominated by the landed aristocracy, who owned large plantations even though they lived in houses in town. Depleted by the Civil War, the aristocratic society declined and by 1925 was definitively supplanted by the commercial middle class. The New South arrived later in Texas than in Henry Grady's Georgia and Lillian Hellman's Alabama. Decisive change came to this tiny town with the discovery of oil and the metropolitan expansion of Houston, only fifty-five miles away. Foote learned this history not from books but above all from tales told by relatives. As Foote has remarked, "I have heard tales of the beginnings of Wharton from the earliest years of my life."[10]

Foote's family history, as well as much of Wharton County's, begins with the life of his colorful great-great-grandfather, Albert Clinton Horton, who was the first lieutenant governor of the state of Texas. Born in Georgia in 1798, Horton moved to Alabama in 1823, where he was elected to the state senate from Greensboro in 1832. Heeding the call for settlers in the Texas territory, he migrated there in 1834, settling on a plantation of 2,200 acres.

The next era of Wharton's history is very important in Foote's plays. Extending from 1865 to 1925, it may be designated the postwar-Victorian period, when many of Foote's closest relatives were born, grew up, and died. They are the models for leading characters in plays set around 1900 and up to the 1950s, like *The Trip to Bountiful,* since these elderly persons lived their formative years in that period. In his plays Foote alters the real models, like his grandfather Albert Foote, making him more sympathetic. Sometimes the playwright makes the character worse than the model, like his father's sister Lily Dale. These changes seem to reflect Foote's personal feelings toward the persons portrayed.

Foote has spoken of "the aristocratic way of life" that he saw the last of as a child. He saw it pass away, heard it mourned, and finally accepted it as gone.[11] This aristocratic era shaped manners, the outward expression of moral beliefs that is described in Foote's plays. It was a fabled time. Foote, like Katherine Anne Porter, looks back continually to this period, with the aim of regarding it truly. Unlike Porter, Foote presents a fuller gallery, because he describes carefully contemporary Texans, such as those oil-rich heirs of the 1980s in *Dividing the Estate* (first performed in 1989).

After the end of slavery, agriculture passed through lean years, but Wharton County, with its long growing season, resumed intense farming by 1900. Cotton was the primary crop. The economic prosperity of the town of Wharton depended heavily on the success of the cotton crop, as manifested in the selling price of the product itself. In El Campo, another town in Wharton County, cotton was the main moneymaking crop, and because land was cheap in the 1890s, many newcomers became cotton farmers. Foote remarked that on his return from New York City, he always asked: "How's the crop?"[12] Besides King Cotton, the land produced sugarcane, rice, corn, watermelons, and other crops. Rice, first planted in 1900, eventually became the principal product, making Wharton County its leading producer in Texas. Filling out the diversity was the cattle business. Pierce Ranch, begun by cattle-raising pioneer Abel Head Pierce, was a large operation. In 1909 the famous Brahman cattle from India were imported and in time became one of the most numerous breeds because of their tolerance of the Gulf Coast weather.

If agriculture flourished, the same cannot be said for industry. The only industry took the form of agriculturally based operations. Cotton gins were started in all settlements of the county, such as Glen Flora and Egypt. In 1909 a rice mill was built in El Campo, southwest of Wharton. The lack of industry differentiates Wharton from the New South of the early 1900s, when slogans like "Where agriculture and industry meet" had visible meaning for the thriving towns of the Carolina Piedmont. The impact of industry was felt less in Wharton than in the Atlantic South.

The railroad was a harbinger of the new industrial age. Until 1881, no railroad passed through the town. After its arrival the growth in population proceeded apace. In that year, the New York, Texas, and Mexican Railway laid a line from Richmond to Victoria, with a station in Wharton and many stops along the way. The Southern Pacific Railway, after buying many smaller lines in Texas, had a depot in Wharton by 1905. Railroad employees were envied in Wharton, not least because they received coveted free passes on the trains. The railroad line permitted Whartonians to reach Houston easily.

Foote's mother, "Hal" (Hallie Brooks), reported to her future husband on August 10, 1914, that she had gone to "the picture show" and visited her Houston aunts, but she also complained that her suitor was not being allowed to call on her anymore. With determination this independent young woman underlined how she felt about the man with whom she would elope: *"I love you."* [13]

An integral part of social life was the pleasure taken in songs, rendered by traveling singers and musical citizens. Popular songs in Foote's plays are often appropriate for the particular moment in the text, like the end of World War I in *1918*. Traveling entertainers gave musical programs at the Ford Opera House and later at the Norton Opera House, a two-story brick building on the corner of Milam Street and Richmond Road. Foote's father loved the popular songs of his youth and would sing them for his own pleasure and the enjoyment of others in a musical voice. In *The Widow Claire* (1982), the character Horace sings "Mighty Lak' a Rose" and "Waltz Me around Again, Willie." On the square near the Norton Opera House was also the Queen Theatre, which was showing silent movies accompanied by local musicians around 1920. In 1929 this theatre switched to "talking pictures," a momentous advancement in entertainment for Whartonians. Foote considered this innovation as the beginning of a new era in *Talking Pictures* (1987), set in 1929.

Related to the social life of Wharton were the institutions providing the educational fiber of its citizenry. The educational side of the county was adequate but not distinguished. Public education began in 1880 when Mrs. Amanda Watts, a widow, received state money for the school she conducted in her home. Choosing the well-respected name of Watts, Foote called the endearing widow of *The Trip to Bountiful* Mrs. Carrie Watts.

In 1898 a red brick schoolhouse was built, and in 1920 a three-story high school was completed on Rusk Street. No institution of postsecondary education existed until the Wharton County Junior College opened in 1946. In Foote's plays, higher education is conspicuous by its absence.

Churches became more firmly established in this era. Always predominant, the Baptists welcomed their first resident minister in 1875. After the Presbyterian church was destroyed by the 1909 hurricane, it was rebuilt in 1912. Other denominations that were strong in Wharton were Methodist, Lutheran, and Episcopalian. Methodists did not play cards or dance. Foote's mother, Hallie Brooks Foote, was the pianist and later the organist for the Methodist church. The playwright's familiarity with the songs she sang and accompanied, such as "Peace Be to This Congregation" in *1918* (1979), testify to the importance of church life and the liking for hymns among the people. Other faiths represented were a Jewish congregation and the Church of Christ. The first Catholic parish in the county was organized at El Campo in 1989.

No one can miss the many funerals and trips to the cemetery in Foote's plays. The first references to the City Cemetery date from 1866.[14] This large, very flat area occupied a site between Alabama and Dennis Streets in the center of the town. Until 1918, most Whartonians attended funeral services. In this close-knit community there were no strangers who passed away unnoticed. Caring for graves was a well-observed custom, acted out repeatedly in Foote's dramas, as in *1918,* when the heroine, Elizabeth, visits the grave of her infant daughter, who died in the influenza epidemic.

From the beginning of settlement of the area, blacks have made up a large portion of the county population. The county census of 1847 recorded 1,315 blacks and 413 whites. Because of the paucity of white children available to play with, "Governor" Horton brought back a white boy from New York City to entertain his son Robert John Horton, the great-grandfather of Foote.[15] In 1891 the black population reached 6,122, and the Wharton County Scholastic Census of 1904 recorded 2,832 black students and 1,806 whites. The Negro School System was established in 1896, and in 1920 a high school was constructed on Rusk Street.

In the postwar era of Wharton, a racial crisis provoked a method to ensure white governance. Because blacks or their white allies gained state and county offices during Reconstruction and held them thereafter, the White Man's Union emerged from the Democratic Party in 1889. Most white males became members, and soon black officeholders vanished. This association, to which some of Foote's kin belonged, was still in operation up to 1954.

A painful chapter in the history of Wharton County for Foote has been the treatment of black convicts. During the last decades of the nineteenth century, Texas counties established convict farms to reduce expenses. In many ways they seemed a continuation of slavery. There were complaints of whippings and inadequate nourishment.[16] In Wharton County, a large convict farm was established on the Pierce Ranch. For many years convicts held there could work off fines at the rate of $7.50 a month. A building with bars on the windows could still be seen many years after; Foote showed such a building to a newspaper reporter. He recalled seeing convict gangs working the fields. When only twelve years old, his father worked as the store clerk on a prison plantation. One of the barracks still stands not far from Foote's home in Wharton, "a chilling barn—a dungeon with rusty bars on the windows," he says.[17]

The notorious reputation of Texas violence can be detected during the early 1900s. There was at least one killing on the courthouse square every Saturday night.[18] As a consequence, the county has honored its sheriffs. At the historical museum a large display portrays the former sheriffs. While attempting an arrest, Sheriff Hamilton Bass Dickson, the most honored in a long line, was killed by a desperado in 1894. The funeral was said to have drawn the largest gathering in the annals of the county. Only six months afterward, an imposing monument of white marble was placed on the courthouse grounds and remains there today.

The practice of whipping, an effort to curtail violent behavior, is especially striking. During slavery times and for many decades afterward, whipping was a popular means of punishment. It was common in schools until abolished in 1914.

The next era is easy to define: commercial times. The Old Wharton period ends in the late 1920s after the death of Foote's Victorian grandfather and the coming of modern business. Previously, members of the landed class, deriving their wealth from the plantation economy, set the character and manners of the community. Now businessmen, reflecting middle-class values with a stress on social conformity and money standards, assumed the direction of all major affairs. The New Wharton lost much if not all of its southern character, conforming to the American pattern. Thus, Wharton steadily adopted the manners of middle America.

The rise of commercial power in the United States, expressed by Calvin Coolidge's slogan "The business of America is business," eventually became visible in Wharton. Photographs from the 1930s show new or brick buildings occupied by various businesses, including the Brooks Building and the Queen Theatre. The Chamber of Commerce erected a large sign in 1935, declaring "Welcome to Wharton." Nearby were automobile companies and new filling stations; the Duck Inn Café offered good meals at the corner of Milam and Richmond Roads in 1938. The town's longest-running society column was written for the *Wharton Journal* by Nan Dean Bennett, one of Foote's cousins who became the wife of Dr. Bolton Outlar.

The new wealth acquired in the United States as a result of industrial expansion soared in Texas because of oil. After the oil boom began in Texas with the Spindletop gusher at Beaumont in 1901, oil was discovered in Boling Field, Wharton County, in 1925. Gulf Coast production more than doubled from 1935 to 1940, and by 1959 more than five million barrels were produced annually in Wharton County.

Though Foote has not written his plays in chronological order, the body of his works covers the history of Wharton County. The earliest references by characters reach back to the pre–Civil War era; numerous plays are set at the turn of the century; others occur in the modern commercial era, beginning around 1925 in Wharton; and some extend as late as the 1980s.

As small as Wharton remained, it felt the effect of urban growth in Texas, whose population was 60 percent urban by 1950. The town's enormous neighbor, Houston, was fast becoming a metropolis, made fabulously wealthy by the oil boom. By 1920, wealth poured into Houston. During this decade the city became the largest in Texas, rapidly becoming the center of the petroleum-chemistry industry in the nation, and maintained that rank.[19] The youthful and ambitious of Wharton migrated to Houston in large numbers. The difficulty of changing from the rural atmosphere to the big city arises for displaced persons in Foote's plays about the 1920s.

For citizens of Wharton, like Foote and historian Annie Lee Williams, the transition from Old to New Wharton was traumatic. There is a strong sense of loss, which, though accepted, is deplored. In a lecture entitled "Wharton—Then and Now" and delivered in 1989, Foote notes that one-half of the stores on the square are now empty. Only one drugstore and one dry goods store owned by a merchant family of the 1930s remain. The second stories that housed the offices of lawyers, like those above his father's clothing store, are empty. There are no movie theatres; the hotels are closed. As the stores were air-conditioned, their fronts were "modernized" by tearing down the porch roofs, which shut out the scorching sun. "The stores have a strange, hybrid look, not of this time certainly, and no longer of the 1890s or early 1900s," Foote remarks.[20]

More sorely missed from the era of Old Wharton are the stately mansions, built in the late Victorian style. By 1946 these large houses were gone. Foote remembers that when Richmond Road became part of the Houston highway, its "lovely old homes" were abandoned. It is now "littered with used car lots, drive-ins and filling stations." A superhighway now bypasses the town, leaving Richmond Road only an alternate route, with its "shoddy ugliness and waste of houses."[21]

What's new in modern Wharton? Foote asks. He answers in the sardonic tone of Flannery O'Connor, who decried "the proliferation of supermarkets" in the modern South. There is a shopping center "of sorts" with a supermarket one block off the Houston highway.[22] Besides this are the Gulf Coast Medical Center, a full-service facility, and a plastics factory owned by a Taiwanese. Wharton's population has grown to 10,000, and the town has its sufficient quota of motels and apartment complexes.

As the Victorian homes expressed the values of Old Wharton, like the sacredness of the family hearth, so the abandonment of these structures reflects the loss of those values and convictions. Foote's plays about life from the mid-1920s to the present record sad tales of marital infidelity, divorce, madness, the misery of spinsters, and family disintegration. What saves this picture from despair and preserves hope, which never vanishes in Foote's plays, is the endurance of strong individuals who adjust and adopt ways of living productively.

It is as important to know the layout of Wharton as it is to visualize Yoknapatawpha County, of which William Faulkner is "sole owner and proprietor."[23] For all practical purposes the information for Wharton given below will provide the same information for "Harrison."

Clustered near the courthouse were four houses of the main families in Foote's plays. They were occupied by his closest relatives, to whom he gave fictional names as Thomas Wolfe did the Gants. In the *Orphans' Home Cycle,* the Thorntons (based on the Hortons) run and live in a boardinghouse. Nearby are the Robedaux, modeled after the Footes. On Richmond Road live the Vaughns (modeled after Foote's maternal grandparents, the Brookses). Behind their house is the home of Horace and Elizabeth Robedaux, based on Foote's parents. This modest house built in 1917 is Horton Foote's residence to this day. Nearby are large pecan trees, which provide the same natural setting today.

Though quite similar to many American towns, Wharton is distinctive, with its own provocative character, history, and society. To say that Old Wharton as seen in Foote's plays was ruled by the landed aristocracy is not entirely accurate. Most of the characters in his works are townspeople, not farmers. It is more correct to say that old-style businessmen with traditional beliefs—like the patriarch of the *Orphans' Home Cycle,* Mr. Vaughn (Tom Brooks)—ran the town until the late 1920s. They exemplified the best virtues of that age. Another exemplar of the old businessman is Horace Robedaux, based on Foote's father, who adores his wife and is scrupulously honest; he is a self-made man committed to hard work.

The southern past continued strong in Old Wharton. That lingering influence appears in the constant remembrances of the dead, seen graphically in the visits to the cemetery. Further, strong guilt continues about the treatment of blacks during the aftermath of slavery, particularly toward convicts.

The Victorian morality of Old Wharton is more exactly termed church-based morality. The moral standards of Old Wharton, seen clearly in Mr. and Mrs. Vaughn, are formed by the Methodist and Baptist churches. The shaping force of those leading Protestant denominations in Southeast Texas is determinative.

The prohibition movement in Texas gives evidence of the strict morality fostered by evangelical churches. As early as 1887, prohibition was strongly supported in the state. There were drives for local option to bar liquor sales, which made many Texas counties dry. The Democratic Party of Texas, supported by the Anti-Saloon League, called for submission of the prohibition question to a referendum, but the legislature of 1909 refused. Prohibition became the national law by 1919, but drinking was widely ignored in the country. Not so by Miriam A. ("Ma") Ferguson, governor of Texas in 1925–1927 and in 1933–1935. During the prohibition era and even afterward, no liquor was served at the gubernatorial mansion during her terms of office. Prohibition is a leading issue and a major goal of many characters in Foote's plays of the *Orphans' Home Cycle,* which take place from 1900 to 1925. The advocacy of prohibition and condemnation of drinking were part of the Progressive Movement, which supported governmental reform; it prevailed in Texas from 1900 to 1938. There is a sharp contrast, however, in the ways of Whartonians. The adherents of church morality believed in hard work. On the other side are those who adopt an unruly, amoral lifestyle, characterized by violations of the rules observed by the church group.

Although Foote is deeply attached to Wharton and indeed has great affection for it, one can detect an ambivalence in his feelings toward the town and some of its citizens. In his early plays like *Wharton Dance,* he is critical of gossip; in later ones, like *Courtship,* he criticizes the prejudice against dancing. In an interview, he denounced the destruction of "fine old Victorian houses," which were being "demolished for fast-food places." [24]

Studying the relationship between the small rural town and the big city is another important likeness between the Mississippi novelist and the Texas dramatist. Faulkner uses his vantage point to indict generally the whole commercial and urban culture of America. Foote's attack concentrates on one big city, Houston, where the civic duty and self-made lives of Old Wharton have been supplanted by the mad scramble of the oil rich for luxurious commodities.

Foote heard its history, the heartbreaks and joys of its people, and saw firsthand the dramas of violence, and the revolt against Victorian and fundamentalist social customs. Formed by the generous, forgiving spirit of his father and the civic responsibility of his maternal grandfather, Foote is compassionate, giving him a unique relationship with his characters, even the hateful and foolish ones. No other American dramatist forgives his unsavory characters so sincerely and consistently. Horton Foote has the right credentials for a playwright of Texas.

2

FORMATIVE YEARS

AND THE CALL OF ACTING

BESIDES the past of Wharton before 1916, Foote grew up in this very real place ensconced among relatives that were as close as the house next door. In his plays, he draws endlessly on his immediate family because he observed their lives so closely during the first sixteen years of his existence.[1] Foote is fascinated by people, how they pass through and surmount the crises of their lives. He heard family tales about the mystery of these lives and possessed an instinct for their dramas. Not an experimentalist, Foote is inspired by the familiar; he continues to question why some people turn out the way they do.

The early years of Foote's life shaped his material. He has expressed this almost fatalistic philosophy in an interview. Foote believes that during the first twelve years, an artist discovers his subject matter.[2] This is not true for some writers; Hemingway found his theme of the lost generation only after becoming a soldier during World War I. For Foote, when he was an integral part of an extended family, these years were decisive. His family did not move to another city, like Tennessee Williams's. Nor did they reside in a big city, like Arthur Miller's. No, for this future playwright, the years of youth, like those of Mark Twain, gave him his best material for a long career of intensely personal plays. He remained in Old Wharton until the age of sixteen, when he left to pursue a career in acting. After one year of studying elocution in Dallas, he took courses in Pasadena, California, and acted in New York City, where he composed his first play, *Wharton Dance,* in 1939.

Of all Foote's relatives, the family that is the most interesting is the Horton line. This ancestry may be called aristocratic without qualification, because of its forbear's distinction as lieutenant governor. It also furnished the most fascinating stories, which provide an endless store of commentaries on human nature.[3]

The most riveting tale of the Horton clan relates the loss of their house, by Governor Horton's son, Robert John Horton, Foote's great-grandfather. Governor Horton left everything to his daughter, Patience Horton, except half of his slaves to his son (*Memoir,* pp. 42–43). According to Foote's great-aunt Loula Horton, the son was incapable of retaining the inheritance after his father died in 1865. Colonel Isaac Dennis, Patience's husband, seized Robert's share with the help of the boy, now an adult, that the governor had brought from New York as a playmate for his son.[4] "Phillips," as he was called, was trained in the law. Through his machinations and the chicanery of Dennis, a lawyer educated in Massachusetts, Robert lost his share of the estate. A newspaper interviewer in 1991 says the theft was done by "Yankee lawyers."[5] Foote has stated that he learned later that this version was unreliable. Be that as it may, Robert's line kept none of the large plantations left by Governor Horton, while the Dennis line gained possession. Descendants of Colonel Dennis resided in Sycamore Grove for five generations, until the house was demolished in 1960, to the consternation of Whartonians.[6]

The loss of Sycamore Grove provided the dispossessed descendants much grist for judging past events. A favorite destination of the dramatist when he is showing Wharton to visitors is the family cemetery at Sycamore Grove. Only a few tombstones remain, but the name that catches the eye is not Horton but "Dennis."[7] When *New York Times* journalist Samuel G. Freedman went for an inspection, he was struck by the forlorn atmosphere of the graveyard, with its tilted tombstones. Foote observed to Freedman, "Let this be a lesson in humility."[8] Like Shelley in *Ozymandias,* he recognizes the pitiful results of human pride.

Because of the lost inheritance, the stage was set for a feud between the Horton and Dennis lines. The former, lacking money and land, would be forced to struggle to keep body and soul together during Reconstruction and afterward. Robert John Horton left Wharton to operate a lighthouse on the Gulf, but after a destructive hurricane, he returned home to raise one son and five daughters. One daughter, Corella, or Corrie, Horton, was Foote's grandmother. In the other line, the Dennis family kept the ancestral property and became prestigious. W. J. Croom, who married Patience Dennis, daughter of Colonel Isaac Dennis and Patience Horton, was county judge, 1886–1888; a town park is now named for Lyda Dennis Croom, daughter of W. J. Croom. The first mayor of Wharton, elected in 1902, was John H. H. Dennis, the son of Colonel Dennis and his third wife, by whom he had five children.[9]

Foote's main source of Horton lore was his great-aunt. Louisiana Texas Patience Horton, given the same name as Governor Horton's daughter (who died in 1863), was called Aunt Loula by Foote. She and her husband, Dr. J. E. Irvin, had a daughter, Mary, who died young. Loula had taken responsibility for rearing Foote's father and was much beloved by her family. This tall, unattractive woman resembles Katherine Anne Porter's Cousin Eva of "Old Mortality," with her sharp appraisals of the past. Aunt Loula loved to tell stories, which she recounted with great gusto if doubtful accuracy. For Foote they were engrossing tales, which furnished material for many plays. He learned from hearing her tales how fickle memory can be. Each storyteller told the same tale in a different way. Foote has remarked that the storyteller would constantly reorganize and shape these family legends. From listening to relatives like Aunt Loula, he gained a valuable insight: "Every version is personal, it's subjective and all of them are telling the truth as they see it." [10]

Aunt Loula's favorite tale dealt with how her side of the Horton family was robbed of its rightful inheritance. She told of how the present occupants of Sycamore Grove stole the house. She considered her own family to be surrounded by crude thieves. "Common baggage," she haughtily intoned ("Seeing," p. 10). When she started on such reminiscent diatribes, her daughter would leave the room while great-nephew Horton remained to drink in all the juicy details.

Another memorable tale told to Foote by Aunt Loula concerned her sister Mary, who married Jim David and died of tuberculosis in West Texas. According to Aunt Loula, Mary appeared as a ghost to relatives. She would be trying to tell them that a buried treasure or oil lay beneath the house ("Seeing," pp. 14–15).

There were many other unforgettable Hortons that Foote knew. His great-uncle Albert Clinton Horton II (1875–1939), a merchant and inveterate gambler, was the only son of Robert John Horton. He was close to Foote's father. Great-aunt Renie Horton (1878-1928) married A. A. Rugeley, proprietor of Rugeley's Drugstore. Robert John Horton's youngest daughter was Lida Horton (1880–1961), who married T. J. Abell, Wharton's postmaster. Finally, the second daughter and Foote's grandmother was Corrie Horton, who married Albert Foote and, soon after Albert's death, C. E. Cleveland, a railroad man stationed in Houston. All of these individuals appear with fictional names in plays of the

Orphans' Home Cycle and in other plays as well, sometimes obviously and other times less distinctly.

Foote's maternal line, the Brookses, though not one of the oldest families of Wharton like the Hortons, was better off. The Brookses offset the fallen status of the illustrious Hortons and gave young Foote the pride of belonging to a leading family. The large residence of his Brooks grandparents lay just behind the home of his parents. Thus, he was in daily contact with his beloved maternal grandmother, Daisy Speed Brooks, and her husband, Tom. Foote was proud that his grandmother became the first secretary employed in Wharton in 1884 and the first to use a typewriter in the county courthouse.[11]

Tom Brooks's ancestral home stood on the Brazos River and impressed Foote as the first abandoned plantation house that he ever saw. Relatives complained that the house had been robbed of heirlooms by filching kindred.

A self-made man, Tom Brooks became a leading businessman in Wharton. After graduating from Texas A&M with honors, he entered the merchandising business in 1886 and married Daisy Speed. Brooks fathered eight children, of whom two died in infancy. He fit the mold of a strict patriarch perfectly. For him the term "Victorian father" is fully justified. He attended the Methodist church faithfully, though he never joined, and frowned on dancing and gambling.

Brooks also became a civic leader as county treasurer, vice president of the bank, and supporter of Liberty Bond drives during World War I. After the war, Bohemian immigrants in the county needed homesites. Brooks bought up much land at cheap prices around the town and made a sizable fortune selling them (*Memoir*, p. 63). Foote remembers vividly the day his grandfather died of a heart attack in 1925, his own presence in the bereaved home, and the large funeral. Foote felt that the magic period when he was the grandson of Wharton's leading citizen was over. In the years ahead, he saw the coming of grim problems to his Brooks relatives, which Papa would have known how to solve. Alas, his kind had been superseded by the new style of businessmen, who neglected their responsibilities to the poor.

If Grandfather Brooks served as a model of success to young Foote, his three sons epitomized the opposite qualities. Besides three daughters—Hallie, Laura Lee, and Rosa (or Rose)—the Brookses had three sons: Tom, Speed, and William (Billy). Foote remembers the ruined lives of "the boys," whom he calls frankly "wastrel sons" (*Memoir*, pp. 12, 150).

Between twenty and thirty years of age when Foote was growing up, they lived shattered lives. Foote observed that many young men in the 1920s found no place to function and develop in the transition from agricultural to modern urban society in Texas. Previously, they had at least been masters of themselves, but now they became slaves of others. They fell into the dissipation of drinking and gambling.[12] This description fits the Brooks sons, though they grew up in town. Like the rural aristocrats, they did not need to become self-made men.

Foote perceives the social change and the effect on the Brooks sons. He is less skilled in applying psychological techniques to understand dysfunctional personalities. In the case of the sons, there was a stern, successful father, whom they were expected to emulate. After Mr. Brooks's death a protective mother tried to rescue her sons from one disaster after another. She lived the last part of her life in Dallas, Houston, and California. Their ruined lives baffled the rest of the family.

Foote's information on his three Brooks uncles shows their strong impression on him ("Learning," p. 72). Tom, born in 1902, married Mabel Horton, daughter of Albert Clinton Horton II, Foote's great-uncle, but this marriage ended in divorce. Tom became an alcoholic; he wandered as a merchant seaman and died at age 48 in a Houston hotel. Speed (given his mother's maiden name) was set up in the clothes pressing business but gave it up and followed his mother to Houston. Arrested for possession of drugs, he remained in San Quentin prison, California, until the age of fifty. Afterward he lived off the family estate until his death in Houston. The youngest son, Billy, went to law school and attempted to start a law practice with the aid of his mother. He was beaten by his alcoholic wife and died at the Milby Hotel, Houston, where his brother Speed also succumbed. These tragic lives affected Foote's observation of human nature, as evidenced by his repeated portrayal of similar dramatic characters.

If the Brooks family was a daily presence to Foote, the Footes were hardly seen at all. As he has remarked, "The Footes were all vague blurs to me" ("Seeing," p. 14). But the inquisitive boy eventually heard a great deal about this line. At first, no one would tell him about his grandfather, nor how he died. Foote spent hours trying to re-create him in his imagination. One day Miss Lily Outlar called him into her parlor, saying she wanted him to know that his Foote ancestors were "a very distinguished, aristocratic family" ("Seeing," p. 14). Indeed the history of the Footes has a fanciful quality, redolent of the Old South. According to family accounts, Foote's great-grandfather John Foote owned a fleet of ships in

Galveston before the Civil War. He made a large sum buying cotton for the Confederacy. After he lost his fortune and died, his wife, Elizabeth, who was descended from the Robedaux of Virginia, opened a boarding-house in Wharton. There she raised a daughter and three sons, one of whom was Albert Foote, the grandfather of Horton Foote.

The Foote family acquired a mixed reputation in Wharton. Two sons, John Robedaux and Stephen Austin—the former a Greek and Latin scholar, the latter a medical doctor—began a newspaper, the *Wharton Spectator,* in 1888, published it for a short time, and sold it in 1910. The daughter, Minnie, Foote's great-aunt, became a highly respected teacher. Foote has spoken of her educational reputation with pride.[13] The photo-graph of teachers taken in front of the Wharton High School in 1907 shows her in the group.[14]

The third son, Albert, who was Foote's grandfather, was described by some as a brilliant lawyer. To others, like Grandmother Brooks, he was a dissolute man who died at the age of thirty-six. Foote's aunt, Lily Dale Foote Coffee, who lived in Houston, had bitter memories of her father, stigmatizing him as a drunkard and a cigarette fiend. Albert became the sole support of his brothers and sister for reasons that Foote says were never made clear to him ("Seeing," p. 198). When he married Corella Horton, the couple moved into Elizabeth Robedaux's boardinghouse. It was not long before the cramped living conditions and quarrels with her mother-in-law led Corrie to depart and to separate from her husband.

The three family lines—Horton, Brooks, and Foote—converged in Foote's parents. Foote admired his father, Albert Horton Foote (called Al). The son was deeply influenced by his father's attitudes and traits and adopted many of his father's values.

As a fervent Anglophile, Al Foote labeled anyone he disapproved of in politics a "Bolshevik" (*Memoir,* p. 65). Foote's father was a "yellow-dog Democrat" who idolized Roosevelt and befriended blacks. He was in truth a contradictory but recognizable southern type: a wild youth, a New Deal Democrat, and a sincere friend of blacks.

From talking with this father about the kindred, Horton Foote noted his father's hard feelings and refusal to speak to his own mother, Horton's grandmother. The playwright has remarked that his father did not dwell on the injustices he experienced while growing up.[15]

Al Foote had to make it on his own in a series of different jobs. He set his mind on work in merchandising. After getting employment at the age of twelve in a plantation store, he clerked in a dry goods store in Glen

Flora during his teens. In Wharton, he started a small pressing shop, then rose to management in a men's clothing store.

Al's next hurdle involved his marriage to Hallie Brooks. Hallie's father was unalterably opposed to his daughter's marriage to Al, whom he considered a hell-raiser. After the couple eloped, Mr. Brooks did not speak to them for a year. When Horton Foote was born in 1916, Mr. Brooks relented, but he never fully forgot the elopement in succeeding years.

Because Al Foote had to strive so hard to secure a home and family, he knew how to value them. He and his wife were totally absorbed in each other, never being separated for a single day in their married life. Although Hallie was asked to join the social round as the daughter of a leading citizen, she preferred to remain at home in her husband's company.

As the first son of his parents and a grandchild who received boundless affection, Foote benefited from the adulation and interest of many adults. As he says himself, "I was the only grandchild for over five and a half years. I knew all the adults loved me. I was the center of the world." [16]

One of his favorite stories, told by his Brooks grandparents and great-aunt Loula, described the fate of a man tortured by the Ku Klux Klan, which was active in Texas during the 1920s. Alleged to be having an affair with his mother's black cook, this fellow was grabbed in broad daylight, tarred and feathered, and turned loose on the square. Later Foote explained how this man's ordeal remained in his thoughts: "When I was older and went to the picture show alone one night, I had to pass his house. I would see him sitting on his gallery and I would try to imagine what it was like being tarred and feathered and set loose on the courthouse square. . . . I imagined his house was haunted and I would get past it as fast as I could" ("Seeing," p. 5).

Foote did not experience the reality of death in his secure existence until Grandfather Brooks died in 1925, when Foote was nine. Foote was taken to his grandmother by his mother, who said, "Little Horton's here" ("Seeing," pp. 14–16). Only when Grandmother Brooks embraced him did Foote realize the deep loss. He has said that ever since, this event is the one toward which he has been groping as a writer: "Until then life was magic." He never felt so secure as he did when he was the grandson of "one of the richest families in town and my grandfather was the most respected man in town." [17]

The impact of Grandfather Brooks's death did not end with the funeral. Grandmother Brooks, dressed in mourning, kept the town custom of daily visits to her husband's grave. She was often accompanied by her grandson, who learned about the people buried in the cemetery. Foote later remarked that when he was growing up, people talked about the lives of the dead, who were almost as alive as the living. Furthermore, unlike today, time was allowed for grief: "We're less allowed our grief [today], and I don't think it's a good thing." [18]

Death may have hovered over the community, but Foote's boyhood was rife with vigorous living. He spent much time roller skating and horseback riding. When Foote was only seven, his uncle Billy ("Brother") Brooks presented him with a horse, which he called Minnie, after the heroine of the popular song "Minnie the Moocher." Foote's idea of fun after school was to race Minnie down unpaved roads. Mr. Wilson, who lived across Richmond Road from Grandfather Brooks, ran a cotton gin, which was located at the back of his property. Foote's playmate during these years was the Wilson boy. He and Foote enjoyed playing on cotton bales in the storage shed and jumping up and down in wagons of cottonseed. They also formed clubs with older boys whom they joined in digging caves, climbing trees, and building clubhouses. Foote recalls that about this time he was reading *Tom Sawyer,* whose activities around Hannibal were very similar to his own ("Seeing," p. 3).

Amid these carefree escapades the ominous Colorado River flowed by. Every two years it flooded, the water reaching to the porch of Foote's home. During these inundations, he and his parents would have to reach town by rowboat, a ride that delighted the townspeople, as evident in photographs from 1900 to 1925 that show large crowds in boats floating by. The river was not to be trifled with. Although Foote's father fished in it, young Horton was not allowed to go near it, and he did not. By the time Foote was growing up in the 1920s, all reasonable people feared the river because of its suck holes and water moccasins. Foote was reminded all too often of the dangers of the river by the wailing sirens that announced another drowning.

Foote entered the adult world at the early age of eleven, when he began to work at his father's small haberdashery on Milam Street. If Foote had become acquainted with women and their ways through his mother and Grandmother Brooks, he received just as intimate a knowledge of men's lives from working beside his father. Foote went to his father's store most afternoons after school and during the summer months. The longest and busiest day was Saturday, when he remained at the store until eleven at night. Most of the customers were black men, accompanied by their wives or girlfriends. Foote had a chance to encounter a cross section of society in this meeting place of town and professional men. Besides the black customers, there was a steady stream of white visitors. Old men would come to pass the time. His father would sometimes implore his son, "Don't leave me alone with them or I'll jump out of my skin." Foote listened to their discussions about the prospects of crops and their arguments over politics.[19]

Nearby were three drugstores, favorite rendezvous spots of men who would spend most of the day inside, swapping stories and playing practical jokes on each other. In his father's store, Foote heard country speech, which was quite different from his family's, and he came to know and like all kinds and classes of people. He acquired a democratic fondness for people.

In a town of the 1920s like Wharton with no college to stimulate mental activity, the chances for intellectual development were limited. Reading provided Foote's first resource. At an early age he became an avid reader. His favorite book was *Miss Minerva and William Green Hill* (1909), by Frances Boyd Calhoun, a southern classic known by boys of Foote's generation. This story of a mischievous orphan who comes to live with his old-maid aunt is an updated *Tom Sawyer,* set at the turn of the century. Living in a small community, Foote could identify easily with this boy's life. He also could feel at home with the easy relationship of white and black children, a major element of the book. Along the same line, *Tom Sawyer* and *Huck Finn* delighted Foote. He read and reread these humorous stories with their many passages of southern dialect, both black and white. Among the books that Foote remembers most fondly is *David Copperfield,* another tale of an orphan. Foote also became interested in the novels of Willa Cather, whose compassion for a Bohemian girl's adversities on the frontier in *My Ántonia,* as well as the touching portrayal of Neighbor Rosicky in the story of that name, show Foote's liking for such moving tales ("Seeing," pp. 13–14).

At the age of fourteen, Foote advanced to a more adult level of reading when he joined the Literary Guild and the Book of the Month Club, which were then more "high class" in their offerings, he notes.[20] At this time he enjoyed popular novels like *Grand Hotel* and also read John Galsworthy's *Forsyte Saga,* Arnold Bennett's *Old Wives Tales,* and Noel Coward's *Private Lives* (*Memoir,* p. 140). A friend of his mother's disapproved of the Literary Guild's selection of *Candide.* Voltaire's radical little satire was considered unwholesome, but Foote was not prohibited from reading it ("Seeing," p. 14).

The church played a large part in the life of young Foote. He has pointed out that "we were Methodists and Episcopalians at that time" ("Seeing," p. 19). That is to say, his mother's family were devout Methodists while the Hortons of his father's family were Episcopalians. The Brooks grand-parents were indeed strict Methodists, who did not permit his mother to dance. They differed from the broad-minded Episcopalians of the Hor-ton tribe, who played cards and danced, a trait seen in his father's love of dancing. Hallie Brooks Foote, a devoted Methodist, had the strongest in-fluence on her son's religious upbringing. Both mother and son would later become Christian Scientists. At an early age Foote was taken to Sunday school, where he heard all the Bible stories. Foote has retained them well. He remarks: "To me the Bible is a wonderful storytelling de-vice that tells much about the family. From the word go Cain killed Abel, stole his birthright, and it took years before there was forgiveness."[21]

A new kind of entertainment arrived during Foote's youth that pre-sented art to him in striking and dramatic form: silent movies. Like Ten-nessee Williams and Edward Albee, Foote became a habitué of the movie theatre, which usually lacked the artistry of the legitimate theatre but showed him the infinite possibilities of drama. Movies were not in far-away cities but easily accessible at the Queen Theatre. Moviegoing be-came Foote's most pleasurable pastime, and he went to see his favorite stars whenever possible. The arrival of "talkies" brought modern life to Old Wharton. Foote also saw talkies in Houston. Driven to the big city by his uncles to see *The Singing Fool*, he watched his father sob when Al Jolson sang "Sonny Boy" to his dying son. When Foote went to visit his grandmother in Houston, he always liked going to the picture show ("Learning," p. 71).

The other innovation in popular entertainment that arrived in the 1920s was radio, and Foote was as much a devotee of radio as he was of movies. This medium brought the outside world directly into the homes of Wharton, as television would thirty years later. Foote enjoyed the pop-ular singers and knew all their songs. Rudy Vallee, Kate Smith, and Bing Crosby were his favorites. He also listened to the comedians on shows such as *Amos 'n' Andy* ("Seeing," p. 21).

Foote made the crucial decision to become an actor while very young. At an early age, he heard his parents describe how a gray-haired man named Mr. Armstrong received a call one day in the fields of Mississippi to go preach in Texas. On questioning, his mother replied that such a call came not only to Baptists but also to Methodists and Presbyterians. A few years later, when he was twelve, he became convinced that he had heard the call to be an actor. Until this time there had been no actors in Wharton and certainly none in his family. He saw actors only once a year when a troupe performed in a tent and came by his father's store. One morning, he says, "I awakened with the sure knowledge that I wanted to be an actor; more, that I was going to be. Of that I hadn't the slightest doubt" ("Seeing," pp. 18–19). He then announced this intention to his startled family. Foote's parents had serious questions about their son's choosing such a dubious vocation. There were sharp clashes with his father about Foote's ambition, but these were not prolonged. Neither parent refused his choice of a career ("Pasadena," p. 33).

At the age of fourteen, Foote read in the Houston newspaper that a talent scout from Hollywood was coming to the city to give screen tests. Foote persuaded his grandmother Brooks and one of her sons to drive him to an interview. During the appointment, there was no discussion of a screen test but only of lessons, including tap dancing lessons. This representative of motion pictures looked very "unHollywood" to Foote, sounding as if he had never left Houston, Texas ("Seeing," p. 21).

Foote was fortunate at this juncture to enjoy the support of two women involved in the theatre. He credits Eppie Davidson for encouraging his interest. Mrs. Davidson arrived at Wharton High School to teach speech and dramatics while Foote was a student. Over a period of three years she cast him in all the plays, amounting to three a year. In her speech delivered to a Wharton High School assembly on April 3, 1963, she introduced her prize pupil. She recalled that Foote cheered everyone else on. He lacked skill with hammer and nails but earned their pardon as he made the audience forget all about staging defects, such as walls that leaned askew.[22]

Eppie Davidson has described how Foote won a much admired award at the state tournament. Her acting class entered a one-act performance in the state One-Act Play Contest. Foote took the leading part of a college student who confessed that he was addicted to drugs. When a judge asked Mrs. Davidson if he was really addicted, she replied that he was only acting. "In that case," the judge decided, "we are going to give him the Best Actor Award" ("Seeing," p. 20).

Foote also received support from Nan Outlar, who wrote the longest-running society column for the *Wharton Journal*. She had seen plays in New York and sympathized with Foote's burning desire to become a Broadway star. Foote considered her sophisticated and glamorous because of her acquaintance with the theatre. Nan Outlar lived in a house across Richmond Road from Grandfather Brooks's residence; she and Foote saw a lot of each other and talked endlessly about the theatre. Nan joined Foote in the activities of the Wharton Little Theatre. Its very presence in a town with a population of only three thousand is exceptional, showing that Foote had more opportunity for theatrical experience than one might expect. He took every chance to act at the Little Theatre.

Foote's graduation from high school early in the summer of 1932 when only sixteen years old forced a decision about the training he desired. He had heated discussions with his parents. Worried about their son's ambition and the unpredictable vocation of acting, they tried to get Foote to attend college for two years before taking such a decisive step. When Foote adamantly refused, they compromised, agreeing to send him to drama school if he would take a year off to work. They hoped that during this time "the madness would pass," Foote says.[23] Since Grandmother Brooks was moving to Dallas at the end of the summer to assist her two youngest sons, the would-be actor joined her there. Foote enrolled in the Woodrow School of Expression, where he studied not acting but elocution, under the direction of a Miss Woodward, who sympathized with his dream of becoming a movie actor. He also ushered at the Majestic Theatre, seizing the chance to see the current movies again and again. One of these was Philip Barry's *Animal Kingdom*, with Leslie Howard and Ann Harding. Foote retained one well-turned line of dialogue from this talkie: "Who but you, Daisy, and strangers are honest with me ever?" ("Seeing," p. 23).

Following the interlude in Dallas, Foote's parents, true to their word, sent him to the Pasadena Playhouse in California. They chose this widely advertised acting school, near the film capital, not because of its superior reputation for instruction in acting but rather because they believed it would provide a wholesome atmosphere. Agreeing to send his son away to acting school, Al Foote was placed under financial stress in 1933, when the impact of the Great Depression was strongly felt. Later, Foote tried to recapture in plays the truth of this time, not just the statistics, when people were faced with "overwhelming financial obstacles" ("Seeing," p. 27). Many weekdays, Foote's father would end the day with no more than $2 in the cash register. When Al Foote would see his three sons awaiting supper at the table, he felt moved to reopen his haberdashery in hopes of making a few more dollars. Preoccupied with his desire to attend acting school, Horton Foote could hardly appreciate his father's financial anxiety. In order to accrue the funds for his son's two years of training, Al Foote was obliged to sell the only real estate held in his own name. Sacrificing the invitation to invest in an oil pool—which succeeded— he sold his rental house for $3,000. If his father regretted the loss of a large profit from investing in the black gold of Texas, he never said so ("Seeing," pp. 25–26).

Foote took the bus to California in the summer of 1933. This odyssey from sheltered Wharton to the great world came early, at the callow age of seventeen. Of his arrival in California, Foote's "most lasting memory" is the sight of endless orange groves. They have now vanished, he notes, recalling Randall Jarrell's reference to them in "The Lost World" ("Seeing," p. 30).

In Los Angeles the Texas relatives materialized to welcome Foote. His great-aunt, a sister of Grandmother Brooks, and her husband listened to him tell about all their relatives back home. Their slight means, however, prevented them from taking Foote in for the night. In his room at the local YMCA, lonely and homesick for the dusty cotton fields, this seventeen-year-old knew for a certainty that he "would never fully go back to that life again" ("Seeing," p. 32).

By the time Foote arrived at the Pasadena Playhouse, this theatre-cum-acting-school had been in operation for seventeen years, since 1916. The artistic director was Gilmore Brown, who had been a minor actor in western theatres. He had capitalized on the vitality of the "Little Theatre" movement. The Pasadena Playhouse became recognized as one of the foremost community theatres in the nation, praised for its classic productions of Shakespeare. It was considered a stepping stone for actors on their way to a Hollywood career. When Foote matriculated at the school, "community theatre" was a misnomer because most often professional and semiprofessional actors were brought in from Los Angeles for the main-stage productions.

In the classes for theatre students at the playhouse, practical training was the guiding principle. The school advertised, "Training is not confined to theory. Students learn by doing!" ("Pasadena," p. 33). Foote took classes in fencing, scene design, and styles of acting, from nine till five. He was discouraged by much of the training that was offered. Having no talent for drawing, he made little progress in stage design. Even the play rehearsals were frustrating. He was thrown into Roman comedy, of which he had no knowledge. To make matters worse, Foote was informed that he would have to get rid of his southern accent or he would never be any kind of actor. The young Texan learned that he hailed from a part of the country disdained by sophisticated people. To correct his accent, Foote took private lessons from a diction instructor. Blanche Townsend's method was to have him repeat Hamlet's speech containing the phrase "trippingly on the tongue," which almost ruined Shakespeare for him forever. The one class that Foote thoroughly enjoyed was theatrical literature. The instructor, who took a special interest in him, was passionate about plays as literature and was always willing to talk about novels, poetry, and short stories.

The stage productions that Foote attended more than met his expectations. Though he had seen amateur productions of popular plays, he had not experienced the thrill of great plays performed by professional actors. On the main stage of the Pasadena Playhouse, he saw Molière's *Bourgeois Gentilhomme*, Synge's *Playboy of the Western World,* Lynn Riggs's *Roadside* with Victor Jory, and Wilde's *Salome* with Lee J. Cobb as Herod.

The climax of Foote's play-going was his introduction to Eva Le Galienne in Ibsen. When she came to Los Angeles in the spring of 1934, Foote's grandmother Brooks, who was visiting two sisters, took him to see the great actress in a matinee of *Hedda Gabler*. He has never forgotten her entrance as this sinister New Woman, in a short skirt, with her hair bobbed, smoking a cigarette. He found her "extraordinary." The play made "a deep and lasting impression on me," Foote says. That evening he and his grandmother saw Le Galienne again in *The Master Builder.* According to Foote, he has seen many fine theatrical productions since then, but none have made "the lasting impression on me that these first Ibsen plays did" ("Pasadena," p. 38). In fact, the future playwright would never stray far from the intensely felt realism of modern drama. After his exposure to Le Galienne, Foote abandoned his dream of being a movie actor and set his sights on becoming an actor in the legitimate theatre.

The impact of Le Galienne on Foote's thinking did not end with her performances. He learned of her theatrical philosophy from *At 33,* the book she published at that age, which his grandmother bought for him. This influential personage in American theatre had become famous in such plays as Molnar's *Liliom.* She could have continued a successful career in the commercial theatre but felt that an actor could only reach full potential in the great plays of the classic and modern repertory. She opened the Civic Repertory in a run-down theatre off-Broadway in order to perform Chekhov, Ibsen, and modern European classics. Here, to be sure, Foote encountered a woman of the theatre who believed in high artistic standards and had chosen the hard road of defying commercial pressure.

Foote found his last year at the Pasadena Playhouse to be satisfying. As seniors, he and his classmates were placed in charge of the Recital Hall Theatre for the season. They were cast in four plays. In addition, they handled scenery and costumes and served as stage managers. In these productions, Foote willingly painted scenery and assisted Janet Scott with direction. Sometimes he worked all night long. Some students objected to the time spent not acting. Miss Scott, who had acted in New York, advised Foote that in theatre one needed all the skills possible "to survive" ("Pasadena," pp. 40-41). He first took the role of Ernest in *The Importance of Being Earnest*. Always conscientious to keep his parents informed, Foote sent them the Pasadena Playhouse program of *Lady Windermere's Fan* dated March 30, 1935. He bemoaned having to wear "a full dress suit" in the role of Lord Augustus Lorton: "I hate the darn things and heaven knows how I'll ever get it on, but get it on I must" (HFC).

In the summer of 1935, Foote was invited by his diction coach, Blanche Townsend, to join the Rice Players, a stock company on Martha's Vineyard. With him came his best friend, John Forscht, and Joseph Anthony, later a successful Broadway director and a close acquaintance. Passing through Wharton en route, Foote received $50 from his hard-pressed father with a final admonition: "When this is gone, don't ask for any more because I won't give it to you" ("Pasadena," p. 41). In the lean years that followed, while seeking work as an actor in New York, Foote did not ask for more.

At the summer stock theatre, Blanche Townsend chose to produce Paul Green's *No \qCount Boy*. This comic one-act about a Negro youth with a taste for fantasy who claims to have visited many faraway places opened a new door for Foote. It revealed to him the value of his familiarity with life in the South, an asset he would utilize in works for theatre, television, and motion pictures. Foote was given the title role, for which his southern accent came naturally. Because black actors were not used at that time, all members of the cast performed in blackface. The play was a huge success, presenting rural blacks, who were entirely unknown to the audience. Foote found this folk play a relief from the unrealistic characters and situations of the usual artificial Broadway fare performed in summer stock. Foote also took the role of Marchbanks in Shaw's *Candida*. He had written his parents earlier from Pasadena on April 16, 1935, that his was "a part I've always wanted to play, and one

I've worked on for a long time" (HFC). When Foote's summer job ended, he and his companions from Pasadena left Martha's Vineyard, determined to try their luck as actors in New York.

As Foote proceeded to New York, he could look back to youthful years of undeniable progress, the by-product of steady habits as well as talent. Born into an intimate family deeply rooted in Southeast Texas, he had made crucial decisions for his life as he chose the uncertain way of an actor. He had succeeded in leaving his birthplace, shedding the protective cocoon of family and hometown and entering the great, wide world.

Foote carried with him to New York excellent resources for artistic creativity. The family lines from which he emerged were rich in dramatic potential. The Hortons offered an engrossing epic, with their origin in the antebellum South. The Brookses, suffering through the shattered lives of three wandering sons, supplied tragedy, giving Foote a firsthand knowledge of the pain that human beings could experience. Not least, the Footes, with the separation of husband and wife and the premature death of the former, offered stark melodrama. Foote joined a rich tradition of droll yarn-spinners and inventive narrators from the South (including Texas), revived in his own times by Lyndon Baines Johnson, who could tell hilarious jokes in a drawl that expertly exploited the vernacular style.

Foote also exhibited personal traits, such as soft-spokenness and small-town sociability, which would give him his own individuality. These qualities might detract from the sensationalism admired in the theatre but would nevertheless stand him in good stead. He won over many with his temperament. In fact, he possessed an amiable manner, exceptional even among actors. Foote's friendliness originated in a sincere concern for other human beings. Truly, he could be called a kind man. Add to this a democratic approach to people of all sorts, and the net result is an engaging individual who would be admired for his humanity.

From the beginning, Texas has been a place open to change, and not just from agriculture to commerce. The world of entertainment has affected the state's culture strongly, as is reflected in Foote. Popular entertainment gave the people of Texas a new look at the world and themselves. Firmly anchored in a rich past, Texans like Foote could exploit it and current life to create new forms of American amusement.

3

FINDING A VOCATION

FROM ACTING TO WRITING

D URING Foote's first years in New York, from 1935 to 1942, the nation passed from peacetime Depression to wartime excitement as the United States entered World War II after the Japanese bombing of Pearl Harbor on December 7, 1941. Foote gave up the goal of being an actor and embarked on a career as a playwright. His experiences and continued training as a professional actor, valuable though they were, did not meet with the success of his writing for the stage. He composed three dramatic works, apprentice pieces necessarily, but highly prophetic of the subject matter, themes, and directions he would pursue for many years. Foote arrived in New York when the Stanislavski Method of acting and the political protests of Clifford Odets set the prevailing tone. As Foote entered the lively theatrical world of New York at the still malleable age of nineteen, he would immerse himself in both movements.

Foote's first year in New York would be the most rootless of his life, when merely keeping body and soul together was a constant struggle. He, John Forscht, and their friends, seeking employment as actors, rented a cheap apartment at 142 MacDougal Street, in Greenwich Village across from the Provincetown Playhouse, which had sponsored the first successes of Eugene O'Neill ("Pasadena," p. 44). Foote informed his parents on November 19, 1935, that he had obtained a part in *Provincetown Follies,* starring Beatrice Kay and Barry Oliver. It was running at the Provincetown Playhouse before being taken "up Town" (HFC). Foote also took odd jobs like working as a busboy at a restaurant, from which he returned in the evening with leftovers for his starving friends. Because his mother described tasty meals that made Foote ravenously hungry, he asked her to omit these passages from her letters.

Foote took advantage of the cultural attractions of New York, which broadened his acquaintance with the fine arts. One Sunday, he treated himself to the symphony for the first time and wrote his parents on November 19, 1935: "I enjoyed it very much." On the program were Beethoven's Seventh Symphony and one by Schumann conducted by Otto Klemperer. Foote also went to a Van Gogh exhibit, which he enjoyed. To see all the canvases at the museum would take several trips, he added. Impressed by Van Gogh's devotion to his art despite little remuneration, Foote noted that the collection was valued at $1 million, but in the artist's lifetime he "only sold an amount of twenty-five dollars" (HFC).

Foote became habituated to "making the rounds," asking for whatever bit parts were available ("Pasadena," p. 44). Daily he entered the agents' offices up and down Broadway and the side streets from Thirty-ninth to Fifty-seventh Streets. He asked about casting at the Theatre Guild and by the Shubert Theatre. Many times there was nothing but a curt shake of the head. Foote obtained his first acting job as a fourteenth-century scissors grinder in an industrial film ("Pasadena," p. 46). It lasted three days, paying $15 per day.

Despite his paucity of funds, Foote managed to attend theatrical performances. He learned how to wait till after intermission and then scurry in to take an empty seat. He remembers seeing Lillian Hellman's *The Children's Hour* and Judith Anderson in *The Old Maid* in 1935. The latter play was presented at the Empire Theater, a lovely building now torn down, Foote laments ("Pasadena," p. 47). In January 1936 he was delighted with Pauline Lord's performance in the dramatization of Edith Wharton's *Ethan Frome*. Foote admired "the truth and the beauty" of the life that this exquisite actress brought to the stage ("Pasadena," p. 48). Stark Young, the well-known theatre critic, who became a close friend of Foote's, also extolled her performance.

Foote's wanderings as an unemployed actor took a more purposeful turn in 1936 when he enrolled at the School for the Stage and became indoctrinated in the Stanislavski Method. Fortunately for him, Rosamund Pinchot, a beautiful actress whom he had met at the Pasadena Playhouse, wanted an acting partner for her scene classes at the school. Backed by a wealthy family of New York, she offered to pay for Foote's instruction. After seeing Pinchot and her partner in a scene from *Candida,* the Russian directors of the school questioned Foote about his previous education. Tamara Daykarhanova, who had been the leading lady of Balieff's Chauve-Souris company in Russia, had opened her own studio in New

York. She and her associates shook their heads when they heard of Foote's previous training. They felt that he could correct his deficiency by taking technique classes at their school.

Although Foote soon lost the financial support of Rosamund Pinchot and was obliged to find odd jobs again, he followed the Russians' advice. His teachers were Vera Soloviova and Andrius Jilinsky, who had acted at the Moscow Art Theatre. These fervent apostles of the Stanislavski Method explained enthusiastically the revolutionary technique. The principle on which the method was based, striving for authenticity above all, proved congenial to Foote, who practiced it not only in acting but also in his subsequent writing of plays. According to Jilinsky, in acting there should be a stress on psychological accuracy of the character and concentration on inner feelings. To further the method's intense realism, he demanded true-to-life movement and speech. The actor uses emotional recall of a dramatic moment. In his emotional memory, the student relives a previous incident. It might be kissing a girl for the first time. The actor goes through the emotions in rehearsal but most intensely in performance. The name for this famous and successful method is emotional realism.

The 1930s was a period of revolt both in American acting and society, and the Stanislavski Method linked Foote to the revolutionary spirit of the time. The method helped transform theatre in America just as the New Deal of Franklin D. Roosevelt was changing the economic system. Foote remarks that those who adopted the new method felt "we were in all ways turning our backs on the past" ("Pasadena," p. 54).

The newly found commitment to emotional realism would shape Foote's direction in his career as a dramatist. He believed that the aim to be truthful was the finest one possible. That meant he would strive above all to discover the truth in people's lives without arguing for a social program, such as Odets's call for the unionization of labor in *Waiting for Lefty*. Foote's appreciation of the domestic drama, exemplified by Ibsen's *A Doll's House,* would hold Foote essentially to this genre throughout his career as a dramatist. He would not be drawn into the varied departures from realism that many American dramatists, such as Elmer Rice, Thornton Wilder, and Tennessee Williams, would attempt. Foote learned what he believed in and could do effectively. Henceforth, he would maintain that conviction regardless of the changing theatrical winds.

From 1936 to 1939, while studying at the School for the Stage, Foote slowly began to find more acting jobs. In the fall of 1937 he got his first taste of Broadway, when he was approached by Warner Brothers, which was starting to produce Broadway plays, for a small part in *Swing Your Lady*. He began rehearsals but, to his humiliation, was dismissed before the production opened. Afterward, he had more success. He became a supernumerary in *The Eternal Road*, Max Reinhardt's epic of the Jewish people based on biblical stories. Next, Foote was hired by the Maverick Theatre of Woodstock, New York, to take eight roles during the summer of 1937. There he got the chance to play the part of Mio in Maxwell Anderson's *Winterset*. Foote had seen Burgess Meredith twice in this role and considered Meredith's performance "electrifying" ("Pasadena," p. 57). Foote had a chance to learn firsthand Anderson's theory of tragedy. That optimistic writer believed that the one faith of the theatre was the belief in human progress. In the tragedy based on the famous Sacco-Vanzetti case, the hero chooses forgiveness over revenge. Mio changes for the better, responding to a high moral impulse. This play rejects the despair expressed in the naturalistic plays of O'Neill, like *The Iceman Cometh*.

Foote obtained acting jobs outside New York. In 1938 he wrote to his father that he was acting away from the city. Plumbing was minimal— "no bath tubs." The director was nice and Foote heard that "he likes me." That pleased Foote "because there's nothing so unharmonious as working against a director." [1]

Foote always kept in close touch with his parents. His mother kept him "well posted," he wrote to his father on Father's Day, 1938. "But I guess there isn't a thing she can't do well. Right?" After encouraging his father about his business, Foote paid him a tribute: "I can't tell you how much I appreciate you." He wrote that he realized every day "how grateful" he should be "for such sane and loving parents." But he also wrote that words don't mean much and added, "I hope I can show you by my actions how much I love you" (HFC).

Foote's life was soon to turn toward playwriting. He remembers that "between acting engagements I would have to find part-time work, usually ushering in a movie house, and in many ways I expected this to be the pattern of the rest of my life" ("Pasadena," p. 60). All that changed when he began his association with the American Actors Company. In 1938, Mary Hunter, a fellow student at the School for the Stage, conceived the plan for a new company, using as its nucleus her acquaintances at that studio. Original members included Agnes de Mille, Jerome Robbins, Mildred Dunnock, Lucy Kroll (who would become Foote's first and only literary agent), Joseph Anthony, and Foote himself. The formation of this company was auspicious for Foote, since it gave him the opportunity to write plays.

Mary Hunter was a talented woman, dedicated to the cause of better theatre in America. Tennessee Williams wanted her to direct *You Touched Me!* in 1943 because she was "the most intelligent woman I have ever met."[2] Older than most students at the school, she was ten years Foote's senior. Born in California, she had become friends with Agnes de Mille and, in New Mexico, with Lynn Riggs, author of the successful play *Green Grow the Lilacs* (1931). In Chicago Hunter joined an experimental theatre group and was hired for a part on the radio program *Easy Aces.* When NBC moved the program to New York, Hunter came along. She had her heart set on directing but realized that because a female director on Broadway was rare, her chances were slim. She began to think then of a nonprofit theatre with art as its criterion. Daykarhanova's School for the Stage was dedicated to the ideal of group acting espoused by the Group Theatre. All at the school subscribed to its goal. After rehearsing students in a play about the Brontë family, Hunter invited several to join the American Actors Company in the spring of 1938. Foote found this company much to his liking. He wrote to his father that he was joining "the American Actors" after leaving the show he was currently performing in: "That gives me a change and I always enjoy it."[3]

Mary Hunter enunciated the purpose of her new company in the preface to Foote's play *Only the Heart,* performed by its members in 1941. It is worth quoting at length.

The American Actors Theatre was founded in 1938 by a group of young theatre people for the kind of experimental development that the creative artist in every field must have and that is most difficult to achieve in the theatre, as none of its arts can be practiced in solitude. Most of the original members shared a common technical training in one of the best teaching methods in the theatre, that of the Moscow Art Theatre passed on to us by its outstanding teachers, Tamara Daykarhanova, Andrius Jilinsky, Maria Ouspenskaya, and Vera Solovieva.

With this in our pockets (and very little money, I might add) we brought together a group of actors, dancers, choreographers, designers, and technicians to begin a non-profit theatre that would give a consistent chance for young talent to develop, a chance otherwise impossible to attain in the very city which is the heart of the theatre as an industry and art.[4]

The main purpose of the company was to depict the many cultures of America, which were being overlooked in the centralized theatre of New York. Hunter emphasized this aim: "Our primary intention was the uncovering of our cultural roots, and since the members of the company represented almost a regional survey of the United States, the sources were rich and varied."[5] Critics recognized the depiction of America's geographic regions. Curtis Pepper of the *New York World-Telegram* wrote of the company: "They breathe American in appearance. The actors have scored again in frankly presenting a play of the American scene with force and charm."[6]

Mary Hunter's wish to exploit areas of American culture that had been bypassed appealed to Foote. He had enjoyed acting in Paul Green's play about rural blacks of the South. The American Actors Company built a stage above a garage on West Sixty-ninth Street and began rehearsing plays by Lynn Riggs, E. P. Conkle, and Paul Green, all exponents of the folk drama, which coincided with the regionalist approach of the company. Members were asked to do improvisations based on life in their own part of the country to arrive at a collective meaning of "American." Foote chose to show the experience of a family caught in a Texas hurricane. A native of the Gulf Coast, he could testify to the realism. Agnes de Mille, the choreographer, was present to see *Gulf Storm* and spoke casually to Foote in words that proved to be prophetic: "You seem to be in touch with some interesting theatrical material. Did you ever think of writing a play about it?" ("Pasadena," pp. 63–64).

Using the same Texas material, Foote wrote *Wharton Dance* in 1939, the "first one-act play ever written and produced by American Actors Company."[7] It was performed in 1940 along with one-acts by Paul Green and Thornton Wilder. At one time Foote wrote that he no longer had a copy of the play, but to the best of his recollection it was "very improvisatory, based on a real situation," using the names of boys and girls from "our crowd" at his high school ("Pasadena," p. 64). Later he recovered the manuscript.

Since Foote still thought of himself primarily as an actor, he wrote this play of thirty-one typed pages as an acting vehicle for himself. "David," played by Foote, heads the cast of fifteen, speaks first, and gives the main thematic speech. Robert Coleman of the *New York Mirror* praised the piece and Foote's acting ("Pasadena," p. 64). Another reporter wrote a story comparing Foote to Noel Coward, who was then known for writing plays in which he took the starring role. Foote remarks that he did not in any way think of himself as another Noel Coward, but that he realized that one sure way of acting was to compose a play with a good part for himself ("Pasadena," p. 64).

Wharton Dance is an interesting play because it shows that Foote has returned to his hometown in his thoughts despite his new residence in New York. At the age of twenty-three, he goes back seven years to high school life. Now he see its pettiness; he attacks small-town gossip, a common subject of such contemporary writers as Sinclair Lewis. The provincial atmosphere causes the lead character, David, to seek escape.

Here, as in his other first plays, Foote is very much a social critic. Yes, he is a regionalist, depicting life in Texas; a close observer of small-town life; and a character analyst, like Sherwood Anderson. Yet he takes the same viewpoint as the social critics, such as Odets, whose plays he knew well, and Maxwell Anderson, whose *Winterset,* an attack on antiforeign prejudice, he admired. In fiction, Foote resembles Sinclair Lewis, the critic par excellence of the small town, though Foote lacks that novelist's satirical gift. Foote's social criticism was present from the beginning and continues. He is a playwright who acquired his essential mentality early in his career. Just as he did not waver in the type of understated drama he wrote, so he did not essentially alter his role as a constructive social critic. Here he did not forget his first model, Ibsen himself, who launched social criticism.

Wharton Dance records the life of adolescents in Wharton. Set in the present (of 1939), verified by such music as a "jumpy arrangement" of "Sweet Papa's Gone" (p. 24), Foote presents people he knew. Three teenage couples with names like "Vard" and "Hulia" (the Spanish pronunciation of "Julia") are gathered at the foot of a staircase leading up to a dance hall. The action has a simple structure. The crowd is awaiting the arrival of another couple, Lyda Belle and Bill, who are seeing each other secretly. While waiting, they engage in conversation with others who arrive for the dance.

Lyda's mother, Mrs. Neal, is dead set against her daughter's choice of Bill. One character says that there will be "a funeral" if she hears that Lyda Belle has been going out with him. The crowd must wait on Lyda

Belle before they enter the dance, because if she is not with them, "the old hens" will report her to her ever vigilant mother, always on the alert to hear gossip about her daughter (p. 2).

In the last scene, the subject of small-town gossip reaches its peak when Lyda Belle and Bill finally show up. The girls are overjoyed that Bill has given her a ring and promise to keep it for her so that her mother will not know about it. The boys also offer to help Bill in any way they can. Lyda Belle mounts the stairs to the dance without Bill, to prevent the chaperones from seeing her arrive with him. As a parting defiance to the nosiness of others, Hulia declares, "I wouldn't have missed being out here making the natives stretch their necks for anything" (p. 27).

Foote shows ambivalence toward Wharton. And, like many artists, he left his hometown. He differs in that he kept in contact and continues to return home.

Although *Wharton Dance* is deficient in dramatic art, it shows Foote as he explores the kind of material that interests him. The play also reveals a clear talent for developing intimately known material in dramatic form, strengthened by thematic insight. Foote returns to Wharton imaginatively and gives a detailed account. It is an oppressive town where no free spirit would willingly remain.

Encouraged by the favorable reception of this one-act, Foote laid plans for a three-act play. He took great satisfaction from writing *Texas Town*, a sign that playwriting was the right vocation for him. Even though he knew "little or nothing" about writing a play, not having admitted to himself that he wanted to be "a playwright," he felt "a certain security about accomplishing my task" that he had never felt in his years as an actor ("Pasadena," p. 65).

When Foote began to write plays seriously, he sought playwrights that could guide him. He was looking for a style that would help him give shape and meaning to his work. Among the craftsmen he learned from was George Kelly, a popular playwright of the 1920s. Foote referred explicitly to Kelly's satire of amateur theatres in his biographical lecture "Pasadena and Beyond." Foote wrote that Kelly, who satirized little theatres like the Pasadena Playhouse of the 1920s, ridiculed "their desperate earnestness" in a popular play of 1922, *The Torch Bearers* ("Pasadena," p. 34). Foote would have heard a positive estimate of Kelly from his friend Stark Young, the distinguished theatre reviewer from Mississippi. That influential critic of the *New Republic* praised Kelly's realistic diction and wrote favorably of his plays in the 1920s.

Foote's dialogue is ordinary with its laconic phrases such as "Is that so?" and "Yes, I would." It gives his plays the impression of realism. His diction is much more low-key than Blanche Dubois's language, more familiar than the theatrical Mr. Williams'. The truthful, colloquial diction in Kelly's plays, like *The Show-off* (1924), resembles the realistic dialogue of Foote's own plays. Later, on November 21, 1977, after seeing *The Show-off*, Foote commented that the actors brought "a compassion" that was usually lacking (HFC). Foote liked *The Show-Off* and its natural dialogue.[8] Above all, Foote would have appreciated the designation "truthful," used by Burns Mantle in *Contemporary American Playwrights* to describe Kelly's plays.[9] Truthfulness was an ideal for Foote, and Kelly was looked upon as "truthful" because of his direct approach to the troubles in American lives and his condemnation of certain unsavory types, such as the self-centered wife seen in *Craig's Wife* (1925).

Foote returned to his hometown to work on his first full-length play, thus establishing a pattern that he would repeat for the rest of his career. He replenished his creative resources by seeing his family and friends. Like Faulkner, he had a hometown to revisit, but unlike that Mississippi writer, Foote did not resume full-time residence. On this occasion, at age twenty-four, Foote found that his two brothers, whom he remembered as boys, had become young men. He felt closer to Tom, the older, who soon followed him to New York, hoping to become an actor also. As a member of the Air Force, Tom was later killed on a flight over Germany in 1944, a tragedy from which Foote's family never fully recovered.

The youngest brother was John Speed, who did not share Foote's love of family tales. His passion was for country-and-western music. As a boy he would listen to his favorite singers on the radio for hours, tapping his foot and pretending to play a guitar. His son, Tom Brooks II, named after the dead brother, inherited the love of country-and-western music.

During Foote's stay at home for a couple of months in 1940, he completed *Texas Town,* which is replete with the life that Foote had known in Wharton. Foote played the part of Ray, thus assigning to himself the lead role, as he did in *Wharton Dance.* The gubernatorial campaign was the biggest news in Texas. W. Lee ("Pappy") O'Daniel, who had been elected governor in 1938, was running again. This flamboyant businessman, who made his money from a milling company in Fort Worth, had become well known for his radio program featuring the Light Crust Doughboys, a string band. "Pappy" enlivened his campaigns with its music. During his second campaign, this popular governor came to Wharton, singing songs like "Beautiful Texas" on the courthouse lawn. In *Texas Town,* Foote included much talk by the townspeople for and against the unnamed governor. In the late fall of 1940, Foote returned to New York with the completed manuscript.

Foote makes progress in his depiction of Wharton in *Texas Town.*[10] He includes actual facts about the governor's visit. Here Foote portrays more mature persons than the teenagers of *Wharton Dance* and examines a more pressing subject, the booming oil industry and its power to lure young people away from hometown moorings. Keeping up with local developments, Foote presents the impact of oil on the town. He also indicts the older generation for keeping the younger generation imprisoned in the plantation life of the past. He still sees his town in a negative light.

Foote's changing view of Wharton is indicated by the name he gave the town. In his first attempt at drama, he labeled it explicitly "Wharton." Then he dropped that name and in *Texas Town* did not identify it at all. He mentioned Houston but avoided the name "Wharton," showing that he wished to move away from literalness. In *Out of My House* he mentioned Houston, Dallas, and Texas, but again the actual setting was not named. Then in *Only the Heart* (1943) he called the town "Richmond," which is the name of a real town between Wharton and Houston. He named the town "Richmond" also in *The Chase* (1952). Finally when he wrote his one-acts for television in 1952–1953 he used the name "Harrison" and called his collection of these plays "Harrison, Texas." This name was taken from a once prosperous plantation community founded by Burr Albert Harrison, whose home was built in 1865.[11]

Like *Wharton Dance, Texas Town* protests against small-town provinciality. The overriding theme is the determination to escape the soul-destroying existence and find a new life elsewhere. Even though Foote does not name the place, we learn more about his objections to Wharton. The play was performed in the spring of 1941 by the American Actors Company under the direction of Mary Hunter at the Humphrey-Weidman Studio Theatre on Sixteenth Street in Greenwich Village. In this compelling play, which takes place in a present-day drugstore, Ray Case is the twenty-three-year-old protagonist, the same age as Foote. Ray has lost his job with the local oil company because he advised some "Bohunks" not to sell an oil lease on their land to Damon, an unprincipled buyer. Desperate to find work elsewhere, Ray accepts a hard but promising job with an oil crew in Baton Rouge. When his mother learns of his plans, she surreptitiously informs the employer, Mr. Reems, that her son would not be the man for that job.

Ray's girlfriend, Carrie, is torn between spending the rest of her days married to a local druggist or joining Ray in seeking a new life. She resolves this dilemma by asking Ray if it is right to stay and look up to liars and cheaters. "We've just begun to fight," she proclaims (p. 3-19), and implores him to learn about the new opportunities in oil and sulfur. Taking her advice, Ray decides in the end to move to Houston and to send for Carrie when he can. In the first version of the play, Ray is killed in an automobile accident as he flees the town.

Texas Town resembles other plays of this time in portraying the individual's search for himself, seen in Odets's *Awake and Sing!* (1935) and Anderson's *Winterset* (1935). In Odets's *Golden Boy* (1937), the young boxer wants to become a violinist but is killed in a car accident, like Foote's hero, as he flees the commercial pressures of the sport. Writers coming after 1940 took the same theme. It appears in Tennessee Williams's *The Glass Menagerie* (1945) as the autobiographical Tom Wingfield leaves home in search of a freer life for himself. Foote also selects this theme, giving it a more hopeful ending in the second version of *Texas Town,* as Ray does not die in a traffic accident. Foote is more successful in portraying the minor characters of *Texas Town* than in developing the central plot of flight. Several male and female characters have their own stories to contribute, which serve "as a kind of counterpoint" to the principal one, Foote notes ("Learning," p. 75). They present convincing reasons why Ray and Carrie should not remain in the stultifying town. Foote thought the urge to flee the small town was "a bit like [Sherwood Anderson's] *Winesburg, Ohio.*" [12]

Ray's confidant, Doc, is a failed physician who cut a patient so badly that he bled to death. Doc then descends to drinking in the back room of the drugstore. He begs Ray not to repeat his unfulfilled life and tells him there are people around who still have "faith and hope in this world." They seize the opportunities around them, instead of being kicked around (p. 1-29).

In *Texas Town,* Foote includes a woman from the decadent Old South, reminiscent of the old-fashioned sisters in Paul Green's *The House of Connelly* (1931). Mrs. Case, Ray's mother, cannot tolerate her son's desertion

of his hometown, saying that he belongs in the birthplace of his ancestors. Mrs. Case is supported by her other son, Tucker, who hates his
brother and his repudiation of his hometown. Tucker will stay where he
grew up. Taking the other side, Doc condemns Mrs. Case's disparagement of Ray to the oil crew boss, charging her with dooming him to a
miserable future.

Foote does his best writing with the comic old men who gather at the
drugstore daily. Here his talent for salty dialogue comes into its own. Pap
and Judge deride the campaign of the governor, whose rally they nevertheless attend. They enjoy the string band and its rendition of "Beautiful Texas," but not the political rhetoric. Judge says the governor promised to give the old folks a pension but did not. What is more, he says,
the governor backs the president's radical social program. Even though
Digger Neal, an old crony, likes the governor, Judge praises Digger for
standing up to his ruthless creditor, Damon, whose mortgage foreclosure
will force an old black man named Hannah to leave his home. The
"Southern white man" is getting kicked around by too many folks, Judge
says (p. 1-26). When Digger and Hannah hear that Judge has taken over
the mortgage, the two of them break down and cry together. Judge remembers fondly "the old days" of the town but does not welcome the
sights of New Wharton: "Paved streets, brick buildings, chamber of commerce . . ."—no more saloons (pp. 3-14 to 3-16). Judge and his cronies
furnish the spice of comic relief, which Foote handles to good effect.

The reception of *Texas Town* was favorable, for the most part. Foote was
overjoyed by the "marvelous" review in the *New York Times* by Brooks
Atkinson, the most respected critic of the New York theatre. Foote was
excited by Atkinson's accolade, "an engrossing picture of small town life"
("Learning," p. 77). The dean of New York theatre critics called Foote
"highly inventive" as a playwright but lacking as an actor in the lead part
of Ray.

Also attending the performance were Clifford Odets and Lee Strasberg, a director of the Group Theatre and an exponent of the Stanislavski
Method. Florence Odets, sister of the playwright, came backstage afterward to tell Foote that her brother and Strasberg had liked the play and
the actors ("Learning," p. 76).

Foote's encounter with a Broadway producer proved less encouraging.
Edward Choate, the representative of Shubert Brothers, took an option
on *Texas Town* and discussed it with Foote. The purpose of Choate's

meeting, according to Foote, was to impress on him the way to make a large sum of money. Choate suggested changes, which Foote attempted half-heartedly to execute. The results were disappointing to both Choate and Foote ("Learning," pp. 77–78).

Choate put his view in a different light when he wrote to Lynn Riggs, inviting him to collaborate. Choate said that Foote had been struggling to rewrite the play. In the first version, the hero dies at the end in a car accident, but since that lacked inevitability and seemed too melodramatic for this kind of play, Foote made the victory over "environment" purely a mental one that could have been arrived at any time. In the revision there is no climax because there is no vital incident building toward one. Choate added that unfortunately this defect had arisen after Foote had shown the actions of the minor characters "so successfully."[13] In any case, the beginning playwright was confronting the power of the commercial theatre as he embarked on his career. Foote could not escape this reality in the world of American theatre.

It was not long after the performance of *Texas Town* that Foote began another play. Because he now thought of himself as a playwright, he did not insert an acting part for himself in *Out of My House* (1942). He had received sufficient encouragement from knowledgeable judges and had experienced enough self-satisfaction to make this crucial shift in his plans.

Out of My House is a series of four one-acts, unified by a developing central character, Jack Weems.[14] The sequence of plays signals Foote's liking for this form, for he would choose it again in the nine-play *Orphans' Home Cycle* (composed 1974–1978) and a trilogy of one-acts, *The Roads to Home* (first presented 1982). Foote's third play was performed in January 1942, just after the United States entered World War II. It was performed by the American Actors Company at its studio on West Sixty-ninth Street under the direction of Mary Hunter. Foote helped stage the play but took no role.

Out of My House presents Foote again as a dramatist of social protest. This play in fact comes as close as he ever does to joining the movement of economic reform. Centering on persons who congregate at a sleazy restaurant, the plays are held together by an angry young man who yearns to leave his hometown. Jack Weems is a drifting habitué of Tell Miller's restaurant, whose main complaint is against the snobbish aristocracy of the little town. Jack, like others in the one-acts, is acutely class-conscious; he takes sides with the downtrodden but rising Bohunks, who he predicts will overthrow the old-time residents.

In the first one-act, "Night after Night," Jack defies the local aristoc-racy, such as it is, by defending the despised Bohunks. When a snobbish couple fresh from college ridicule Clara, the Bohemian waitress, for her clumsy dancing, Jack reprimands their rudeness. Tom Sloan, the con-temptuous male student, calls Jack "common boy," provoking him to draw a knife. Jack yells, "I'm as good as they are, Clara too" (p. 1-19).

The second play in *Out of My House*, ironically entitled *Celebration,* ap-pears to depart from the main plot, Jack Weems's protest against social wrong, but in fact advances it by giving stark evidence of the aristocracy's internecine feuding. The scene now shifts to the home of "Red" Mavis, who is celebrating the homecoming of her brother and sister from col-lege. The besotted Red is an overpowering personality, even if repulsive. Divorced from a man pronounced to be "trash," she can also celebrate with the Negroes on this June 19 because they both gained their free-dom on "Juneteenth," emancipation day for the slaves of Texas (p. 2-11).

In the fourth one-act, *Behold a Cry,* the hero delivers his protest against capitalism to his family. The plot is based on family legend, centered around two brothers who are loosely patterned after Foote's uncles. Back in his shabby home, Jack argues with his brother, Ford, and their mother. Ford condemns Jack's whole aimless life. Jack gives as good as he takes, saying that Ford will do anything for money, even marry banker Thomas's homely daughter. This kind of existence can't continue, Jack insists: "Stealing from each other . . . hating each other all for a little land, a little money." He denounces the old stock who can't pull out like the Ne-groes, nor stay and really work like the Bohunks. He's glad the Bohemi-ans will take over because "We deserve it" (p. 4-15).

Jack hears the answer to his anguished protest from a completely un-expected source, his grandfather. In Grandfather Robedaux's impassioned speech we get the best writing of the play. Banished from the shop he operated for fifty years by the heartless banker Peters, the old man makes his own protest against what has happened in this corner of Texas. People came from all over the South, wanting to escape aristocratic domination, but unfortunately they built their own aristocracy here. After a short while, the newcomers to Texas were "afraid to think of other men, afraid to be kind." These settlers were good men at first, but then they tried to hog it all. They were forced to live in their own hells or turn them into paradise. Robedaux claims to be glad they can't move anywhere else be-cause now they must make the best of what they have: "They have got to awake. They have got to see things as they are." Finally the old man enjoins Jack to carry his message to all. As confused and rambling as this "cry" is, it expresses the stirring idea of creating a new paradise in Texas because there is nowhere else to go.

The story of Jack Weems ends on a note of strong resolve. This dispirited man takes heart from the guidance of his grandfather. Thinking of those like himself who have lost their faith in a better life, he repeats Robedaux's rallying cry, "Your hunger is my hunger, your loneliness my loneliness" (p. 4-20). Convinced that he has not been wrong in condemning the selfish taking on "these five streets," he declares to the old man, "Your words have given me the strength to do." Next, he will deliver this message to his friends at Tell Miller's restaurant. Quietly approving, old Robedaux says, "From my house it has begun and there's no stopping it" (p. 4-21). The double meaning of the title, *Out of My House,* now becomes clear. It includes members of old Robedaux's house as well as those from the dramatist's store of memories of the Brooks household.

Behold a Cry significantly views Texas as a new place, breaking from the exclusive background of the South. Foote shares Jack Weems's vision of a promised land, a new society, where all residents can find a better life. With democratic fondness for people, he foresees this future for Texas.

This one-act reveals the influence of *Awake and Sing!* Odets's play, first performed in 1935, had received a successful restaging in 1937 by the Group Theatre. Though Foote disliked *Waiting for Lefty* because it was too overtly political, he praised *Awake and Sing!* He was "greatly moved" by its indictment of the capitalist system in human terms.[15] The clearest parallels between the plays of Odets and Foote are the two grandfathers who attack economic oppression and the grandsons' subsequent determination to reform the system.

The critical reception of *Out of My House,* produced at the Provincetown Playhouse in Greenwich Village, was greater than Foote had attracted heretofore. Mary Hunter in her foreword to *Only the Heart* stressed the human element in the work and indicated her dislike of such agit-prop as Odets's *Waiting for Lefty* (1935). She wrote that the American theatre should not be a medium for economic schemes but should "fuse elements of flesh and blood experience and thus open up the audience's own understanding." Hunter further reminded audiences of the play's focus on the South, which had been called the nation's number one cultural and economic problem by President Roosevelt.[16]

Under the heading "Those Southern Blues," Brooks Atkinson wrote that the first three acts lacked luster, saving his accolade for the finale:

"The play reaches a stunning last act. It is vibrant, glowing, and bitterly realistic" (*New York Times*, April 8, 1942).

Foote was especially pleased with Atkinson's praise of *Behold a Cry*. He has noted that because of Atkinson's earlier favorable recognition of *Texas Town*, all nine of the daily reviewers in New York attended the opening of *Out of My House*. Many were complimentary of *Behold a Cry*, but none so enthusiastically as Atkinson, who felt that "the last of the plays was the best writing I had done so far" ("Learning," p. 78).

Foote's plays for the American Actors Company are very important in his career because they record the solid apprenticeship of a playwright. From the composition of his first work, *Wharton Dance*, to *Out of My House*, Foote made steady and impressive progress. One notices real advancement from the improvisation of *Wharton Dance* to the dramatic skill of *Out of My House*. Furthermore, Foote deals with provocative themes, which show a penetrating mind investigating life in America of the late 1930s, a complex period at the end of the Depression. He picks up the vital social thought of Odets and adapts it to his own use.

In his first plays, Foote speaks in the voice of protest even if he does not espouse such controversial causes as unionism and the exoneration of radicals, like Odets and Anderson, respectively. In *Texas Town* there is a deeply felt aversion to the monotonous, frustrating life of the small town. Ray's angry tone adds a sharpness and aggressiveness to the language and family conflicts that would lessen in Foote's later writings, which are not permeated with the same tone of social protest. Jack Weems, another angry young man, despises the class hierarchy of his home region. He defends those, like the Bohunks, who are discriminated against by the corrupt aristocracy. Though we may not recognize this class in Texas as genuine aristocracy, since it lacks the age and distinguished background of Virginia gentry, it is an aristocracy nonetheless, based on the plantation economy, that feels superior to the rest of the community.

In his first plays, Foote proves that hope will animate his thought. The situations he dramatizes, like Jack Weems's disillusionment with the selfish grasping of his town, could end in despair, but they do not. Even though *Celebration* concludes with the Mavis family's hitting rock bottom, it is only the second play in the series. The next two give cause for hope, especially the last, in which the hero determines to correct the social and economic wrongs around him. Foote reflects the positive outlook of Odets, Anderson, Wilder, and Saroyan. Similarly, the optimistic Harold Clurman of the Group Theatre believed in the efficacy of cooperation;

he would not stage Paul Green's *The House of Connelly* (1930), which showed the failure of the New South, until the dramatist wrote a hopeful denouement. Mary Hunter disliked "darkness or morbidity" in contemporary plays.[17] Nor did Foote adopt the bleak pessimism of O'Neill, which had lost some of its appeal in the 1930s, a decade when the New Deal strengthened belief in a better tomorrow.

When Foote took the decisive step from acting to writing, he made portentous choices about what he would and what he would not write. Just as he had chosen to adopt the Stanislavski Method in his own acting, he chose methods, forms, and subject matter in his writing. These choices resulted from the tastes, preferences, and skills of a playwright with unshakable convictions. First choices are always important because they tend to persist, and the choices Foote made are no exception.

The new playwright showed a particular affinity for one-acts. They were popular when he first arrived in New York, and he himself acted in a number of them, such as *The Coggerers,* by Paul Vincent Carroll. The American Actors Company always included an evening of one-acts in its seasons. Foote has remarked that the three-act plays in which he acted lacked the force and impact of the shorter form, given by the unities of time, place, and action.[18] He was more successful with his one-acts, like *Behold a Cry* in *Out of My House,* than the more loosely crafted and longer *Texas Town.* The one-act would provide an ideal form for the television plays that Foote would later write. In a recent collection of his one-acts (1989), Foote has observed that they have enabled him to explore material he could not in the longer form.[19]

Besides dramatic form, Foote was making choices about favorite subjects, inevitably extracting them from his close observation of life in Wharton. The material that he chose and continued to treat with variations includes the problems of adolescents and small-town mores, like malicious gossip and its consequences and the need for secrecy in concealing behavior from parents. The individual's search for himself, seen in the struggles of Ray Case, reappears in the saga of the *Orphans' Home Cycle.* That series of nine plays centers on the search of Horace Robedaux, a self-made man, to make a life of his own after the death of his father and the abandonment by his mother. Foote also demonstrates a recurrent liking for the comedy of family inheritance. The two sisters of *The Girls,* the third one-act in *Out of My House,* present a ludicrous exercise in futility as they conspire to inherit their rich aunt's estate.

As Foote looked for the raw material of his plays among his closest relatives, he made choices also. He soon identified the lives with the most dramatic potential. Although there are suggestions that the heroes of *Wharton Dance, Texas Town,* and *Out of My House* are semiautobiographical, since they are approximately Foote's age and, like him, decide to leave home, this playwright is not inclined toward dramatizing his own personal life. He does not have the autobiographical bent of O'Neill. Like other dramatists, rather than the familiar autobiographical novelists, Foote is interested in others, people whom he knows intimately but can observe objectively as other human beings, like actors on a stage. The family configuration that is most noticeable consists of a widowed mother who is anxious about her sons in *Texas Town* and *Behold a Cry.* It corresponds closely to the family of Grandmother Brooks, who was a widow with three troubled sons. The selection of the unusual name "Robedaux," which was the maiden name of Foote's paternal great-grandmother, Elizabeth Robedaux Foote, underlines the use of close kindred here. It should be noted that Grandmother Brooks's father, like Grandfather Robedaux in the play, continued to live in her home after Mr. Brooks died in 1925. The problems of the Brooks household—what was to become of the three sons, the interaction of the people living there, and the inheritance of Mr. Brooks's large estate—provide rich material for plots and thought. Foote's skillful modification of this material to suit his dramatic purposes indicated that he would find his best material for character study among his closest kindred and that he would in time use his own father and mother as models for the central characters of the *Orphans' Home Cycle.* He would transform the real persons, without forgetting the riddles of their lives.

By 1942, Foote had joined the circle of young, aspiring playwrights in New York, which included Tennessee Williams. Foote had benefited from the sponsorship of a vigorous acting company, discovered what he could write plays about—his sector of America—and received critical encouragement from Brooks Atkinson, the leading drama critic. Now it was time to move from the sheltered playhouses off Broadway to the glittering theatres on Broadway.

4

TEXAS PLAYWRIGHT ON BROADWAY

AND TENNESSEE WILLIAMS

WITH his recognition as a new playwright, Foote set his sights on Broadway. It was the great age of the New York theatre from 1945 to 1960, when the most influential voices were Tennessee Williams and Arthur Miller. The theatre was highly competitive but receptive to new talents. Except for three years of writing for television, 1950 – 1953, Foote entered unreservedly the contest for Broadway success from 1944 to 1954. It would be the period of his most intense participation in the Broadway theatre, always his destination. In the company of serious playwrights, he adapted to changing styles while preserving his own individual voice. He changed from the prewar socially conscious drama of Clifford Odets to the personal drama of Tennessee Williams, focusing on the emotionally crippled of society who made their separate peace, which was realistic but far short of perfect. At the same time, Foote joined the focus on the personal, typified by *The Glass Menagerie,* but he steered clear of the po-litical protest of Arthur Miller, who carried on the tradition of Odets. Foote's special contribution was his application of the inner problem to the life of Wharton. This specialization enabled him to speak originally about the American scene.

In his first full-length plays, Foote had joined the social protest move-ment. This type of play was not congenial to Foote, as can be seen in the indigenous regional material of his hometown. He also showed a pen-chant for the individual's search for himself seen in *Only the Heart* (1944) and would turn further in that direction. This new trend concentrated on those crippled by destructive blows in childhood or by hostile soci-ety. Modern life was hard, and individuals had to adjust the best that they could. In plays by Inge, ordinary people found a way to endure. In *The*

Chase (1952), *The Trip to Bountiful* (1953), television one-acts, and *The Traveling Lady* (1954), Foote wrote moving plays about persons beaten down by emotional problems.

Foote took the momentous step to Broadway with *Only the Heart* (1944), his third full-length play and the last composed for the American Actors Company. He began writing it in the summer of 1942 while working as an elevator operator in a Park Avenue apartment building. It was first entitled "Mamie Borden" after the leading character, but the actress who was sought for the part, Hilda Vaughn, felt that the title would be confused with the murder case of Lizzie Borden, which was the basis for *Nine Pine Street,* a popular play of the 1933–1934 season. Vaughn suggested "Only the Heart," taken from a poem by Heinrich Heine: "They flourish and flourish from year to year / And only the heart is withered and sere."[1] Despite Foote's opinion that the new title was "much too flowery" and had nothing to do with the play, he acquiesced because he wanted her for the part ("Learning," p. 82). On December 6, 1942, this play opened at the Provincetown Theatre, which had been rented for two weeks. Because the American Actors Company had run short of funds, it could not pay the actors or playwright.

The off-Broadway tryout of *Only the Heart* earned some critical praise from Lewis Nichols of the *New York Times* and others. Jacques Therie, who introduced himself to Foote as the George Kaufman of Paris, wanted to transfer the play to Broadway. At Therie's invitation, Foote took the script to Hollywood, where he was unfavorably impressed by screenwriters like Billy Wilder, who contributed to the revision. Foote was not convinced that the play was improved. He later remarked, "Whatever raw power it originally had was diluted."[2]

With the assistance of Helen Thompson, who was a fund-raiser for the Group Theatre, *Only the Heart* opened at the Bijou Theatre on April 4, 1944. Among the list of illustrious angels were Katharine Cornell, Howard Lindsay, Eva Le Galienne, Thornton Wilder, James T. Farrell, John Gassner, and Lynn Riggs. It had a run of six weeks, through the generosity of one backer. Foote had to agree to take no royalties. In the new version of the play, the time was changed from 1934 to 1921. Because Pauline Lord, an actress highly admired by Foote, did not believe the role of Mamie was right for her, it was played by June Walker, a well-known comedienne. Mildred Dunnock, who had acted with the American Actors Company and was to appear frequently in Foote's plays, played the part of Mamie's sister.

Only the Heart, like *Texas Town,* also tells the story of an individual's search for herself through fleeing the confinement of small-town life.[3] Julia Borden leaves Richmond, Texas, and begins a new life in Houston. She is accompanied by her husband, Albert, who chooses love for his wife over loyalty to his mother-in-law. This play, like the drama of Ray Case in *Texas Town,* ends with hope for a better life. Despite the importance of the young couple, the play is dominated by the mother, Mamie Borden, a new woman of Texas. It is her play. This comic oil speculator gives the play its principal interest. She had been anticipated in *Texas Town* by a comic character, also named Mamie, who proudly reported her oil strike to women in the drugstore.

In *Only the Heart,* Mamie provides the humor, which is considerable, given that she is onstage almost continually. Her speech is country Texas and contains the kind of dry humor that Foote would continue to cultivate. Mamie allows that "I reckon we could stand anything if we had a few oil wells" (p. 29), and when her daughter Julia becomes engaged, Mamie tells Julia's sister that Julia is no longer a baby: "Nope. We got a grown woman on our hands, India" (p. 27).

In the following passage, Mamie kibitzes as Julia gives her future husband a lesson in dancing. These lines provide a sample of her characteristic language, which makes generous use of ludicrous comparisons in the tradition of southwestern humor. Like George Kelly, Foote writes vernacular dialogue with ample portions of earthy humor.

> Mamie. He just don't like it. He just don't. Like me, don't like it. You can tell by the expression on his face.
> Julia. Everybody's so awkward at first. Isn't that so, Auntie?
> India. Yes. It is.
> Mamie. I declare—look at Albert. (She laughs.) He looks like he's being drug to the firing squad . . . don't look so pained, son.
> Julia. You're doing fine, Albert.
> Mamie. You're like me, Albert. You got no more sense of rhythm than an old horse. (pp. 27–28)

Only the Heart gives Foote a chance to develop his humorous bent. It would have been a great loss if he had not seasoned his plays with this sense of humor. Compared with his contemporaries, only Williams shows an equal gift for idiomatically humorous lines.

The play ends happily as the daughter asserts her independence of the overbearing mother, choosing not to live a life enslaved to her mother's money. As a businesswoman who cares only for financial success but wishes to become closer to her daughter, Mamie resembles Regina of *The Little Foxes,* which had played successfully in 1939. Appropriately in 1921, rather than 1900, the woman with a talent for business has been able to engage in a life of business. This businesswoman manages cotton farms, speculates in oil, and takes pleasure in all her business enterprises.

The motif of oil fever is one that reappears in Foote's plays, notably *The Oil Well* (1953). Unlike in *The Oil Well,* in *Only the Heart* there is a strike and Mamie can look forward to astronomical wealth therefrom. Foote, however, thinks that the dream of oil, whether realized or not, is a will-o'-the-wisp. The oil money does not bring Mamie happiness. As the poem by Heinrich Heine states, material prosperity abounds; "only the heart is withered and sere."

Only the Heart fiercely attacks the obsession with work, a theme that Foote repeats in later plays, like *The Old Beginning* (1952). When India talks about the new belief in peace forever after World War I, Mamie retorts that none of these foolish ideas are needed. "There's one idea that's good enough," Mamie says, "and it's been in the world long as I can remember. Work and tend to your own business" (pp. 37–38).

Mamie is a materialist, unashamedly interested in accumulating more and more possessions. She enunciates her philosophy openly to her idle husband, Mr. Borden. Referring to the prosperous times after World War I, she tells him that all are making money as fast they can. "I'm gonna see that Julia gets all there is to get," she says. "Things you can see and touch and feel, things that are there, ready to take care of you no matter what your husband does, or what happens" (p. 31). Despite the time of the play after World War I, this play has relevance to World War II, when it was produced. Like all alert playwrights, Foote has one eye on the interests of contemporary theatregoers. Mr. Borden says that, during the war, people talked of "cooperation" and doing differently if they were spared, but now they are "grabbing" again (p. 32). Like Wilder in *The Skin of Our Teeth,* performed during World War II, Foote is asking people to remember afterward their resolutions made during the war.

Mamie represents a narrow, provincial attitude found in Texas. She dislikes a college education and praises the Ku Klux Klan's punitive actions against women like her husband's Bohemian mistress (who was black in the first version). Revealing its power in the Texas of 1921, the Klan runs her husband's mistress out of town.

The unmarried sister, India, typifies the woman who has been prevented from marrying her sweetheart. In India's case she becomes a schoolteacher, sings songs like "Oh, Promise Me" (p. 27), and remains bitter because of her disappointment in losing the man she loved. He was considered worthless by Mamie, who opposed the marriage. India, however, cannot bring herself to condemn the drunken, broken man that her lover has become. India is a stereotype of the 1930s, 1940s, and 1950s who appears in O'Neill's *Ah, Wilderness* (1933) and Inge's *Picnic* (1953). Julia, on the other hand, has a chance for a happier life since she rejects her mother's domination, leaving home to make her own life.

The best feature of this play is the indigenous material. Mamie is a genuine Texas type: the humorous, vigorous woman who speaks her own mind about the need for oil money and admits her own loneliness. Her diction is natural and authentic. Telling Julia and Albert she wants them to get married, she exclaims frankly: "Nothing would make your old mama happier" (p. 18). Furthermore, she preserves her optimistic spirit. She does not look with blank, despairing eyes when all have left her. Instead, she thinks about the oil strike. She has money, which is her "happiness" (p. 72), and she will resume her work, which is both her salvation and her curse. The spirit of this woman remains alive.

Foote makes an advance as a Texas playwright by his creation of Mamie Borden. Mamie is unforgettably Texan with her country diction, lust for oil, dislike of higher education, and crass materialism. She represents the Texas businesswoman post–World War I. To capture Texas character, the writer must bring to life an unmistakable type. Foote does so with the bossy Mamie of Richmond, Texas.

This was Foote's first Broadway play. The critical reception of *Only the Heart* was mostly negative. The dislike went from tepid to harsh as the play moved from the Provincetown Playhouse in 1942 to the Bijou Theatre in 1944. Regarding the first production, Lewis Nichols called Foote "the minnesinger" of "Texas morals, attitudes, and family life" (*New York Times,* December 7, 1942). When Nichols reviewed *Only the Heart* on Broadway, he had nothing good to say. The company had an advantage in its less formal production by not trying to be too professional, which it lost by moving uptown. Nichols censured the play for being "talky, old fashioned, and dull" (*New York Times,* April 5, 1944). Wretta Waldorf (*New York Post,* April 5, 1944) noticed that in the

Provincetown Theatre version, Borden's mistress was a Negro, which made the Klan more plausible.

Of six reviews on April 5, 1944, only two could be called favorable. Burton Rascoe of the *New York World-Telegram* said that young people could be saved from many a disaster by attending the performance. He called the play "absorbingly interesting and satisfying." Ward Morehouse of the same paper said Foote revealed a talent for both construction and characterization. Some critics compared Mamie Borden to the domineering mother in Sidney Howard's *The Silver Cord,* in which the bloodsucking matriarch wrecks the lives of her two sons. Other evaluations were strongly negative. Howard Barnes of the *New York Herald Tribune* called *Only the Heart* "a dreary domestic drama." John Chapman of the *New York Daily News* said that not since Tallulah Bankhead in *The Little Foxes* had he seen a woman he would so like to "bat down." Not amused by June Walker's dialect, he said she could be from "Texas, Iowa, or the Erie Canal." As usual, Foote had his admirers, but not enough to make the play a hit. Detractors canceled the favorable reviews.

Only the Heart, nevertheless, brings to the forefront some fresh Texas flavor. Mary Hunter, who directed the play, wrote that "in southern life the observer can find in the sharpest focus the conflicts in our social patterns that affect us all." She believed that the character of Mamie could be drawn more sharply because of her "southernness." There is "the power of personal recognition in the turn of every phrase, in the flavorsome humor," she wrote. Hunter stressed the positive qualities: "The atmosphere throughout the play is found through the illumination and pointing up of the familiar, never through darkness or morbidity."[4] Foote, sharing Hunter's optimism, shows in his plays a hopeful viewpoint.

It must be said that Foote's first venture onto Broadway ended unsuccessfully. The climax of his writing for the American Actors Company amounted to a setback in his career, but the newcomer had showed originality in subject matter. He was an artist who knew his own mind, pointing the way to an unhackneyed investigation of Texas manners.

When Foote was writing plays for the American Actors Company, he became acquainted with Tennessee Williams, who exercised a constructive influence on the plays that Foote would subsequently compose. Williams had received the Group Theatre Award in 1939 for *American Blues.* He brought his play *You Touched Me!,* coauthored with Donald Windham, to Foote's company, seeking a production. Though this never materialized, Mary Hunter directed one of Williams's one-acts, along with others by Paul Green and Thornton Wilder, in 1943. Williams was gaining a reputation for his sensitive vignettes of troubled individuals existing on the fringe of society. Foote thinks that Williams has written some of the most effective one-acts ever performed in the theatre.[5]

Foote's contact with Williams intensified from 1943 to 1945, marked by some interesting developments. When Foote came to Hollywood in July 1943, he saw a great deal of Williams. At this time both men were learning the craft of playwriting. In a letter from St. Louis dated April 5, 1943, Williams had suggested that they cooperate while in Hollywood. Williams wanted their workplace to be "in the vicinity of a summer playhouse and a beach and let us determine to work on one big problem (that is, one each) and not a lot of little pieces so that when the summer is over we shall have something significant completed." They could also edit each other's work. "It would be an interesting experiment to supervise the other's revisions," Williams suggested. "I think good professional criticism is half the battle—and I have never really had it."[6] This shows that Williams respected Foote's plays sufficiently to seek Foote's advice on dramatic composition. Later Williams would cooperate in such a fashion with Carson McCullers on Nantucket Island in 1946. In the evening each read aloud to the other the day's work.[7]

On April 24, 1943, Williams offered to criticize a play of Foote's when he returned to New York from St. Louis. He asked Foote: "Are you going to let me see 'Michael Strahan' when I return?" Williams wrote that he was "very anxious" to see what Foote had done with it: "I have great faith in the ultimate script and think you should devote the summer to it if it isn't right yet." Williams probably refers to "Marcus Strachan," listed as "Never Produced Script" in the McJunkin Inventory (HFC).

In the same letter, written with his characteristic wit, Williams stressed his energetic support of the American Actors Company, which he hoped would fill the crying need in New York for an "art theatre." Regarding the conflict between art and commercialism that Foote had experienced with Edward Choate, Williams came down hard in favor of art, which would have influenced Foote at this formative time of his career when he was turning over in his mind the twin appeals of art and commercialism. Williams wrote, "I wish you could think of a title that would mean 'Art Theatre,' as distinguished from commercial, without saying exactly 'Art Theatre.' The most palpable and discouraging fact in the New York theatre is that no art theatre is in existence at the present time. You promise to establish one and you have already taken notable steps in that direction—why not let the emphasis be modestly but plainly focused on that object and accomplishment." In effect Williams was saying to keep the same name that the company had established but to preserve art as the guiding light, not the almighty dollar. In a letter to Donald Windham, Williams used the name "Playwrights Company" instead of American Actors Company.[8] Williams in his forthcoming plays would keep sight of art while benefiting as well from commercial success, a combination that Foote would not realize.

Always keeping his eye on the big picture, Williams imparted to Foote in the same letter his advice about the theatrical scene. Looking to the future, he advised him to keep "your ear to the ground and concentrate on honesty till you know what is coming." Williams believed that the prospects for a new theatre after the war were excellent: "We must remember that a new theatre is coming after the war with a completely new criticism, thank God. The singular figures always stand a good chance when there are sweeping changes" (HFC, April 24, 1943). Williams must have been thinking of himself. It was a prediction proven true. In retrospect it can be seen that Williams had in mind "a new plastic theatre," combining the screen, music, and lighting, as he wrote in his notes to *The Glass Menagerie,* defining the inner drama.[9]

In a letter to Donald Windham, Williams reported that Foote had arrived on the coast to work on *Only the Heart.* Williams complained that he had had Foote on his hands "for the last 24 hours." He was bathed "in sweetness and light which has such a withering effect upon my spirit," Williams reported. "But I bore up bravely realizing that he probably believes in his sentiments more than I do."[10] Williams experienced mixed feelings toward the man who not only had liked his one-acts but also had helped him find short-term employment as an elevator operator in 1942 when Foote himself also operated an elevator.[11] Williams could not fail to recognize Foote's "niceness however one is capable of responding inwardly." But he "couldn't bear it more than one night." Williams's most crushing verdict after one more day was "Horton is more like a pineapple ice-cream soda than ever."[12]

Neither did Williams care for *Only the Heart,* which was in competition with *You Touched Me!* for production by Mary Hunter's company. He preferred Mary Hunter to Margo Jones as the director for *You Touched Me!* because "Mary is the most intelligent woman I have ever met."[13] He hoped that Mary Hunter would stage *You Touched Me!* but believed that she favored Foote's play. This clash caused Williams to express his distaste for Foote's ingenuousness. He wrote Audrey Wood, his literary agent, about Foote: "It was not very smart of me to introduce him to Margo, for he is just as ingenuous as she is and I think he is much closer to her idea of a playwright. I regard Mr. Foote with a somewhat uncharitable reserve." [14] In fact Williams found his ingenuousness "spurious." [15] Here the paranoid Williams clearly misjudged Foote, who later stated that he was truly "in awe of Tennessee" at this time and "had no idea he was resentful." [16] Williams had a basis for noticing Hunter's fondness for Foote, because they had been collaborating for some time. As it turned out, Hunter did choose to produce *Only the Heart* on Broadway in 1944, which delayed any production of *You Touched Me!* until 1945. After Mary Hunter called Williams to apologize for not getting his play on the boards, Williams informed Windham that "where they really fell down" was putting on *Only the Heart* in the first place when everyone knew it had no chance of success. [17]

The incompatibility of Williams and Foote throws light on the writing style of the latter and explains why Williams had the success on Broadway that Foote failed to achieve. For Williams, Foote's ingenuousness was alienating. The young man from Texas came across as naive and artless to Williams, a disillusioned observer of human nature. Williams's mordant sense of humor and witty speech are the antithesis of Foote's sincerity and honesty. The latter's folksy manner was the opposite of the former's sophistication, which would prove congenial to the taste of a metropolitan audience accustomed to the witty chatter of Noel Coward's *Private Lives* (1931) and the debunking jabs of Robert E. Sherwood's *Idiot's Delight* (1936). The contrast between a sharp-tongued observer of social misfits and an advocate of warmhearted ties, expressed in unadorned, plain vernacular, identified a quality in Foote that would frustrate his advancement on Broadway.

As for Foote's appraisal of Tennessee Williams's drama, Foote's preference was clearly for *The Glass Menagerie,* which captured not only the conflicts but also the attachments within a family. Foote remarked later that Williams's *The Glass Menagerie* was his favorite; Foote looked at this play in his own way, perceiving a virtue in Amanda Wingfield not appreciated by critics. When he saw Pauline Lord take the part, Foote noted Amanda's attempt "to bring order and meaning into the Wingfield lives" ("Learning," p. 84). The plays that followed Williams's first success were "a little overwrought for my taste," Foote remarked.[18] He was referring to the series initiated by *A Streetcar Named Desire* (1947), with its shrill language and high-pitched emotion. On the other hand, Foote called the early one-acts of Williams the most effective one-acts ever written.[19] Foote was an admirer of Williams's first dramatic writings, from which he learned much.

While in St. Louis visiting his mother and Dakin grandparents, Williams wrote Foote on April 24, 1943, about his work on the script that would eventually become *The Glass Menagerie:* "I have been working with tigerish fury on 'The Gentleman Caller,' it has become a fully-developed play almost of the usual length. It has at least one part in it for you and maybe two, if you can imagine such a thing" (HFC). Williams refers to the two male parts of Tom Wingfield and the youthful Jim O'Connor.

Foote followed the progress of *The Glass Menagerie* very closely. He recalls: "Tennessee gave it to me to read. He thought the part of Tom was right for me. . . . I said I was no longer acting but I was directing at the Neighborhood Playhouse and would very much like to do the last section of the play with The Gentleman Caller, as I felt I could not adequately cast the mother."[20] He staged only the candlelight scene. Williams gave Foote permission, but two days before the scene was to be performed, someone told Williams how much he had liked the rehearsal. With a stricken look on his face, Williams replied, "I've just sold the play to Eddie Dowling" ("Learning," p. 86). Foote recalls that Williams nevertheless "allowed me to continue and present my production of The Gentleman Caller section of the play."[21] Foote staged this excerpt in 1944 before the Chicago premiere on December 26, 1944. At the premier of *The Glass Menagerie* in New York on Saturday, March 31, 1945, Williams importuned Eddie Dowling to supply Foote with one house seat.[22] From that time on the contacts between the suddenly successful Williams and the still struggling Foote ended. After Foote moved to Washington in 1945, he chose to direct a play by Williams at the King-Smith School.

The impact of Williams's new type of play on Foote's own dramatic composition was long-lasting. Williams sought to understand "the fugitive kind" and to portray them with compassion. Here was the kind of drama inherently appealing to Foote. On the minus side, Foote would never attain the poetry of Williams's language, the brilliance of his symbolism, or the stunning drama of his big scenes.

During the six years that Foote belonged to the American Actors Company, 1939–1945, he formed a close association with leading figures in the world of dance. Foote met Agnes de Mille, a major artist, in 1939, when the company was rehearsing her *American Legend*. From his acquaintance with de Mille, Doris Humphrey, Valerie Bettis, and Martha Graham, he absorbed their seriousness of purpose. He has commented: "Certainly at this period of dance, there were no playwrights being produced that could equal the seriousness of purpose and the storytelling talents of Graham, Humphrey, and [Anthony] Tudor" ("Learning," p. 80).

Out of Foote's meetings with dancers emerged several works. In April 1944 he composed "Daisy Lee" for Valerie Bettis and Bernardo Segall, which was performed at the 92nd Street UMHA. The next year he codirected "The Lonely" with Martha Graham and wrote another more realistic piece for dance, "Good-bye to Richmond," both of which were given at the Neighborhood Playhouse. In 1943, Foote read *The Desperate Heart,* a poem accompanied by the dancing of Valerie Bettis very successfully at dance recitals throughout the city ("Learning," p. 80).

In this dynamic time, dancers were enchanted by the avant-garde seen in the modern dance of Martha Graham. Valerie Bettis was a strong proponent of the nonrealistic theatre and dance. The experimentalist John Cage composed music for her dances. Though Foote was open-minded in approaching the nonrealistic preference of modern dance, in retrospect it is clear that he leaned toward the realistic mode and away from experimental techniques. Foote notes that in watching the anguish of Martha Graham's art, he and others found the less subjective manner of Doris Humphrey more accessible ("Learning," p. 79). Foote made use of his experience with music and dance in his own way. It can be seen in the hymns and popular songs sung by many characters in the *Orphans' Home Cycle.* The liking for dance appears also in *The Dancers* (1956) and in glimpses of couples dancing, as they pass wraithlike by the characters of *Courtship.* Texas composer Carol Hill wrote the music and lyrics for *The Dancers* (HFC, November 21, 1977).

After the American Actors Company disbanded, Foote was left without a place to perform his plays. "It was a lonely feeling," he recalls ("Learning," p. 88). When *Only the Heart* closed in 1944, he turned from Broadway to teaching. Sanford Meisner asked him to teach the second-year acting students at the Neighborhood Playhouse Theatre, which, like the Pasadena Playhouse, combined training in acting and production of plays. Foote was commissioned to compose one-acts combining the three disciplines of the school: acting, dancing, and music. He wrote *Miss Lou, The Lonely,* and *Good-bye to Richmond.* With the choreographic assistance of Martha Graham, these pieces were produced at the Neighborhood Playhouse in 1945.

At this time Foote continued to receive inspiration from Martha Graham. The same could not be said for the advice he received from a very successful Broadway director. Howard Lindsay, at his townhouse in the Village, counseled the aspiring playwright to follow his example. At a tryout of one of his plays, Lindsay did not look at the actors, but rather at the audience to detect boredom. What's more, he never put people in his plays that "you wouldn't care to entertain in your own living room" ("Learning," pp. 87–88). The conflict between artistic and commercial goals was a subject that Foote could not escape.

While teaching at the Neighborhood Playhouse, Foote had the good fortune to meet his future wife, who became his friend, business assistant, and lifelong companion. Their meeting was fortuitous. Because teaching did not supply adequate funds, Foote took a job managing the Doubleday Bookstore in Pennsylvania Station. Lillian Vallish, a student at Radcliffe College, was taking a semester off to work in New York. Foote hired her to work with him on the night shift. "She loved writing and books, and we soon became inseparable," he observes ("Learning," p. 87). After her graduation, the young couple was married June 3, 1945. Lucy Kroll preserved a clipping from the Wharton newspaper, which reported that Foote and "Miss Lillian Vallish of Mount Carmel, Pennsylvania, were united in a quiet marriage ceremony, June 3 in New York" and that "a wedding reception was held at the home of Mrs. Valerie Bettis of Dallas and New York." [23] Among congratulations were notes from Nan Outlar and Margo Jones, who wrote that she was glad Foote got married (HFC, July 1, 1945). The union was indeed a happy one, which lasted until Lillian died in 1992. They became the parents of four children: Barbara Hallie (born March 31, 1950); Albert Horton III (November 7, 1952); Walter Vallish (December 5, 1955); and Daisy Brooks (July 3, 1959).

At this time in his career, Foote was looking for further guidance in composing plays about Texas. He had learned that he did not want to continue in the way of Odets's drama of social protest. Foote's models would be George Kelly's plays of ordinary Americans and Tennessee

Williams's inner emotional dramas. In the fiction of Katherine Anne Porter he discovered a way to approach his Texas background. This accomplished writer from Central Texas, who was twenty-five years Foote's senior, wrote about an older Texas in her collection of three short novels, *Pale Horse, Pale Rider*, first published in 1939. Among writers of Texas whom Foote eschewed was the popular preserver of Texas legends, J. Frank Dobie, of whom Foote has said that reading about his Texas is like reading about a foreign country.[24] Porter, however, took pains to tell her stories in a careful, artistic style; she did not perpetuate the clichés of romantic cattle drivers in Texas, as did Dobie, but rather gave her personal interpretation of the life she had known, seeing in it universal truth. In Porter, Foote found a Texas writer who had written according to the highest literary standards. Born and bred in Texas, she showed how to be an artist and an authentic Texan as well. Porter could teach him about creating art.

Foote's wife, Lillian, introduced him to Porter's writings before they left New York in 1945. At her prompting, he read *Pale Horse, Pale Rider* and was delighted with it. He has commented: "It had a profound and lasting effect on me. Here it seemed to me was a supreme prose stylist, yet with no trace of artifice. No local colorist and not sentimental about the past and yet using the past and the region of her birth to create her imagined world" ("Learning," p. 90).

Foote decided not to take the direction of Lynn Riggs and Paul Green but rather to take that of Porter. The American Actors Company had been devoted to the plays of Riggs and Green and had performed Riggs's *Sump'n Like Wings* and Green's *Shroud My Body Down*, in which Foote played a part. Foote, however, did not wish to be "a regionalist" in the style of Riggs and Green. Their dependence on dialect and quaintness was "defeating" in Foote's view and "limited them terribly." At this time Foote began to discover Porter and felt that hers was much more the direction he wanted to take.[25]

What Foote admires most in Porter's writing is her truthfulness about the past and her region. He has singled out for praise "Old Mortality," the first novelette in *Pale Horse, Pale Rider*. She "does not take sides, does not tip the scales, but tries to be truthful."[26] Foote stresses Porter's truthfulness also in "Noon Wine," the second story in *Pale Horse, Pale Rider*. Porter has described how she used the sources for this story in an introductory essay printed in Brooks and Warren's *Understanding Fiction*.[27]

According to Foote, she gets the facts and then runs them through her imagination, but she always tries to be "truthful." [28]

William Humphrey and William Goyen, like Foote, carried on Porter's truthful exploration of Texas culture, according to Don Graham. An important critic of Texas literature, Graham discusses Porter's treatment of class. Graham says that if Texas writing was about anything it was about class. Mr. Thompson in "Noon Wine" can't stand "low-down white trash families." In this story Porter writes one of the best delineations of class structure in the South, Graham states. Porter did not repeat the clichés that Zane Grey and others did about Texas. [29]

In the case of "Katherine Anne," as Foote calls her, the influence has been long and comprehensive. She is the author that he harks back to most often in naming influences. Only recently, some forty-seven years after first reading *Pale Horse, Pale Rider,* he terms her "the great influence on me." [30] Foote values her detached view of the past, which he strives for in the personal dramatizations of his family. Like Porter, he can see those individuals with irony, since they themselves lack self-knowledge. He is too much an admirer of truth to wax sentimental about the past. After internalizing Porter's spirit, Foote turned more noticeably to his own personal past. This change appeared in his next plays, those written for television, and in later ones, those in the *Orphans' Home Cycle.*

In this interlude, after *Only the Heart* had closed and Foote was marking time, he continued his close acquaintance with Stark Young, who corresponded with Foote about a new play on March 1, 1946. Young also suggested to Foote that he could lecture at the King-Smith School in Washington (HFC, letter dated July 15, 1946).

Following his work at the Neighborhood Playhouse, Foote accepted an offer to administer another acting school in Washington, D.C. His friends Valerie Bettis and Bernardo Segall, who were moving to the King-Smith School there, made him the proposition. He agreed if allowed to use the school's theatre to perform his plays. Along with his wife and Vincent Donehue, a director-friend future collaborator on television, Foote undertook the full-time running of this school and the formation of its theatre for the next four years, 1945–1949.

Foote found his stay at King-Smith to be fruitful. As he repeatedly showed during his career, he wished to get away from the commercial pressures of New York periodically. These breaks allowed him to renew his creative energies and make plans more dispassionately for his development as a playwright. In Washington, he directed plays by Lorca, Sartre, Ibsen, Chekhov, Synge, and Williams, an impressive list of the best modern playwrights who gave him a solid grounding in the greatest drama of the twentieth century. Additionally, Foote wrote four one-acts, which were performed at the school theatre. These included *Homecoming,* later given off-Broadway, and *The Return,* the precursor of a dramatic monologue, *In a Coffin in Egypt* (1980). The duties of teaching, directing, and running a theatre, however, left little time for completing full-length plays. In 1949, Foote returned to New York because he felt the urge to resume his professional career on Broadway.

CHAPTER

5

RETURN TO BROADWAY: *THE CHASE*

BACK in New York, Foote benefited from the services of his literary agent, Lucy Kroll, who became a close friend. Their correspondence, which began in the 1950s and extended throughout his career, is
the best source for following chronologically his career as a playwright.
On March 21, 1956, Kroll stated that she had been involved in "Horton's
professional life" for "some twenty years" (HFC).

Lucy Rosengardt Kroll graduated in 1933 from Hunter College and in
1934 married Nathan Kroll, musician and film producer. She served as
coproducer of the American Actors Company from 1937 to 1944 and as
literary agent for Warner Brothers Studios from 1942 to 1944. After teaching drama for two years at Hunter College (1944–1945), she established
the Lucy Kroll Agency in 1945.[1] Her clients included Horton Foote, actress Kim Stanley, and others. She corresponded with Bette Davis and
Helen Hayes, whose letters she sent to Foote. Kroll died in 1997.[2]

With renewed purpose, Foote was ready to attempt Broadway for a second time with *The Chase* (performed 1952), a psychological drama about
a Texas sheriff.[3] Having worked on the play at his wife's family home in
the quiet countryside of Pennsylvania, he had copyrighted it as an un-
published dramatic composition in 1948. He entered it in a playwriting
contest. One of the judges, Herman Shumlin, said he would have no
trouble winning, but Shumlin wanted Foote to withdraw it for Shumlin
to produce. Foote granted this request, but Shumlin never "got around
to it," Foote recalls.[4] After revision, *The Chase* opened on April 15, 1952,
at the Playhouse Theatre on Forty-eighth Street. Indicating the outstanding talent that Foote could now attract, this production starred John
Hodiak, an exciting newcomer to the movies, and Kim Stanley, an ex-

cellent actress and close acquaintance from Texas. José Ferrer, whose acting and directing talents were acclaimed, directed.

Before the opening night of *The Chase,* Foote wrote an article entitled
"Richmond, U.S.A." for the *New York Times,* giving theatregoers a fore-
taste of the play (April 13, 1952). Again he had used the setting of Richmond, a town north of Wharton. In the play it is located in "Jackson
County," which is in fact to the south of his home county.

Foote comes closer to the theme of *The Chase* when he discusses how
a heartless society can crush the emotional life of its members. He reviews the evolution of that society. In his writing, he has concentrated
on "the problems of the upper and middle class and old land-holding
aristocracy." He saw the last of the aristocracy go when he was a child.
The middle class now reigns supreme—"their thinking, their tastes, their
culture." They seldom meet "the tenant farmers, the servants, the day laborers," who surround and serve them. But they do meet in *The Chase,*
"brought together by the dehumanization of one man, Bubber Reeves,
and a sheriff struggling to escape dehumanization."[5] Even though the
sociological tone harks back to the class warfare in *Out of My House,* this
play concentrates on the inner emotions of the two central figures, the
fugitive from justice and his compassionate pursuer, the sheriff.

Despite the local setting, Foote enlarges the ramifications of the action. He wishes to go beyond the parochialism that he disliked in the
pieces by Green and Riggs. In "Richmond, U.S.A.," Foote writes that
he likes to think of his plays as "a moral and social history of Richmond."
He chooses "problems which are specific" to this particular section "and
yet will have some meaning for the outside world."[6]

The Chase deals with a major subject in an original way. Here we have
the story of a Texas sheriff who, unlike the stereotype, wants to save a
criminal's life, not end it by killing. Sheriff Hawes seeks to end the chase
after the fugitive, which started when he was a boy at risk and continues
now. Killing the escaped prisoner will not end the chase for others like
him but will only perpetuate it. In this anti–Western, Foote spells out his
dissent from the movies. He refuses to glorify the use of violence to exterminate the criminal. Foote's refutation of the use of violence among
Texans and other Americans was a timely topic when *The Chase* was
written in 1948 and performed in 1952. After World War II, Hollywood
was trying to regain its dwindling audiences. There was a return to the
popular genre of the Western in John Ford's trilogy, starring that hard-
riding, fast-shooting hero John Wayne. Along with a gutsy, Patton-like

Henry Fonda, Wayne appeared in *Fort Apache* (1948), which told how the U.S. Cavalry defeated the Indians in West Texas after the Civil War. This film was followed by *She Wore a Yellow Ribbon* (1949) and *Rio Grande* (1950), which dealt with the same material, also glorifying the violent repression of the Indians. Relentless killing was the way to solve the problem of those who broke the law in this country. The action takes place in Texas, accentuating the image of that state as the place where officers of the law carry out splendid exploits, solving the problems of society once and for all with bullets.

It is important for an understanding of Foote's plays to recognize that in *The Chase* he remains a social critic, not a naturalistic determinist in the school of Dreiser, O'Neill, and Miller. Though the character of the young prisoner suffers from the mindless, cruel treatment of society, Foote wishes to attack the harmful behavior of that society with the purpose of reforming it. He does not reveal the pessimistic attitude of the determinists. Foote follows Ibsen the social critic of *A Doll's House,* not Ibsen the naturalist of *Ghosts,* in which the hero is the helpless victim of bad heredity and corrupt society. In *The Chase,* Foote again takes aim at society's wrongs toward the individual and indicts its chase to punish. There is first a denunciation of cruel punishment, that is, the whipping of Bubber Reeves, when a boy. There is condemnation of his vindictive punishment as an adult, desired by the vicious deputy, Rip, and the lyncher Damon, an unprincipled businessman. But even in this mean town, there are signs of hope in the sheriff's attempt to save the young man's life. The corrupt citizens of this town are guilty of inhumane acts. It is not an impersonal environment, in the manner of naturalism, that produces a pitiful victim, but rather evil, willful acts that are cited for correction.

Bubber is Foote's first major character with a criminal record, the result of a self-image that he was born bad. He is whipped by his mother and the previous sheriff. He becomes vindictive against everyone and kills a man. Next, the town of Richmond chases him when he returns from the penitentiary. He is made worse by upper-class persecutors like Edwin Stewart and Hawks Damon.

When Bubber Reeves, whom Sheriff Hawes had sent to the penitentiary, escapes and returns to Richmond, determined to take revenge on his captor, the sheriff will not satisfy the town's demand that he be shot down like a dog. Nor will he second the foul-mouthed deputy, Rip, who wants Reeves's life. Making every effort possible to save Bubber's life and return him to prison, as the law requires, Hawes above all does not want to kill him. Tragically, when the sheriff corners the fugitive in his wife's shack by the river bottoms, Bubber brings about his own death, which he himself yearns for by this time. Hawes thinks wrongly that the unarmed but advancing Bubber intends to kill him and shoots wildly. Accidentally he does what he tried his utmost not to do. There is no satisfaction in this killing.

Bubber does not fit the preconception of the depraved criminal. We understand eventually what made him the enemy of society that he has become. His inconsolable mother, who does all in her power to save her son's life, tells how Bubber, who loved fishing in the river, was told as a boy that he was born bad. When he did wrong, all "Old Sunshine," a former sheriff, could advise was whipping. Mrs. Reeves did whip him, wishing now her hand would drop off from the beatings. She even dressed him like a girl so he would remain at home. Of course Bubber retaliated violently at the first opportunity.

What did Bubber learn from the streets of the town that made him go wrong? Mrs. Reeves asks. Sheriff Hawes says that does not matter now, but she replies that it matters to her. She hopes that the son soon to be born to Hawes's wife will be chased as her own has been. When Hawes gets a telephone call from another distraught mother who cannot control her son, he exclaims, "How does it start? How does it end?" Only one positive answer is given. Hawes agrees to talk with the son of this mother who is at her wit's end. Dixie Graves's boy has gotten into trouble, and Hawes says in five years we may have another Bubber on our hands. He will try, nevertheless, "to talk some sense into him" (p. 60). In any case he will not resort to violent punishment like whipping. Furthermore, killing a criminal like Bubber, it is implied, will not stop the chase of other lawless youth. Violence only begets violence.

And what part do the townspeople play in the making of the hapless criminal? The villains in this melodrama are Bubber's fellow townsmen, who want him killed by any means available. Edwin Stewart lets Bubber take the blame when he himself has stolen money from the cash register. Old Sunshine's laughter when informed of this subterfuge supports Mrs. Reeves's protest that the law protects the upper class unfairly. Now Edwin is mortally afraid that Bubber will kill him in revenge. When Hawes refuses to place a deputy at his home because he cannot spare a single man, Edwin sees to it that Hawes does not get the bank loan he sorely needs to purchase a farm as a refuge from the sheriff's job.

Bubber's most implacable enemy is Hawks Damon, a despicable leader of the town who is a recognizable type—a fun-loving joker who will resort to the harshest measures when provoked. Damon, who bets that Bubber will not return to Richmond, seeks to end Bubber's life when the escapee robs his store. Damon demands that the sheriff hunt Bubber down and kill him or the sheriff will suffer loss in the next election. Damon recruits a mob of gun-carrying men, who stop cars and search the river bottoms, intending to lynch Bubber. Damon declares to the sheriff that "the good people" of the town will make sure that Bubber will bother them no more, no matter what it takes (p. 50).

In the extensive condemnation of the larger community, represented by Damon and Edwin, the hunted criminal is the product of a vicious and cruel society. Bubber is hardly responsible for turning out as he has. The guilty society will exterminate him, however, and then boast of its actions. Neither does it give any help to end such "a chase"; this society pursues a member not responsible for what he does. Foote is not a thoroughgoing naturalistic writer, since he offers hope in the person of Hawes, who attempts to construct a better society. In this play, however, Foote comes as close as he ever does to taking the view of naturalistic determinism, like Theodore Dreiser in *An American Tragedy* (1925).

In *The Chase,* Foote goes beyond the simplistic view of character taken by George Kelly in *Craig's Wife* and other plays as composed merely of personality faults. Here Foote shows a real awareness of a corrupt society, of how it shapes Bubber Reeves and extinguishes his life. Foote does not show a familiarity with sociological analyses of American society, nor with novels like Sinclair Lewis's, nor even Lillian Hellman's plays describing socioeconomic influences on businessmen. But in *The Chase* he begins to consider the larger society and to attack it for inhuman treatment of its vulnerable members. This change adds to the complexity of characters like Bubber Reeves. In *The Chase,* Foote shows the ability to change and adopt new ideas by giving greater attention to the larger society, which can have a destructive effect on the individual's development.

Foote does not show a strong talent for social criticism. When he emphasizes it too heavily, as in the attack on the lynch mob of *The Chase,* it seems artificial. He must keep it incidental, as it is in Williams's plays, not made the main subject as in Miller's.

Probably Foote found the inspiration for this play in an event that had occurred during the same time in Wharton. On Christmas Day, 1945, Sheriff T. W. "Buckshot" Lane was holding the outlaw Pete Norris in the Wharton County jail. When Norris pulled a gun, the sheriff, whose nickname implies the desire not to kill, hurled himself at the prisoner but did not kill him. Norris shot twice, one bullet grazing Lane's cheek. The prisoner was then killed by a deputy.[7] According to Marion Castleberry, who has interviewed Foote extensively, *The Chase* was loosely based on this incident, one of the most violent moments of Wharton's history.[8]

The Chase, which ran for thirty-one performances, was more success-ful on Broadway than *Only the Heart.* Lucy Kroll reported to Foote for the week ending April 19, 1952, that it had grossed to date $15,801.75, with a royalty for Foote of $1,280.18. Unfortunately, the critics showed their lack of insight by considering it no more than a Western onstage. Reviewers who liked the play gave most of their praise to the actors. Jim O'Connor of the *New York Journal American* (April 16, 1952) en-joyed "the excitement" and acclaimed the stage debut of John Hodiak. John Chapman in the *New York Daily News* of the same date called it "a psychological Western" or a Texas version of Sidney Kingsley's *Detective Story,* a Broadway hit of 1949.

Influential critics like Walter Kerr and George Jean Nathan reacted very negatively; the latter considered the play warmed-over melodrama.[9] Strongly disapproving was Brooks Atkinson, who was beginning to find Foote's plays not to his taste, after praising the earlier ones highly; he had favorable comment only for the character studies, which had a literary flavor. Atkinson felt that the Western without the ethical point would have been preferable and that *The Chase* was neither the one nor the other. By the middle of act 3, Atkinson wrote, little drama was left in this "melodrama" (*New York Times,* April 16, 1952).

A recent analyst of *The Chase* has recognized Foote's point, which con-temporary reviewers missed. Marian Burkhart writes that violence is dis-credited. She correctly sees the play as a commentary on the American myth of the individual who achieves justice single-handedly through the use of violence. It is a gloss, unconscious or not, on *High Noon* (1952), she states. That film was a popular Western starring the epitome of Texas bel-ligerence, Gary Cooper. Burkhart argues that the film justifies violence. In the play, on the other hand, the sheriff is admirable because he does *not* want to shoot the criminal but wants simply to return him to prison.[10]

In *The Chase,* Foote reveals himself as a dramatist able to look critically at American values; he sees a more humane approach in Texas. Foote is on solid ground in arguing that the use of violence will not work. The chase after wayward young men will continue. Sheriff Hawes understands what not to do: no more whippings or public executions outside the law.

As a compassionate man of law who wants to reform the criminal, Hawes will start early with the young offender and communicate with him.

Foote turned *The Chase* into a work of fiction, publishing it as a novel in 1956.[11] Having become a work of 274 pages rather than a 60-page play, it is a much fuller story. The adaptation is interesting, but not an artistic improvement, since it is wordy and much of the action is overwritten. The fictional narrative provides a fuller picture of the town of Harrison. We learn that some townsmen make money by going into rice farming and oil leasing, though hundreds have made nothing. The layout of the town is filled in. According to Sheriff Hawes's description, filling stations have replaced imposing old homes.

The etiology of Bubber Reeves's degeneration is expanded so that the causes become clearer. We meet his father, a weak, ineffectual man overshadowed by Mrs. Reeves, who now emerges distinctly as a protective mother. Thus, we see the harmful consequence of an overbearing mother and a submissive father on a son. Mrs. Reeves tries again and again to buy her son out of trouble, wanting to pay for the secondhand car he stole rather than accept his assignment to the state prison farm by the sheriff. Feeling that he is inherently evil, Bubber believes the pronouncement by his Sunday school teacher that his sister died as punishment for his bad conduct.

Learning more about the lives of other townspeople, we hear about the fast lives of young couples. When they get together, there are crude jokes about violence and marital infidelity. Edwin Stewart cries when he hears that Hawks Damon is sleeping with his wife. The deputy Rip is even more despicable than in the play. He would have allowed a Negro held in jail to be lynched and wants to be sheriff solely for the excitement. Sheriff Hawes looks forward to a happier life in the novel. He quits his job and moves to a cotton farm. In the end he holds his newborn son and retires to peaceful sleep.

This novel received some perceptive evaluation, though no one mentioned its similarity to Western movies. Anthony Boucher in the *New York Herald Tribune Book Review* (February 6, 1956) considered it powerful as a novel of character, "studying the moral and psychological problems of violence." W. J. Smith in *Commonweal* (March 15, 1956) said that it went beyond being a mere thriller: "psychological melodrama—perhaps describes it better."

In 1966, *The Chase*, starring Marlon Brando and Jane Fonda, was made into a film, surely its worst version. Producer Sam Spiegel saw an analogy between the madness of the small Texas town and the anger that led to the assassination of John F. Kennedy in 1963. With the screenwriting assistance of Lillian Hellman, Spiegel intended to make a socially conscious movie about the collective immorality that can lead to violence. Spiegel and Hellman correctly perceived a social dimension in *The Chase;* their interpretation strengthens the deduction that Foote was becoming more aware of the larger society and its evils in this work than he had been in previous ones like *Only the Heart.* Foote, however, disliked the Peyton Place melodramatics added by Hellman. "I wasn't too happy with her," he understated.[12] He was learning the bitter lesson of what could happen to a serious drama sold to the commercial media.

Arthur Penn, director of *The Chase,* wrote an angry letter on February 14, 1966, to the drama department of the *New York Times,* contradicting what a reporter wrote about Lillian Hellman in an article appearing the preceding Sunday. He mailed a copy to Foote. Penn complained about the interviewer's version of his discussions with Sam Spiegel, the producer, with regard to Hellman's screenwriting. Hellman had recommended Penn to Spiegel, who then asked him to direct it. Penn wrote, "I did not say, 'I did it out of friendship. It's her first play since she was politically blacklisted.'" He went on to praise Hellman as "a distinguished playwright" who needs "no acts of charity performed on behalf of her work. She is a much sought after writer" (HFC).

Penn's compliment to Hellman directly contradicts Foote's displeasure. As a result of this painful experience with Hollywood filmmaking, Foote learned a lesson: "If you sell your work to a studio, they own it. That's why I would never do it again. That's the last time I did it."[13] In time, Foote became a producer of his original screenplays like *Tender Mercies* (1983), thereby not having to worry about producers ruining his scripts.

Bosley Crowther, a sensitive and respected critic of the *New York Times,* wrote a devastating review of the movie. He called it "a picture to leave you cold" with its clumsy attempt to combine the civil rights theme and *Peyton Place* scandals. "It has an ending that was not in Mr. Foote's play but was evidently inspired by a very tragic occurrence in Texas in 1963," Crowther wrote. In the film the young man based on the character Bubber is killed by a gunman, who is then brutally beaten by the sheriff, thus reducing the sheriff to the level of the enraged townspeople, Crowther observes (*New York Times,* February 19, 1966). Despite the negative judgments of Foote and Crowther, this film has remained popular and is considered a trailblazer in subject matter, because of its exposure of society's guilt.[14]

In Foote's first phase as a dramatist from 1941 to 1952, he did not produce a hit as had Williams, Miller, and Inge during the same period. Foote had tried sensational drama like *Texas Town* (1940) and *The Chase* (1952), full of noise, suspense, and excitement, drawing on what the public expected in Texas material, but still he had not achieved a real success. If he could not satisfy the public in this way, then he must satisfy himself and write about the world that he knew best: small-town, ordinary life in his hometown of Wharton, which was in fact the "Richmond" of *Only the Heart*. He must write what he was comfortable with. Going in this direction would disappoint those critics who deplored his lack of theatrical excitement and the highly dramatic climax, achieved by Williams in *A Streetcar Named Desire* and Miller in *Death of a Salesman*. Foote relies on a reservoir of memories and thoughts about his origins, as many novelists do. His strongest feelings and convictions arise from this world that he thoroughly understands—where he was born and where his forbears lived out their lives. He takes the view of Faulkner, because this place furnishes Foote with enough material to write about for the rest of his career and draws from the depths of his feelings about the people he has known intimately.

Foote made progress in this phase of his career in his theory of truthfulness. In the 1930s he had absorbed thoroughly the concept of truthful acting conveyed by the Stanislavski Method. The Russian teachers had made him a convert to this ideal of realism. In practice it meant acting that demonstrated the truth in a character's life, like Nora's humiliation as a doll by her husband and others. Foote would always strive for natural speech, true to the spoken word he heard in Wharton. Further he discovered the aim of truthfulness in the fiction of Porter.

Finally it should be said that Foote, unlike some other artists and writers, *believed* unquestionably in the possibility of *discovering* truth *and* rendering it honestly and comprehensibly in realistic forms. It was not impossible to do, as the surrealists would argue. Therefore, his understanding of truthfulness and how he developed his own theory can be traced directly to the Stanislavski Method and to his admiration for Katherine Anne Porter. This idea of truthfulness would direct him unerringly in his future writing regardless of what seductive trends might arise in the years to come.

CHAPTER

6

THE GOLDEN AGE OF TELEVISION

FTER failing to produce a hit on Broadway, Foote enjoyed his first
real successes with the plays he composed for television, which became a significant component of that medium's Golden Age. This con-
noisseur of the media, an early fan of radio and movies, now had the
chance to launch a new dramatic form, the television play, and he seized
the opportunity with enthusiasm. From 1952 to 1954 he composed ten
plays for Fred Coe's noted *Philco Playhouse* and earned a celebrity status
that he had never attained in the legitimate theatre. Foote's professional
career was indisputably launched with his television plays, which rescued
him from what could have been a dead end in his writing. Looking back
at this era, he regrets its untimely demise, when live television was supplanted by taped plays filmed in Hollywood, saying, "You just have to
shut that out of your mind." Terry Barr, a student of Foote's whole career, considers this period its high point. He calls it Foote's "glory years
of writing." [1]

Aside from the fact that live television offered an ideal form for a playwright like Foote, with its balance of popular appeal and serious intent,
what gave his television plays an advantage over conventional works
like *Only the Heart*? First, he hit upon the concept of the single setting
for all his television plays, a town that he now called "Harrison, Texas."
Foote took an original step by choosing the same setting for a series of
plays, not short stories. Use of the same town as a setting was a technique that had previously been used in fiction famously by Sherwood
Anderson in *Winesburg, Ohio,* by Faulkner in his sage of Yoknapatawpha
County, and by Edwin Arlington Robinson and Edgar Lee Masters in
poetry. Foote knew of Anderson and Faulkner and admired especially

70

the works of the Mississippi genius. Of course there were many series on television that had the same setting, such as Andy Griffith's comedies set in Mayberry, North Carolina, but like earlier series on radio, these cannot be called serious art. With the setting of Harrison, Foote discovered the element that elevated his dramatic writings from the undistinguished to the noteworthy. His "Harrison" plays make his works worthy of much greater interest.

Along with the single setting, the town of Harrison changes the nature of the television plays. Foote, in the introduction to his one-act plays set there, speaks of his "mythical town." Some critics refer to the universality of Foote's and others' writings, but for the former it is more accurate to speak of their mythic quality. Myths deal with archetypal patterns recounting fundamental human repetitions, like the search for a father exemplified by Telemachus's search for Ulysses. Foote observes that he himself is a fifth-generation Texan who has heard of the lives of his relatives over and over. He seeks to find the "patterns" in these accounts to bring some order out of the chaos, as Katherine Anne Porter said she was trying to do in her writing.[2] In the middle of life, she notes, we are confused and cannot know where we have been or where we are going. Out of this inchoate matter, art seeks to create orderly form.[3]

Foote, in his plays about Harrison has the same aim. Thus, some of the television plays detect patterns, like the father-son conflict in *The Old Beginning* and the overwhelming urge to return home in *The Trip to Bountiful*. These patterns or cycles evoke deep responses in audiences because they have felt them also, as have countless previous generations. The mythical dimension of the Harrison plays for television expresses implicitly the same mythical quality dramatized more explicitly in Wilder's *The Skin of Our Teeth*. The angry conflict between the father and son in *The Old Beginning* treats a battle similar to that between Mr. Antrobus and Henry in Wilder's play.

Finally, a reason for the success of Foote's teleplays is their short, one-act form. Designed as one-hour shows, they were the equivalent in drama of the short story in fiction, with which many critics have compared Foote's one-acts. Foote admired the one-acts composed by Tennessee Williams in *American Blues* (completed in 1939 but not published till 1948) and esteemed those by Sartre and Beckett.[4] The one-act was a happy choice for Foote at this time in his career. It eliminated the talkiness and complications of longer works like *Only the Heart* and *The Chase*. Foote early on appreciated the unities in plays because they enforced a discipline on his playwriting. In his television one-acts, he sometimes dropped the unities, but he maintained time limits that continue the effect of the unities. Foote liked the one-act form because it enabled him to cover material that he could not in the longer form.[5] In practice this meant that he could concentrate on one facet of a town's life that would be insufficient for a full-length play.

After a decade of floundering, failing to make a hit on Broadway, and not achieving financial success, things changed greatly for Foote as he entered the world of television. He began writing for television with the *Gabby Hayes Show*, a children's program (October 1950–December 1951), in late summer 1950, after Vincent Donehue called him about writing historical pieces for television.[6] The new television writer earned larger amounts of money than for the preceding stage plays. It was Foote's first introduction to television and led to his resignation from a teaching job at the American Theatre Wing (Lillian Foote, HFC, undated letter, 1953).[7]

The expectations of television brought about a marked change in Foote's writing. Because television shows were above all designed to depict the lives of modern people, saying to them "This is your life," Foote necessarily shifted predominantly to recent times and low-key incidents, rather than relying on the exceptional moment of excitement demanded in the theatre and seen graphically in *The Chase*. This change was appealing to Foote because he felt very comfortable with middle-class American life.

The chance to write for television was a godsend for Foote. Fortunately for him, the industry was headquartered in New York, where he resided. He was welcomed by the television world, by its management, writers, and audiences. He was allowed the freedom to create the works that became his first really successful plays. Like the careers of many other writers for television, such as Paddy Chayefsky, Foote's career as a writer for television and movies began with the series of plays that he composed for the *Philco Television Playhouse* in 1953.

Foote's transition from the theatre to television was momentous for his future. He could henceforth concentrate on the ordinary events of life, not the sensational ones. This change meant that he would be censured again and again for failing to achieve theatrical excitement and for composing plays that were allegedly slight, lacking in weight and substance. The demands of the small television screen that distributed fare to the home audience explain this change in his dramatic writing. When Foote began to write television plays, boiled down to one hour, he settled on the characteristic dramatic mode that he would use for the remainder of his career.

Replacing the American Actors Company for Foote was the *Philco Television Playhouse,* which began in October 1948 and became the sponsor of his television plays. This series produced live dramas on television and was managed by Fred Coe, a young man from Mississippi. Coe is a central figure in the Golden Age of Television. As the forceful and creative producer of the *Philco Playhouse* and the *Goodyear Playhouse,* he grasped the great potential of original one-hour shows presented live. His belief in this form and in the stimulation of writing for television provoked an outpouring of what were essentially serious plays staged before the television camera. Coe's encouragement of high-quality drama established the reputation of writers such as Foote, Paddy Chayefsky, Tad Mosel, Sumner Locke Elliott, Reginald Rose, and others. Actors who got their start in television drama included Kim Stanley, Eva Marie Saint, and Steve McQueen. Two outstanding directors were Vincent Donehue and Arthur Penn, who directed some of Foote's best offerings on television.[8]

Coe fiercely protected his stable of writers and was always on guard against sponsors' interference. Foote liked Coe very much because Coe gave him freedom and encouraged him to explore his native material. Coe gave a start to many budding playwrights, encouraging them to please themselves and not to write according to formula.[9] Under the aegis of Coe, Foote was given the opportunity to learn the craft of the television play. His influence on other playwrights such as Chayefsky, Mosel, and Locke Elliott is fully substantiated by their testimonies of appreciation. Foote was also fortunate in having as director for some of his television plays Vincent Donehue, with whom he had established the theatre workshop of the King-Smith School of Creative Arts in Washington during the 1940s. Donehue directed five of the seven teleplays that Foote wrote for the *Philco Playhouse.*

A leading spirit in the *Philco Playhouse* was Paddy Chayefsky. His play *Marty* and his comments on television drama provide an illuminating introduction to the dramas that Foote wrote for the same playhouse. Chayefsky spoke for the group of playwrights contributing to the *Philco Playhouse.* He compared their plays to short stories, calling them "small" plays, but not in a pejorative sense. He rejected the label "kitchen drama," arguing that they dramatized the lives of people "out there in the audience" and contributed what any artist is supposed to: "some sort of understanding." He held that the job of the artist is to give his audience "some insight into its otherwise meaningless pattern of life." Chayefsky and his associates, like Tad Mosel in *The Out-of-Towners,* were saying, "This is your life, this is what's going on, and this is one shred of understanding about your life."[10] Chayefsky believed that is why drama was important.

Chayefsky contended that plays for the small screen were correspondingly small in scope and intimate in subject matter, but not to be demeaned for all that. In those days "a kind of miniature work" was required, "the equivalent of a short story." He added that a writer could take any impulse and make a show of it.[11] One created character, and that became the plot. Typically, *Marty* is a modest drama about a young unmarried butcher whose mother insists that he find a wife.[12]

There was a fertile interchange of ideas among the writers for *Philco Playhouse.* Sumner Locke Elliott says they learned from each other and that he himself learned "a lot about simplicity" from Chayefsky.[13] The latter received his first inspiration to write for television from Foote. After seeing *The Trip to Bountiful* on *Philco,* Chayefsky called it "a lovely simple play laid in the South."[14]

Foote does not probe psychological depths. His television plays indicate that he not only lacks the inclination to delve so deeply but further thinks that it is out of place in his type of drama. Chayefsky agrees; he does not go deeply into the characters' latent homosexuality in *Marty* since the play was a comment on the social values of the time.[15]

In these television plays, Foote demonstrates a much surer grasp of dramatic craft. The discipline of writing for television, with the assurance of production and a favorable reception, was surely beneficial. The plot does not wander, and the point of the play is sharp and effectively made. As Foote said, he found writing for television very rewarding, though demanding. It was an apprenticeship that he needed. It schooled him in his craft and showed him the subject matter that was right for him.

In the preface to *Harrison, Texas: Eight Television Plays* (1956), Foote makes clear that he wishes this work to be considered as serious art, not written to meet the demands of a commercial medium. The teleplay was not presented to exploit the commercial value of the actor. Changes were made for the good of the production, not to please some sponsor.[16] Foote says that this is "my familiar country"; the people are "my people." He goes on to say, "I write of them with affection, certainly, and I hope with understanding" (p. viii). Analyzing the plays, he says that they share one or two common themes: "an acceptance of life or a preparation for death." In *The Midnight Caller*, both themes operate because the various characters "are involved with an acceptance of life and a preparation for death" (pp. viii–ix).

Foote composed nine television plays from late 1952 to early 1954, the bulk of them being written and produced in 1953. *The Old Beginning*, produced November 23, 1952, on the *Goodyear Television Playhouse*, is the first of Foote's plays to be set in Harrison, Texas. The archetypal pattern is the father-son conflict evident in many of O'Neill's plays, such as *Long Day's Journey into Night*.

The father-son conflict of this play attracted the attention of psychiatrists. Lucy Kroll reported to Foote that the Psychiatric Institute of America thought that *The Old Beginning* should be shown to psychiatrists concerning "the father-son complex." Although this play dramatized a psychological problem confirmed by professional psychiatrists, Kroll wrote to Bette Davis, who had been intrigued by Foote's television plays, that "Mr. Foote did not employ one technical or scientific word in this script and yet its truth and power, met the test on such a high level" (HFC, April 10, 1953).

A Young Lady of Property on April 5, 1953, was a first-rate television play. Foote's second Harrison play appeared on the *Philco Playhouse*. Here he achieved the human drama that he had strained for but had not realized theatrically in his full-length plays. It received the best review of any of Foote's television plays from the usually disapproving critic of *Variety* (April 8, 1953), the widely consulted trade magazine of television. For this reviewer, the script was "topnotch." Calling the piece a "mood" play, the reviewer said it opened with a mood and sustained it until the last fadeout. This play has had a long life in amateur productions.

What makes this one-act so emotionally moving and, yes, dramatic is the heroine's battle with her fears. Wilma, one of Foote's semiorphans who has lost her mother, is afraid that the woman about to become her stepmother will reject her. To her best friend, Arabella, she describes how a woman was shut up in a house that became covered with vines and died at the age of seventy-three. She is fearful that might happen to her.

A typical teenage girl, Wilma is anxious about her future in Harrison and dreams of becoming a Hollywood actress. As the play opens, she nervously awaits a letter from a movie agent to take a screen test. Hanging around the post office, she tells her father, Lester, that Mr. Delafonte is "giving screen tests in Houston for people of beauty and talent." Caustically, he tells Wilma that the screen tests are "a lot of foolishness" and says, "You're not going to Houston to take anything" (p. 57). Next, she learns that her father plans to sell the house her mother left her. With her luck, she laments, she will not get married and will never have a family.

What is it that Wilma must do to save her life? The house she expected to own as a young lady of property seems lost. Under pressure, she acts very courageously. Deciding she does not want to be rich and famous in Hollywood, she announces, "I want to stay in Harrison." Then jumping up, she cries, "I'm going to see old lady Leighton. She's the one that can stop [Lester from selling the house]" (p. 80). She does go to this dreaded future stepmother, whom Aunt Gert told her not to see. The climactic scene is not staged as Fred Coe argued it should be. Foote held to his view that this dramatic meeting should be related by Wilma to Arabella, as it movingly is. When Wilma told Mrs. Leighton that her mother wanted her to own the house, the compassionate woman cried. She persuaded her husband-to-be that Wilma should keep the house. Having reached this decision, the trio of father, daughter, and stepmother all cry. From now on, Wilma calls Mrs. Leighton "Sibyl" and will attend her wedding.

Even though the last part of this one-act is moving, it is not sentimental. Wilma's fearfulness returns as she goes back with her friend to the house she now owns. Will there be life in the house again? she worries. That was what she missed even when swinging on the porch with her mother, awaiting the return of her gambling father at four o'clock in the morning. Wilma's longing for "the life in the house" (p. 87) recalls the wish of Emily in *Our Town* to relive the daily joy of watching her mother fix breakfast. Such precious moments are what Wilma hopes to relive in her childhood house. Arabella reassures her, saying that there will indeed be life in the house once more. In the last lines, Wilma speaks of the enormous pecan tree, planted when her mother was born. "I can't put my arms around it now," she says (p. 87). Wilma will gain strength from this reminder of her mother.

A Young Lady of Property received a glowing review in *Variety* (April 8, 1953). The reviewer called it one of the season's major highlights for the *Philco Television Playhouse*. This show was a personal triumph for the lead, Kim Stanley, who was aided by "the topnotch script." Fred Coe's production skills make this "one of the most enjoyable plays in the Philco series."

A Young Lady of Property attracted the keen interest of Bette Davis. Lucy Kroll informed Foote on April 10, 1953, that this intelligent actress had been much impressed with the television play and Kim Stanley's performance. Miss Davis felt that Foote had "the quality of truth" and could reveal the inner life of characters more than any other single writer of the day (HFC). *A Young Lady of Property* was considered for transfer to Broadway. Kroll wrote Barrett Clark, executive director of Dramatists Play Service, on April 22, 1953, that she had received two offers by Broadway producers to stage the play, but that never happened.

The Oil Well, produced May 17, 1953, on the *Goodyear Television Playhouse,* shows keen insight into the distinctive life of Texas. Here Foote finds a compelling subject, oil fever—the dream of great riches by a sudden discovery of oil—and treats it incisively. This is a classic subject of Texas, which became the largest oil-producing state in the nation and retained that rank as oil production increased continually. Foote takes a popular subject of Texas, as he did with the contest between prisoner and sheriff in *The Chase;* but in *The Oil Well* he goes beyond the typical treatment of striking it rich, as he presents a failure. He shows himself to be a perceptive critic of the Texas psyche, giving an understanding of oil fever to those who have never been to Texas.

The oil fever takes its toll on the Thornton family. Knowingly shown as country people, they still prefer the porch steps rather than chairs and make telltale grammatical errors. Good country people who have been raising cotton for forty years, they have lived through the oil booms of 1925 and 1938 but have not discovered oil on their land. Will, the father, has always dreamed of an oil strike. He says, "I want to die rich" (p. 98). When prospectors believe that his land contains oil, the raging fever seizes him again. His two children are consumed by the same passion. As the signs become stronger, they plan what they will do with the great sums of money, like the dreamers of Duerenmatt's Guellen. By contrast the mother, Loula (recalling great-aunt Loula), wants nothing to do with drilling for oil. She puts her confidence in cotton, which is slow but sure. When Will abandons the cotton crop in hopes of striking oil, she undertakes the plowing of cotton herself to keep bread on the table if the well comes in dry. At the end, when the drilling is unsuccessful, it is Loula who sustains her husband. The rock in the family, she consoles him. Realizing that he needs hope to live, she sustains his never dying belief that oil will yet be found on his land.

This play is most successful for the insight it gives into the oil fever that has permeated the lives of many Texans. Belief in oil replaces religion for some. This substitution can be seen in the religious words that Will and

others use in speaking of oil. He says that one must keep "faith" in striking oil (p. 99). When his faith is not rewarded, he laments that it is not
fair, recalling in other contexts that when faith in God is not rewarded
by material prosperity, many become cynical and protest that life is not
fair. When the prospectors offer to buy leasing rights from Will, he happily sees this as "a sign" that he will now strike oil (p. 118). Will's fifth
cousin Mamie Bledsoe, who resembles the oil-mad Mamie Borden of
Only the Heart, makes a "prophecy" that this time Will will surely strike
oil (p. 122).

Conspicuously, Loula does not use religious terms in her speech, indicating that faith in oil has not replaced her religious faith. The religious
terms used demonstrate that this oil fever is a debased form of religion.
It corrupts the spirit and finally annihilates. At the end, the tragic Will,
who still suffers from the fever, must keep hoping but admits that his
"heart" is broken (p. 129). His spirit in fact will not survive this final
blow.

The hope of gaining great wealth by an oil strike throws light on
the Texas passion for gambling, which Foote showed in *The Chase* and
brings up again in the plays of the *Orphans' Home Cycle.* Will Thornton
will not sell his mineral rights on the land to H. T. Mavis for $100,000
because he wants to "keep on playing in the game until we get everything that is coming to us" (p. 110). The gambling obsession harks back
to the frontier days. This gambling instinct among Texans has been renewed by the discovery of oil. Foote identifies a malady that lies deep in
the Texas soul.

The climactic scene of the oil drilling brings together many of the leading ideas in this play. As the Thorntons wait impatiently, the scene of the
drilling takes on a diabolic cast. Harrison turns out en masse, showing
how the fever touches more and more townspeople. The influence of the
town mounts. Will is drained of all energy, not having slept for weeks.
This sickness has strained Thelma Doris's nerves so much that she cannot bear to go outside to watch. The comic Mamie, having taken a plane
from Louisiana to be on hand for the oil strike, gives the best speech of
the play when she arrives: "I took a plane to Houston so I'd get here in
time. Then I hired me a taxi to bring me straight out. Cost me fourteen
dollars and eleven cents. The taxi man says, 'Why are you going to Harrison in such a hurry? Is there a death in your family?' I said, 'No, there's
no death. There's an oil well.' 'Yours?' he said. I said, 'No, but in the family. A sweet dear cousin of mine. My fifth'" (pp. 121–122).

The religious feeling appears grotesquely in Mamie. She remembers when her well came in dry twenty years ago. She cannot understand why the well of "a good Christian woman" could come in dry. Horace, her husband, has been cured of the oil sickness, saying they have plenty. Mamie, however, points out that Gertrude Barsoty has plenty too and never goes to church but has oil wells by the hundred "and all of them producing" (p. 122). Foote demonstrates a gift for satire in his ridicule of the person who thinks her Christian faith should ensure an oil strike. The greed for oil money overshadows an individual's loudly proclaimed religious faith.

The Oil Well, featuring E. G. Marshall and Dorothy Gish as the elderly couple, was given a lukewarm assessment in *Variety* (May 20, 1953). The reviewer called the finale poignant as Marshall (playing Will Thornton) tries to rouse new hope in himself but in his heart acknowledges the futility of doing so. The theme of the play is hope springing eternal in the human breast, this critic said. The show was "no earthshaker" but adequate as a vehicle for fine performances.

Despite the reviewer's disparagement, Foote came as close as he ever did to writing a controversial television play by satirizing and disapproving the Texas obsession with oil in *The Oil Well.* Not surprisingly, it did not run on the *Gulf Playhouse,* which was sponsored by Gulf Oil; on the other hand, it *was* produced on the *Goodyear Playhouse.*

Foote's television plays began to attract some critical recognition by the time *The Trip to Bountiful* and *The Oil Well* were produced on March 3 and May 17, 1953, respectively. Lillian Foote noted that Foote wanted to continue in television, regardless of how much theatrical writing he did because he considered it "a medium of great vitality" that allowed the writer "much scope." He had had no problem with interference with his scripts (HFC, undated letter, 1953).

In his television plays, Foote cultivates new forms such as the camera eye. That is, the action is seen by an invisible character, as in *The Tears of My Sister* and *The Death of the Old Man.* It has much in common with the stream of consciousness, the ultimate technique of subjectivity, by which we enter the mind of the narrator. Cecilia in the first play watches her sister being forced into unwanted matrimony and in her lines keeps crying. The old man (the "camera eye") from his deathbed follows the predicament of his surviving daughter, Rosa, but is helpless to rescue her. This device reveals the inner thoughts and painful feelings of an individual, duplicating the stream of consciousness method.

Foote cultivated more assiduously and successfully his humorous talent in these plays. With a true ear for the amusing idiom of the people he has known, he is expert in catching the unconscious humor of older men like H. T. Mavis in *The Old Beginning*. One woman says that because Mavis never fixes anything, he is "the most disliked person in town." When she is out of earshot, H. T. remarks, "That's gratitude for you" (p. 27). Foote knows comic personages when he sees them.

Foote's annus mirabilis in television is 1953. After finishing this remarkable sequence of plays, he published all but two of them in *Harrison, Texas: Eight Television Plays* in 1956. The eight plays, with production dates, appeared in the following order in this collection: *The Trip to Bountiful* (March 1, 1953); *A Young Lady of Property* (March 15, 1953); *The Death of the Old Man* (July 17, 1953); *Expectant Relations* (July 21, 1953); *The Tears of My Sister* (August 14, 1953); *John Turner Davis* (November 5, 1953); and *The Dancers* (March 7, 1954). Omitted were *The Old Beginning* and *The Oil Well*. These latter two plays do not illustrate the two common themes found in the eight chosen: "an acceptance of life or a preparation for death." When *Selected One-Act Plays of Horton Foote* was published in 1989, *Expectant Relations* was omitted because of its lesser quality, along with *The Trip to Bountiful*, which had become well known in its stage and film versions. Added in the second collection were the two previously absent: *The Old Beginning* and *The Oil Well*, which merited publication because of their superior quality. Of the ten plays listed above, five appeared on the *Philco Playhouse*, three on the *Goodyear Playhouse*, and two on the *Gulf Playhouse*.

These plays for television went on to an extended life. Several were staged as one-acts, notably *A Young Lady of Property*, which distinguishes this work as the best, if we exclude for the moment *The Trip to Bountiful*, which was successfully expanded to three acts. On July 23, 1958, *A Young Lady* was being performed in twelve theatres, according to information from the Dramatists Play Service preserved by Lucy Kroll. On January 23, 1959, Kroll recorded twelve royalties for the work. On April 19, 1960, this play was deemed "enchanting" in London. On May 15, 1960, more royalties were earned for the play. On October 29, 1970, an excerpt was shown on the television series *Guest Scenes for Young Actors*. On February 10, 1984, the "Joanne Woodward and Paul Newman Special" presented an excerpt from the play. Among numerous amateur productions, the play was announced on November 1, 1987, at the Los Angeles County High School, along with *Dancers* and *Blind Date*.[17]

Taken together, these television plays about Harrison, Texas, offer an original look at the real qualities of a small Texas town. Such a town can be petty and narrow-minded but contrastingly big in its generosity and care. Harrison further reveals strong generational conflicts. The older people, born before 1900, differ sharply from the younger in some ways. In *The Old Beginning* the father interferes with his son's desire for independence in business. In *The Death of an Old Man* the younger generation does not take responsibility for the care of the older generation. In *The Dancers* the socially conscious aunt wants her unwilling nephew to better himself socially by dating a girl with high social status. Foote is usually sympathetic with the new generation but also admires the goodness and unselfishness of the older, as in *The Death of the Old Man*. As for the religious character of these plays, it should be noted that, unlike *Ludie Brooks* (1951), they are not overtly religious. The religious subject arises in them essentially as it does in pieces by other playwrights like Tennessee Williams and Maxwell Anderson. There is indirect criticism of a false religion in *The Oil Well*. What is noticeable is Foote's admiration of religious values, especially the value of compassion, seen movingly in the wife's encouragement at the end of *The Oil Well*.

After the high point of writing for Coe's *Philco Playhouse*, Foote continued his association with this much admired producer. Foote wrote other plays in the years when live television produced in New York was on the wane, as television moved to filmed plays made in Hollywood. This shift marked the decline of television drama, as commercial sponsors decided what would be shown to sell their products to a larger market. The decline of artistic quality took place inevitably, proving the judgment that television became "a vast wasteland," much to the chagrin of producers with high standards, like Fred Coe.

The ten plays written by Foote during the Golden Age of Television represent a solid, important accomplishment. As a unified, original body of plays, they are an outstanding achievement. Here Foote writes the equivalent of a collection of short stories set in one place, like *Winesburg, Ohio*. Like short stories in a collection, they are condensed, artfully presented, and coherent.

CHAPTER

7

THE TRIP TO BOUNTIFUL

THREE VERSIONS

THE television plays that Foote composed during the Golden Age of Television gave him the success that he sorely needed. But we have not recognized the work that set the crown on this achievement. *The Trip to Bountiful* was the only television play by Foote that advanced to the legitimate stage. Conceived as a full-length stage play, it was first produced on the *Philco Television Playhouse* on March 1, 1953. Later, on November 3, 1953, it premiered on Broadway, running thirty-nine performances.

Like Gore Vidal's *Visit to a Small Planet, Bountiful* transferred from the small screen to the large stage, and like Paddy Chayefsky's *Marty,* it advanced from television to the big screen. Foote's television play became an excellent stage play. In 1985 it achieved popular success as a film. Why did *Bountiful* achieve this renown? It benefited, to be sure, from the performances of two distinguished actresses in the lead part, Lillian Gish on television and stage, and Geraldine Page in the film.

Bountiful made its way through the three media by virtue of its inherent assets as well. In this special work, Foote dealt with three subjects that lifted it above others. It captured the mythical pattern of coming home; it utilized the jarring contrast between big-city life and a simpler way in the country, thus exploiting the assault on urban absurdity. It also stressed the human need to belong to a family, a house, a town. Not the least of the reasons that it excelled was the presence of three memorable characters, providing enough roles to give the work depth and substance: the pathetic mother, Mrs. Watts; the gabby wife, Jessie Mae; and the defeated husband, Ludie. *Bountiful* drew deserved applause in its three forms, but it reached its best realization in the theatre because of the superior art and thought in that version.

Foote's best contribution to television was *The Trip to Bountiful*. He combined the material of Chayefsky and his own interpretation of modern life. In fact, Foote's career for television, stage, and film was definitely launched with this television drama. Starring Lillian Gish again in the leading role, the play went on to Broadway in 1953, where it received critical praise, but not popular acclaim because of its seemingly slight plot. The audience missed the customary dramatic scenes. Later it became an excellent film in 1985. In making the difficult transition from television to the stage, Foote showed new talent and ability. Although *The Trip to Bountiful* was not the success that all playwrights seek, it was Foote's most successful play to date, with its insight into the trials of modern urban life, particularly adjustment to change. As Foote has noted, he has not had the sudden success, financial nor popular, of his contemporaries like William Inge.[1] Foote's rise has been slow but sure.

Both the public and the critical response to this television play were enthusiastic. Chayefsky exclaimed, "Boy, that's how to do television!"[2] Lillian Foote sent quotes from *Variety* to a correspondent in 1953, which said that with his television plays, "Oil Well, Trip, etc.," Foote was building "a fictional Texan world" approaching the stature as well as the volume of Faulkner's Mississippi work, "asserting more vigorously and hopefully the theme of man's dignity, which Faulkner too often approaches negatively and to the point of obscurity." Describing Foote as "a fine and important creative writer," the reviewer commented, "It's good to have him in television."[3]

Lillian Gish was an early supporter of television because she liked to participate in innovations. She considered Fred Coe "the father of the medium."[4] Gish also became a dedicated backer of Foote. In her autobiography (1949), she wrote that after Foote's television play about a woman looking for "her lost spirit" was shown, the CBS president phoned the head of NBC to say, "Tonight television came of age." She also noted that it was the first television film that the Museum of Modern Art requested for its archives.[5]

The television version of *Bountiful* is printed in *Harrison, Texas* (1956) and in *Horton Foote's Three Trips to Bountiful*.[6] Although the expanded play is the best of the three versions, the main outlines of the work stand out clearly in the teleplay and show why this production attracted much attention.

In the first act of the television version, set in the Wattses' cramped Houston apartment, we learn of Mrs. Watts's situation: her hometown of

Bountiful and her family line are coming to an end. Mrs. Watts's perse-cutor, Jessie Mae, opposes her hymn singing and is interested above all in the government pension check received by her mother-in-law. The brief look at Ludie, the son, describes his face as covered with "defeat" (p. 36).

After the television production of *Bountiful,* Lucy Kroll engaged in en-ergetic correspondence with regard to its enlargement and transfer to Broadway. Barrett H. Clark, executive director of Dramatists Play Ser-vice, wrote her on April 10, 1953, about publishing a stage version and offered an advance of $750. On April 22, 1953, Kroll enclosed the New York reviews of *Bountiful* with Gish to Clark. She notified him that Foote would begin work on "enlarging" the play and would sent it to him by June 1 so that Clark could publish it by August 1. At this time Kroll also informed Fred Coe, the producer of the television play, that Foote would expand the short television version into a full-length play. Most notably she wrote to Lillian Gish on April 27, 1953, asking her about getting *Bountiful* on Broadway.

On May 14, 1953, Kroll sent Barrett Clark a supportive quote by Gish on *Bountiful.* The famous actress reported that she had telephoned Coe earlier, telling him that he should not be surprised if "the large cities and the country at large" did not like *Bountiful.* "I was so wrong," she said. "When an author can create the character so true and sympa-thetic . . . he has a rare talent. Too often, today, we just see a plot with no real play, only cardboard characters surrounding it." Gish concluded with a final boost: "Yes, we can look to the future of young Horton Foote in any phase of his talents of the theatre with excited anticipation. Hallelujah!" (HFC).

Before *Bountiful* premiered on Broadway, there were high hopes for success among its backers. Lucy Kroll had read it and in a letter to Foote proclaimed it "a lovely and perfect play" (June 30, 1953). On August 28, 1953, she informed Harold Hecht of Norma Productions, California, that *Bountiful* would open September 7 (in Westport, Connecticut), that "it is my conservative estimate that this play will begin a new cycle of true theatre," and that Gish would be acclaimed as "our greatest artist in the theatre today." Lillian Foote reported that the play would be pro-duced by Fred Coe and the Theatre Guild. It would be presented now as first conceived—as a full-length play. After starting in Westport, it would move to Hartford and New Haven and then run for two weeks in Boston before the New York opening (HFC, undated letter, 1953).

On Broadway, *The Trip to Bountiful* predictably received the qualification that would apply to the "small" television play, that is, one that treated an ordinary happening movingly but undramatically. Critics used phrases like "thin plot," "flat dialogue," and "lack of emotional excitement." Walter Kerr of the *New York Herald Tribune* (November 4, 1953) thought that Foote had made "heartening strides" since *The Chase*, but that *Bountiful* remained "a small play," lacking "sustained vitality."

Brooks Atkinson expressed reservations in his review of *Bountiful* (*New York Times*, November 4, 1953), stating that the playwright did not make the play better "by underwriting." Atkinson's complaint of what might be called Foote's objectivity may be compared with Foote's liking for Porter. In an interview, Foote noted that Porter did "not take sides" in writing about characters based on her relatives, that she wanted to "see it as it really was" and could recognize the "irony" between actions and words. Foote said he also wanted to be an "observer" and "objective" in portraying his characters.[7]

Wolcott Gibbs selected for special commendation the comic role of Jessie Mae, played by Jo Van Fleet (*New York Times*, November 14, 1953). With regard to Van Fleet's performance, Gibbs stated perceptively that "altogether it is one of the funniest and most awe-inspiring comments on Southern womanhood I have ever seen."

The exception to these opinions that Foote's play retained the deficiencies of a small television play and thus did not prove convertible to the theatre was the review by William Hawkins in the *New York World-Telegram and Sun*. Hawkins did not qualify his high praise with any invidious remarks about "a small play." He said that the evening would prove to be "an indelible memory" and found that the play became an emotional chase that had "the suspense and tense excitement of the wildest physical contest." Hawkins also had unqualified praise for the dramaturgy. Foote, he wrote, had done the one beautiful thing necessary for a playwright to do: provide "disciplined material for expert actors" that completely captures an audience for an entire evening.

Lucy Kroll was pleased with the reception of the play. On November 19, 1953, she wrote Foote about its staging and advised him to take advantage "of the wonderful press and the audience response to the show" (HFC).

It is necessary to take a fresh look at the stage version of *The Trip to Bountiful* in order to see it not as "a small play" but as one with timely themes that make it equal to other seemingly slight plays like *The Glass Menagerie*. Although this play, about a mother living in a cramped city apartment with her son and daughter-in-law, bears an undeniable resemblance to *Marty,* it goes beyond that work. Not merely an expanded character sketch of an elderly woman returning to her birthplace, this play takes up perplexing subjects, such as the wrenching transition from country to big city and the meaninglessness of chaotic modern life treated by Existentialist dramatists of the day like Eugene Ionesco.

In a relevant article by Foote called "The Trip to Paradise," he gives a revealing clue to the larger meaning of an abandoned town named Bountiful. While passing the vanished towns of Wharton County with his grandparents, Foote as a boy asked why one town declined and another flourished. Enjoying a photograph collection of lost towns in Texas that flourished at the turn of the century, he is glad that it preserves scenes from another way of life. He lists some of the fanciful names such as "Sublime" and "Elysian Fields."[8] The title of this article confirms that the destination in the play can also be termed "a paradise." Bountiful is an idyllic place that harbored a purer life. It is also "paradise" in the sense that it is the heroine's heaven, where she would like to spend eternity. Finally, "Bountiful" connotes the many blessings of paradise.

To underline the idea of lost towns, Foote cites Robert Frost's poem "Directive," which narrates a trip to "a town that is no more a town" (p. 140). This poem describes a modern traveler's discovery of earlier values in an abandoned town, with an old house where people lived "in earnest" and which contained relics of toys belonging to children who needed only the simplest pleasures.[9]

This play features an absorbing central character, Mrs. Carrie Watts. The mother figure, standing alone after the father has died or left home, is an American archetype, seen in Williams's Amanda, Albee's Grandma of *The American Dream,* and Lena Younger of Lorraine Hansberry's *A Raisin in the Sun.* Foote's mother figure has her own personality, necessarily similar to the others in some respects, while differing also.

Carrie Watts is a particular mother, with some typical traits. She is gentle but determined, with the single-minded purpose of an earlier generation. She would have been born around 1890. Though southern in her speech and attachment to a fully remembered place, she lacks the aristocratic pretensions and theatrical flair that make Amanda such a striking lady, transferred from Delta Mississippi to St. Louis. No, Mrs. Watts lacks the qualities of the refined lady. If she can be labeled, it would be more accurate to call her a southern country lady. She is a lady who treats others with respect and courtesy, from the country with little education, an addiction to Methodist hymns (appropriate for one bearing the same name as Isaac Watts), and years of working on the land. All her previous life has furnished a conviction of what is right and wrong, of what is essential in life and what is not, what people need to live anywhere, and a belief in truth, hope, and courage, what Faulkner terms "the old verities" in his Nobel Prize speech. Mrs. Watts is thus qualified to take on the teacher role with her son, like Shaw's Candida with Marchbanks, and to guide him toward a stronger, more confident existence in the midst of adversity. Mrs. Watts, who must make the transition from a simpler time to a different one of dislocation, is a trustworthy mother who offers children of the modern generation guidelines for their unstable lives.

Here Foote again shows his grasp of Texas character in his creation of Mrs. Watts. She has been almost broken in her transfer from a rural community to the metropolis of Houston. Foote recognizes her type, which was common in the state. Not as common was her dogged return home to regain moral strength. She renews her memories of an earlier time and then is ready to live in the city environment, as many had to do in post–World War II Texas.

With Carrie Watts, Foote displays his sense of the tragic spirit, an element in drama going back to *Oedipus, the King,* which Foote admires.[10] The predicament of an elderly, unwanted mother-in-law transplanted to the city leads to suffering. Though she does not die in the end, her difficult life will continue back in the city, living with her son and his wife. If any evidence is needed that Foote is not sentimental, the ending of this play furnishes convincing proof. Happiness does not extend endlessly into the future for the heroine. The solution for Mrs. Watts is resignation to her fate—resolving to get along with her daughter-in-law and adjusting to a bleak life in the modern metropolis. Carrie Watts will face what the future holds with dignity.

Mrs. Watts in the last act names an important value to her son, Ludie, as she regrets what is missing from their life. She says that "the need to belong to a house, and a family and a town has gone from the rest of the world" (p. 124). Clearly she and Foote consider this a value that meant much to people of such a place. The modern world is worse off for having lost the value put on a place that one belonged to. As Flannery O'Connor said about New York literati: "They ain't *frum* anywhere!"[11] Mrs. Watts has no doubt where she is from. Knowing that one is from a definite place gives the individual identity and continuity with previous generations.

Not only does Mrs. Watts find value in a place, but she also remembers people now dead who personified worthy beliefs and virtues. Often in the play Mrs. Watts speaks of her father. Although he blocked her marriage to the man she loved, she remembers his virtues. She tells the sheriff: "My father was a good man, a peculiar man, but a good one" (p. 124).

Mrs. Watts's last surviving friend in Bountiful, Callie Davis, also stands for a belief of another time: working up to the time of death. Mrs. Watts is told by the ticket man at the Harrison bus station that Callie Davis drove her tractor the day before she died. The sheriff says that she died a lonely death all by herself in that big house, but Mrs. Watts, thinking of the cramped apartment in Houston, comments, "There are worse things." When she remarks to the sheriff that people have deserted the fields around Bountiful, he says that Callie Davis stayed on and made farming pay. "She learned how to treat her land right," he says, underlining the reward that comes with proper stewardship of the land, not exploitation (p. 125).

An important blessing that Mrs. Watts receives from the return to her country home is the strength obtained from nature. Having stayed in the concrete environs of Houston for twenty years, Mrs. Watts has lost contact with the soil. She says to Thelma, her traveling companion on the bus, that the first thing she wants to do on her return is to work in the soil of Callie's garden. Then she will live to be a hundred. She tells Ludie that by this trip she has recaptured her strength, which she gained before from the woods, the river, the Gulf, not from people. Many of Foote's strong characters show a closeness to nature. Elizabeth in *Valentine's Day* (1974–1978) will celebrate her newfound happiness by planting sweetheart roses at her new home.

The sheriff helps Mrs. Watts identify the call of a redbird. She wishes she could see a scissortail, which now is much rarer, but at the very end she does see one again: "Look, isn't that a scissor tail?" (p. 134). It is a memory that she can take back to the big city. As her father made this a sanctuary for birds, Bountiful is a sanctuary for its former inhabitant. Mrs. Watts's delight is expressed in sensual detail as she sees and listens to the birds.

Nature gives Mrs. Watts understanding of what happened in the sad lives of herself and her son. She had hoped in the Harrison bus station that by returning to Bountiful she could get some understanding of why her life had become so ugly. With agony she laments to Ludie that they should have stayed to fight because that would have been better than their present joyless life. Then she looks at the cycle of life around her, and that makes her philosophical, as she can be from time to time. The land her father planted in cotton is now grown up in woods. The people left the country for the city, but she thinks that someday the cycle will recommence as people return, farm the land, and then leave again.

The whole pilgrimage that Mrs. Watts makes to her paradise takes on a religious quality. From the beginning of the play, Mrs. Watts has fortified her spirit by singing hymns, which she names to sympathetic listeners like Thelma. She has been singing "There's No Friend Like the Lowly Jesus" as she makes her tortuous way back to Bountiful. Mrs. Watts feels free to admit to Thelma that she did not love her husband, causing Mrs. Watts to wonder if we are punished for doing wrong, though only one preacher agrees with that. When she hears of Thelma's anxiety over her absent soldier-husband, Mrs. Watts recites the Ninety-first Psalm, about the Lord's keeping the supplicant under His wing. The last thing that Mrs. Watts does before leaving her birthplace is to kneel devoutly and let its soil run through her hands. This act has the quality of a sacred ritual. She physically touches the soil of Bountiful, which is indeed holy to her. Made from this dust herself, she is ready to return to dust now that she has regained her dignity. The last words become a "nunc dimittis" to herself as she says, "Goodbye, Bountiful, Goodbye," and leaves this place for the last time.

The proof of the benefit that Mrs. Watts has received from her return to Bountiful can be seen in the effects on her spirit. She regains her sense of humor and can laugh at herself. She discovers the government check that she had believed was lost stuck in her dress. "That's a good joke on me," she says (p. 133).

By this play, Foote clearly aligns himself with those American writers who find their most helpful values in the past, like Wilder, as opposed to those who do not, such as Hemingway. Foote abhors certain aspects of modernity such as alienation and rootlessness. He finds balm not in new ideologies or in revolts from former behaviors, like Tennessee Williams's anti-Victorianism in *Summer and Smoke,* but rather in revivals of past beliefs.

What particular values of the past stand out in *The Trip to Bountiful?* Foote, recognizing an absence of belonging in modern life, like O'Neill in *The Hairy Ape,* believes that the sense of belonging to a place, a family, and a house gave meaning to the people of rural America. This meaning has inevitably been lost in the anonymous life of the big city, which delights the repellent Jessie Mae. The frantic life of the city unsettles migrants from the country, who find no substitute for its spiritual nourishment.

Not least, *The Trip to Bountiful* succeeds as a play because of two other major characters and two well-realized minor ones. The transition from television turned this play for the small screen into a much fuller work, containing the development of character necessary for a major stage play. Reginald Rose in his commentary on *Ten Angry Men* said that in a television play it is hard to develop both character and plot. In his film of *Ten Angry Men,* Rose devoted most of the added time to exploring the characters and the motivations for their behavior.[12]

In the television version, Ludie appears only briefly in the first act. Thus, the portrayal of a stronger character in the third act of the television play is not sufficiently prepared for. In the third act of the stage play, the problem with his job and timidity before his wife in front of his mother are added, which make his change at the end much more effective.

In the third act of the television play, Ludie shows a lack of convincing development. He still speaks in a wheedling tone. After his mother has peevishly torn up the government check and made an apology, Jessie Mae says all is forgiven; Ludie can only beg for "a pleasant ride home" (p. 61). Ludie's development is much stronger in the stage version. He revives his memories of Bountiful when he drinks from the creek. At the end of the play, taking a new stand toward his wife, he asserts: "We've got to stop this wrangling once and for all. You've given me your word and I expect you to keep your word" (p. 134). Finally he announces that all three of them have to live henceforth in peace. The dramatic development of Ludie from passivity to firmness, as a bringer of peace, goes a long way to making this a more fully developed play than it was on television.

If Mrs. Watts longs for a return to her home in the country because of the strains of modern urban life, her son is not so aware of his need. Ludie is one of Foote's defeated modern men, like the unhappy sons in *The Death of the Old Man* who did not succeed in the city after leaving Harrison.[13] We learn that Ludie had been sick, lost his job, seeks a raise, and is reading a book on how to become an executive. His timidity before his shrewish wife marks him as an unaggressive, passive man; he does not resist being ordered around by her.

The most striking change that occurs when Ludie returns to Bountiful is the revival of his memories. In Houston he protested his mother's recollections of Bountiful, although he would join her sometimes, re-calling the song about the mockingbird she sang to him as a boy. Back in Bountiful, where he was born and grew up before his mother sold most of the land to educate him, he remembers. When Mrs. Watts says he looks like his grandfather now, he remembers that, at the funeral, the best friend of his grandfather told him that his grandfather had left an ex-ample to follow. Even after saying that it does no good to remember and refusing to enter the dilapidated house, Ludie remembers that he liked to drink from the creek. That water always seemed to taste better. His last line in fact is a memory: "The house used to look so big" (p. 134).

Back in Bountiful, Ludie remembers the promise made to his grand-mother to name a son after his grandfather. "I would have too," he says, "but I did not have a son, nor a daughter." His friend Billy Davidson, who has four children, asked him, "What do you live for, Ludie?" His answer was an incomplete sentence: "Well, Billy, . . ." He cries out, "Oh, Mama, I haven't made any kind of life for you, either one of you and I try so hard" (pp. 128–129).

Ludie nevertheless finds moral courage, which is the blessing that he receives from Bountiful. He acquires an inner power that enables him to become the peacemaker in a troubled family. At the end, when Jessie Mae begins to argue with his mother again, he reminds his wife that she promised to keep the peace. They are not going to have any more such arguments, he declares, as the two women stare in astonishment at this new, firm Ludie. He tells his mother and wife, "We have to live to-gether and we're going to live together in peace" (p. 134). Foote has re-marked that Ludie derives strength from returning to Bountiful just as his mother does.[14]

The play's attack on urban superficiality would be incomplete without its epitome, the comic but irritating Jessie Mae. Foote shows again, as with Mamie Borden of *Only the Heart,* his gift for caricature. He has com-mented that Jessie Mae has been done many times in southern fiction "but you have to cut through that."[15] In fact she speaks the "southernese" of Welty's wives at the beauty parlor in "Petrified Man." Besides pro-viding many counterpoints to the country-bred, disarming Mrs. Watts, Jessie Mae furnishes the comic relief that is absolutely necessary in this play of modern unhappiness.

Jessie Mae, the worshiper of materialism, is motivated by greed. She is single-minded when it comes to money. When Ludie talks about his mother's dying from heart trouble if she goes to Bountiful, all Jessie Mae can think of is how much it would cost to bring her body back for burial. She is continually preoccupied with Ludie's salary and his keeping his job in order to satisfy her personal needs. Jessie Mae further wants her mother-in-law in the apartment because it frees her from domestic chores and enables her to enjoy personal pleasures, like "Coca-Colas" with Rosella in the drugstore. In contrast to Mrs. Watts's desire to return to Bountiful, Jessie Mae dreams only of going to Hollywood.

Jessie Mae manifests traits that may have kept her childless. Very prudish, she tells Ludie to look the other way when she removes her dressing gown before getting in bed. She has not sought help from a doctor to correct her childlessness, saying that if God wanted her to have a baby, He would have let her. Furthermore she tells Thelma that she does not need a child, since she already has Mother Watts and Ludie on her hands. One concludes that this self-centered woman secretly does not want a child to interfere with her personal life.

Jessie Mae gains nothing from her trip to Bountiful unless it is the satisfaction of Mrs. Watts's promises not to sing hymns in her presence or run in the house. Significantly Jessie Mae is horrified to hear of Ludie's liking to drink the creek water: "I knew a man once that went on a huntin' trip and drank out of a creek and caught something and died." She can think only of heading for the nearest drugstore and exclaims, "I'm so thirsty I could drink ten Coca-Colas" (p. 132).

Besides furnishing indispensable exposition in the play, two minor characters also respect the values that Mrs. Watts finds in Bountiful. Thelma, the wife of a soldier fighting in Korea, proves that among the younger generation affirmation of past values continues. She listens to Mrs. Watts's recollections of Bountiful, appreciates her hymns, and helps to retrieve her purse. She loves her husband very much and, while he is away, stays with her parents, showing that she maintains family ties. Mrs. Watts says significantly that if she had had a daughter, she would have chosen one like Thelma.

Another well-drawn character is the sheriff of Harrison, who is indispensable in Mrs. Watts's attempt to reach Bountiful. He also exemplifies the old values of Bountiful. In the most dramatic scene of the play, Mrs. Watts protests that no sheriff, king, or president is going to keep her from returning to Bountiful. Though the sheriff had ordered that she must remain at the station until her son arrives, he relents after learning of her long-held desire to see Bountiful again. In *The Trip to Bountiful* the sheriff takes mercy on a distraught woman and bends the law's strictness by driving Mrs. Watts out to Bountiful.

This sheriff practices the old virtues that are preserved in the small town. He takes time to listen to Mrs. Watts talk about her father, as Thelma listened. He knows the birds and identifies them to Mrs. Watts. Finally he speaks to Mrs. Watts with old-fashioned courtesy. He always answers her with a "Yes, ma'am" and in his last words goes through a conventional but sincere parting. In return for her thanks, he replies, "I was glad I could oblige" (p. 126).

It was not long after the Broadway closing of *Bountiful* that its backers began to think of a film. Kroll reported to Foote on April 28, 1955, that Coe had talked with Vincent Donehue about making the film, with the latter as director and Coe as producer. Coe believed that *Marty* had broken ground as a film, and Donehue and he believed that *Bountiful* would be "a great motion picture" (HFC). Chayefsky had blazed the way for a television play to be adapted as a film, but it would be thirty years before *Bountiful* would attain its successful reincarnation.

In 1985, *The Trip to Bountiful* was made into a successful movie, starring Geraldine Page as Mrs. Watts, a role for which she won the Academy Award. The film is a superior one and a worthy rendition of the play. Jessie Mae is a more sympathetic character, especially in her romantic attitude toward Ludie, seen most overtly in the last scene, when she walks off arm in arm with him. This version also stresses nostalgia in an effective way, as Mrs. Watts longs for her former home and rejoices on her return to it. The emotion is genuinely moving and not false. Page contributes another quality that enriches her conception. She makes Mrs. Watts a formerly flirtatious belle like Amanda Wingfield in her recollection of dancing when young and her girlish mannerisms when she recalls for the bus station attendant her coming to Harrison: "You know I came to my first dance in this town."[16] This scene offsets the impression that she is merely a sweet old lady. In the movie a bus stop interlude is added appropriately in 1985. A Mexican is present whose incomprehension of English leads to a sneer from a Texan bystander, who thereby condemns himself.

Two individuals involved in making the movie did not strengthen Foote's hope that it could be produced "without sentimentality."[17] Peter Masterson, Foote's cousin who had directed the popular success *The Best Little Whorehouse in Texas,* was the director and had strong ideas about the film's appeal to a larger audience, a view that often brought the author and the director into disagreement. At the beginning of the film, Masterson selected a beautiful soprano voice for the hymn "Jesus Is Calling Me Home," while a young mother chases her son through the bluebonnet field. Foote complained, "That's terrible. Mrs. Watts would never have sung like that." Masterson countered that "she thinks she did" (p. 233).

Carlin Glynn could not keep from feeling sorry for the character she played. She allowed her personal feelings to affect the personality of Jessie Mae, who does not succeed if made likable. Glynn, Masterson's wife, said that she was assigned to play a character who is basically a villain. She decided her "biggest architectural job" in the role was "to embrace her" (p. 238).

The subsequent production record of *The Trip to Bountiful* proves that this work has demonstrated the most staying power of all Foote's creations and the most sustained esteem. *Bountiful* was televised on the *Saturday Night Theatre* in Britain, March 30, 1957. Many productions were given that year in the United States. Rights for its production in Amsterdam were granted June 11, 1958. In 1959 it was performed at Theatre East, New York. An Australian production was given in 1962. After the film appeared in 1985 and won the Academy Award for best actress, royalties showed a new surge. The Dramatists Play Service royalties dated February 10, 1988, show this work far ahead of others, such as *A Young Lady of Property*.

A more recent production of *Bountiful* was praised highly. Ben Brantley reviewed the performance by Ellen Burstyn, well-known actress of the Phoenix Theatre Company, at the Performing Arts Center of the State University College, Purchase, New Jersey (*New York Times,* August 20, 1993). Below the heading "A New Traveler Makes a Classic Journey Home," Brantley recognized "the perniciousness of deracination in an urban society."

Long-term records of performance prove convincingly the worth of a dramatic work, and *Bountiful* is no exception. Here Foote conceives a play rooted in the subconscious because of its archetypal pattern—the longing to return home. This is no longer an obsession, however, as the last scene in both play and movie shows. In the former "she kneels for a moment holding the dirt, then slowly lets it drift through her fingers back to the ground." In the film she only touches the soil with her hands, and as the car drives away, she looks straight ahead, not back at Bountiful.

When I asked Horton Foote on a visit to his home on March 12, 1994, which was his best play, he modestly answered that my opinion would be more valuable. I replied *The Trip to Bountiful*. Now I would add that it is because it catches the deep love of "home"—the first, the childhood home. In the movie *The Wizard of Oz,* Dorothy cries, "I'm home, Auntie Em! I'm home!" At the beginning of the last act, Mrs. Watts says to the sheriff, "I'm home. I'm home. I'm home . . . I thank you." This deep longing for "home"—when prepared for, as it is in this play—is an artistic achievement.

8

CHRISTIAN SCIENCE

IN addition to Foote's professional activities in the theatre, important developments were taking place in his personal life that have a bearing on his dramatic works. He started living in New York City in 1936 and moved in 1956 to Upper Nyack, on the Hudson River, where he built a house. Lucy Kroll was pleased with Foote's letter about the new house, saying that his announcement was "so full of birth and hope." In 1955, Foote had informed her that the building would begin in the spring. There would be enough money earned from his television work to build as quickly as possible.[1] By this time he and his wife, Lillian, had two children: Hallie and Horton Junior. The new location would be a more convenient place to raise their children. Foote moved with his family to New Hampshire in 1966. He returned to New York in 1978 and thereafter divided his time between New York and Wharton.

Even though Christian Science is never mentioned explicitly in Foote's plays, in a literary biography a knowledge of it is needed to understand his activities outside the theatre and who his friends were.

Foote's Christian Science faith became evident in correspondence with his mother. Christian Science is a religion based on the principles of divine healing expressed in the acts of Jesus Christ. It was started by Mary Baker Eddy, who published *Science and Health with Key to the Scriptures* in 1875 and founded the Church of Christ, Scientist in 1879. At services a member reads from the Bible and from *Science and Health*. During Wednesday meetings, members give testimonies. Beliefs of this religion found in Foote's plays include that death is not God's punishment for wrongdoing (in *Courtship*); God desires instead health. Scientists agree that it is unscriptural to say that suffering is God's will. Rather,

God's will is for wholeness and health. Christian Scientists deny the reality of the material world, seen in Foote's antimaterialism. They argue that illness and sin are illusions to be overcome by the mind. Nothing can substitute for compassion. Emphasis is upon healing, primarily of sin, secondarily of disease. Thus Christian Scientists refuse medical help in fighting sickness. The main means of healing is prayer. There are no pastors, but rather "practitioners." Like Foote, this religion does not proselytize. Christian Scientists oppose foreordination, or election of a few to be saved. Because of such tenets, the church has attracted disaffected Protestants.

In the late 1950s when Foote was screenwriting Faulkner's *Old Man* for *Playhouse 90,* he referred to Christian Science in a letter to his mother. He reported that "Brother" (Horton Foote, Jr.) had been ill with the measles and "wanted C. S. to help and showed a lot of courage and faith." He and his wife had to notify the doctors, who were "amazed at how quickly he was up." Since Horton Foote, Jr., was born in 1952, this undated letter was probably written in 1958, when the boy was six years old and Foote was working on *Old Man,* referred to in this letter (HFC).

Foote had mentioned Christian Science to Lillian in letters from Los Angeles, when he was working on the *Playhouse 90* production of *Old Man.* On October 21, 1958, he asked her to order a Bible "the same size as the *Science and Health* the church is getting me [by Mary Baker Eddy]." On October 31, 1958, he wrote his wife that he had attended a Christian Science service the previous night at "Fifth Church." It was "a wonderful meeting" with "an excellent 1st Reader" (HFC).

Foote's mother, Hallie Brooks Foote, was the main religious influence on Foote. She had written to her son about Christian Science at an earlier time. In a letter dated July 7, 1944, she reported that Norton Rugeley had been confined to the hospital in Corpus Christi for two months. She disagreed with the treatment saying, "There is a simpler way for all to know about and how I wish they would practice and learn of Christian Science." On July 3, 1944, Hallie Foote had described the "church service yesterday," when the "second reader" moved to another light to read better but had to relinquish his reading because he had left his glasses in El Campo (HFC).

Hallie Foote's part in her son's conversion to Christian Science is confirmed by her brother in a letter to Foote dated September 13, 1962. Speed Brooks was glad Foote became interested in Christian Science—"Hallie's influence I'm sure." The impact of Christian Science on Foote's plays is not explicit; no Christian Scientists are named in any of his plays, nor is there a consistent avoidance of medical treatment by any of his characters. On the other hand, Christian belief is prominent in his characters' lives, and talk about the church is ubiquitous in his plays. The Christian faith is presented with respect and sensitivity, an approach not common in the works of other American playwrights, such as O'Neill, Williams, and Albee.

Foote's affiliation with Christian Science becomes apparent in indirect remarks from the autobiographical lecture "Seeing and Imagining" (1989), in which he describes wryly the view from his home in Wharton. Across the street is "the huge complex" that is part of the First Baptist Church; to the side is "a small, very small frame building that houses the Christian Science Society" (p. 3). In his plays there is frequently a sarcastic line or two about the dominance of Baptists in Harrison, which was true in many small towns of Texas. In *Lily Dale,* Mrs. Coons, a Baptist, replies to Horace's remark that he is "an Episcopalian," though no such church exists in the rural community where he works. Mrs. Coons says, "Yes, in Harrison they have only a very small congregation"; then she adds proudly, *"I'm a Baptist."* [2] Though Foote is fair and tolerant in naming denominations, it is not surprising, given his Christian Science affiliation, that he sometimes casts a jaundiced eye on other, larger churches, particularly the Baptists.

Foote's first television plays of the 1950s reveal a stronger religious tone than do those he wrote for the New York stage in the 1940s, like *Only the Heart.* The characters are clearly based on religious family and friends. Significantly, one of the first plays composed by Foote for television features an explicitly religious theme. Religious organizations had approached him. *Ludie Brooks* (note the last name of his mother's family) was a piece commissioned by *Religion in Everyday Life* for its series *A Lamp unto My Feet.* It was presented by CBS on February 4, 1951, and repeated on March 13, 1955. The first showing was seen by Fred Coe, who thereafter asked Foote to write original plays for the *Philco Playhouse.*

Ludie Brooks presents the spiritual crisis of a Methodist preacher who has lost the will to pray after the death of his beloved daughter Martha. In the bereaved household we see Daisy, his wife; Mrs. Brooks, his seventy-year-old mother; and Maybelle, Martha's surviving daughter. Mrs. Brooks, the mother, remembers her son's switch from farming to preaching. She thought he should have remained a farmer, but he announced, "Mama,

I've used the plow for the last time. I've had the call. I'm gonna be a preacher." Mother Brooks replied, "Suit yourself, honey, long as it's a Methodist preacher." She adds that when she heard him preach the first time, he was not "a spell binder" but "real sincere." [3] The deeply religious nature of this short play is established at the outset and continues throughout, which makes it very different from the dramas presented on secular programs.

Ludie must overcome his spiritual crisis and regain his faith. A neighbor, Mrs. May, intruding on his privacy as he is trying to pray, tells Daisy that she is anxious about the whereabouts of her son, whom she had not heard from. She wants Ludie to pray with her. Ludie sees Mrs. May, hears how she has endured the blows to her Christian faith, and takes her testimony as the guidance he needs. He will return to the ministry, renewing his faith, and continue his call to be a minister.

Commenting on this religious play, Terry Barr writes that one would think from reading it that the author is very religious, and according to Foote, this is so. Having said that, Barr adds this disclaimer: "Foote maintains that he prefers to keep this religious side from entering his work." [4] This statement must be taken with the qualification that religious questions will nevertheless enter Foote's writing in the future. Barr writes that questions of religion like loss of faith in God and man recur throughout Foote's career. Unlike Ludie, some characters in the plays do not receive the comfort or security of having their prayers answered. [5]

The other early religious play that Foote composed, *The Rocking Chair,* though filled with religious believers and vocabulary, differs significantly from *Ludie Brooks*. Its characters are similarly religious and pious, but the theme is not so overtly Christian. *The Rocking Chair* was written in 1948 when Foote was living in Washington, D.C., and was produced by Coe on NBC in May 1953.

Unlike *Ludie Brooks,* which directly presents the theme of losing and regaining one's Christian faith, this one-act play humorously treats a physician's inability to retire to the rocking chair. It is the story of an elderly doctor, Dr. Ewing, who has announced his retirement several times, only to abandon his rocking chair and return once more to his practice as a physician, beloved by the poor, rural people of the county. His wife is based on Foote's real great-aunt Loula Horton Irwin, the wife of a beloved doctor in Wharton (Dr. Irwin, whose daughter also died). Loula Ewing has finally succeeded in getting Dr. Ewing to sit in his rocking chair on the front gallery as he renounces his medical service of many years. Every time Loula sees a retirement present for her husband, she says, "Thank you, Lord, that means he'll just have to go through with it."[6]

But the doctor's wife cannot ignore the never-ending line of visitors that upset her plans. The Giffords' old yardman, who has no money to pay, comes seeking the doctor. Samuel, an old black man from the country, cannot change to a new doctor's office in town. The doctor is unhappy because "my conscience hurts me when I sit here when I'm needed" (p. 19). Dr. Ewing is a faithful member of the Methodist church who attends prayer meetings. Finally, Dr. Ewing cannot endure the idleness combined with the urge to heal his patients. He leaves Loula in her rocking chair, takes his own inside, and notifies her that he will be back in the evening after visiting Samuel in the country.

Although this television play is not overtly religious in its humorous theme of the inability to retire, it includes a clear preference for one kind of Christianity over another: the caring versus the indifferent kind. A delegation arrives from the Methodist church choir to deliver a present for the retiring doctor. Edna Mae Hooten tells Dr. Ewing that the Lord has blessed him, because he will spend the rest of his days on the porch rocking. When Lucy Jay, another member from the choir, presents him a Bible, Mrs. Ewing observed pointedly, "Why don't the Baptists ever think of things like that?" (p. 14). This play is more typical of the kind of play that Foote would write from this time on than *Ludie Brooks*. He develops a moral theme, the insistent urge to heal those who are helpless, and places it in the mouth of a Christian believer, but he does not treat Christian belief explicitly. His subsequent plays like this prototype nevertheless differ from those of his contemporaries in presenting Christian principles positively. They differ further from those of such contemporaries as Arthur Miller, who, like most modern playwrights, omits religious belief entirely from the thought of his characters. It is no wonder that Foote is highly esteemed in such publications as *The Christian Century, Christianity Today,* and the *Christian Science Monitor.*

Recently, Foote has referred to his own religious commitment. In an interview in 1994, Foote, when asked if he belonged to any religious denomination, replied, "I am a Christian Scientist," as was his deceased wife.[7] He said later that he considered Christian Science a kind of study.[8] James M. Wall, a writer on religion, says that Foote was raised "in bedrock Protestantism" but left the Methodist church "and as an adult converted to Christian Science," a faith little known in the Texas of his childhood, but "one he faithfully follows."[9] In Foote's plays, southern Protestant culture is always in the background, based on his relatives' connection with Methodist and Episcopal churches.

Foote has talked at greater length about his religious faith in two interviews for the *Christian Science Sentinel,* the weekly publication of the church.[10] These interviews throw light on the genesis of his Christian Science faith, such religious beliefs as anti-materialism, the nature of God and human beings, and his opposition to proselytizing. Certain ideas have a clear bearing on his dramatic writings, such as his adoption of the *Christian Science Monitor* as a model. At the time of the second interview, Foote was a member of the editorial board of Monitor Television, which reviewed programming for the television network of the *Christian Science Monitor.*

I mention the *Monitor,* but in discussing issues, Foote is careful not to introduce Christian Science doctrines explicitly. Occasionally, I indicate ideas that may have come from Christian Science, but one cannot be absolutely certain.

In his second interview (April 7, 1991), Foote spoke of the beginnings of his Christian Science faith in 1953. Answering a question from Allison W. Phinney, editor of the *Sentinel,* Foote noted a retrospective of his work from 1953 to the present in Cleveland, Ohio. Shown there were five of his early "television things," nine films, and a current play. "I began writing and began studying Christian Science about the same time [that is, 1953]," he said. "I was touched by these early television plays, how much of what I was learning in Christian Science asserted itself" (2, p. 13). Viewing them, he could see that "this search" for values has always been there.

Of particular interest is the relevance of Foote's comments related to his plays. We note in the first interview (April 27, 1987) with Marilynne Mason, film critic for a Denver, Colorado, weekly, his adoption of the *Christian Science Monitor* as a model for objective but critical commentary. Answering a question about Hollywood's giving moviegoers what they want, he made a contrast with the *Monitor:* "I think of the daily *Monitor* and the job the *Monitor* does in making us aware without preaching." He wished that the circulation were larger, "but I think of all the substance that is there and all the power and I take that as my model" (1, p. 5).

Continuing to stress objectivity, Foote emphasized his dislike of "preaching" or proselytizing. One may conclude that he disliked didacticism. He was wary of any stated thesis or "sense of proselytizing," he said. "As an artist, as a writer, I don't consciously do that." He preferred the policy of the *Monitor,* even though some had said that it focused on things that were "upsetting." He realized, however, "as a Christian Scientist, that it was done to shake me up and make me do my spiritual work" (1, p. 6). The stress on objectivity here repeated the ideal that Foote has admired in Katherine Anne Porter's works.[11]

In these interviews, Foote discussed some religious beliefs derived from Christian Science that reappear in his dramatic works. Of first importance is the condemnation of materialism. One cannot help noticing in his plays the conviction that spiritual belief should replace concentration on the material world. According to Foote, spiritual belief is the key to healing achieved by those sick in body or mind. He told the interviewer, "The one problem that frightens me most about American society is the materialism. I do feel that we have to be alert to this ever increasing materialism" (2, p. 12). Foote expressed his gratitude to Christian Science for emphasizing spiritual priority and giving him "a perspective." He speculated that maybe that is "the great desire behind creativity—to bring some order" (2, p. 12).

In the course of these interviews, Foote expressed certain ideas that have a clear bearing on his plays and films. With regard to dramatic form, he commented first on character change. As a Christian Scientist, he believed that people do change: "It's the nature of drama that some change takes place" (1, p. 4). Concerning the necessity of a happy ending, he said that endings don't have to be happy "to have a sense of encouragement about them." Early on he became "enamored of the courage of people to meet devastating things" (1, p. 7). Again, note his praise of this spiritual quality, as in his plays. Touching on sentimentality in art and especially movies, the interviewer asked, "What can a writer do to nourish spiritual values in a medium that often brutalizes or trivializes with sentimentality, the deeper yearnings of the heart?" Foote answered succinctly but forcefully, "I don't know what you can do, really, except mind your own store" (1, p. 8).

Foote also ventured into larger religious topics in the interviews. On his development as a Christian Scientist, he said, "I'm a devout Christian Scientist. I grow in Science, I perceive more deeply." He continued, "When you surfeit yourself with materialistic things you are apt to get caught up in that. I think spiritual values beget spiritual values, and spiritual values lead you to hunger for more spiritual values" (1, p. 6).

Foote boldly entered the realm of theology when he discussed his belief in God. "Substance means a lot to me," he stated. And that substance "doesn't come from me—that is, I reflect qualities of God." He had been thinking a lot about a play. Insofar as it "manifests certain spiritual qualities, then the better it is." Connecting God's nature with man's, Foote answered the question, "What do you feel about the nature of man?" "Speaking as a Christian Scientist," he replied, he strove every day "to understand more deeply that man is made in the likeness and image of God." To grasp that image you have to know "what God is," which "you could spend infinity trying to find out" (1, p. 7).

The effect of Christian Science teaching on Foote's view of human nature is recognizable in his plays. Keeping in mind Foote's ability to discover redeeming qualities in bad characters, we note his positive outlook. He reported that he knew "the downsides of human nature, but if you look at the overall picture, you see more." To support this generalization, he gave a specific example. Since his childhood he had been aware of "the problem of alcoholism because I had some uncles who were struggling with that." He continued, "I loved them very much," but they were defeated by the alcoholism. He excluded Mac Sledge in *Tender Mercies,* however. Not to recognize those who were not defeated "would be untruthful" (2, p. 8).

Finally as for the healing effect that is central to the Christian Scientist's faith, Foote had this to say. Asked if his films had "a healing effect," he replied, "I've been told that. When I saw some of those early films of mine [in the 1950s], they had a healing effect on me." They were "strengthening and affirming and gave me courage" (2, p. 13).

The following beliefs or tenets are condensed from a Christian Science lecture. These statements are based on an informative talk entitled "Christian Science: The Law of Love," delivered by Kittie Burris, a member of the Christian Science Board of Lectureship, in 1999.[12] The statements given by Mrs. Burris derive from the writings of Mary Baker Eddy, founder of the Church of Christ, Scientist, and the ideas reappear in the themes of Foote's plays. Mrs. Eddy, who cherished kindness, was deprived of her only child because it was felt that she was not qualified to raise him; she was reunited with him only when he was an adult. Mrs. Eddy disapproved of being "argumentative" about a subject, since it caused unpredictable responses.

The adherents to this faith acknowledge God's "forgiveness," a paramount virtue and one of Foote's recurrent ideas. It is the main theme of *The Habitation of Dragons* (1988). Christian Scientists believe in "complete forgiveness." Those who forgive are no longer in the hold of evil. Forgiveness is the cancellation of the negative past; it is not the religion of "sentimentality." Foote's emphasis on forgiveness has a solid foundation in Christian Science as well as in Christianity.

In one's search after truth, the Bible is the constant companion. For the Christian Scientist, *Science and Health with Key to the Scriptures,* by Mrs. Eddy (first published in 1875), is "the pastor" for this religion, which has no clergy. It is the sufficient guide to eternal life. Sickness is a temptation to believe that its cause is "the atmosphere" or some other false reason, not misguided thinking. The antidote is spiritual faith.

The first biblical chapter much used by Christian Scientists, according to Mrs. Burris, is the one quoted by Carrie Watts on the bus to Bountiful: Psalm 91, which begins "He that dwelleth in the secret place of the most High shall abide under the shadow of the almighty." The Christian Scientist believes in the "Father-Mother God"; as a father, God protects, and as a mother, God cares and comforts. Christian Science virtues that Foote emphasizes in his plays include kindness, compassion, and seeing every human being not as sinful and evil but as a child of God.

Foote says that in his writings he does not make a religious statement. "I watch and observe," he says, and he tries to be as objective and truthful as he can to "the human condition."[13] In an interview with Gerald Wood and Terry Barr, Foote answered their query about his religious faith: "I am deeply religious but I never write from that point of view. I don't proselytize." The latter word is used repeatedly by Foote in discussing his religious belief. Wood and Barr report that people who know him say that Foote lives Christianity rather than preaching any particular religious dogma.[14]

CHAPTER

9

PEOPLE AND THEMES

IF Foote is not a philosopher-dramatist like Sartre and does not read intellectual works as Albee does, what is the main source for his plays? It is certainly people, whom Foote listens to and transforms into dramatis personae like Mrs. Watts of *The Trip to Bountiful*. He is not unlike a contemporary novelist, Clyde Edgerton, who fashioned administrators of a small Christian college in *Raney* (1985) from men he had observed himself.

The two most important women in Foote's life were his mother and his wife. The former, Hallie Brooks Foote, wrote to him, giving the news of his kindred and town.[1] Also she expressed some fine sentiments. An important series of her letters to Foote, which he deposited in his collection, tells a lot about their close relationship. Foote was then living in Nyack, New York. In 1962 she wrote him several times in late summer, describing the bumper crop of cotton: "The cotton is something to write about. . . . The gins are going day and night." She said that "not many were in the store" (his father's haberdashery); however, "We're enjoying the bountiful harvest," just the same. She noted, "Dad said we all should be making a million. We hope the results (of this crop) will be coming later."

Soon afterward Wharton was hit by a destructive storm. Hallie wrote Foote, alluding to his play, *The Night of the Storm:* "This has been 'The Days* and *Night* of the Storm.'" She wrote her son in great detail of the damage. After the storm passed, there was no electricity. Hallie and her husband drove out to get "some cooked food." In Hungerford they had "about 6 cups of coffee." Plus, a family "served us toast, jelly and Bohemian (garlic) sausage,—no water—. The Brandl's did a big business & their place surely served well—." Then she commented on the goodness of people in such a crisis, in words that Foote might have written himself: "At times of stress everybody seems so kind, thoughtful & helpful and that checks us always again on how fine people are."

By coincidence, at this time Foote's play *The Night of the Storm* was being shown on television. Hallie had read it in the *Houston Post*. "You'll see from Johnny's letter the public is noticing (your play)," she wrote. John Foote, Foote's brother, lived in Houston.

Next year in the spring, Hallie wrote her son a long description of the flowers. This is the basis for Elizabeth's announcement about the flowers she is going to plant after her marriage in the *Orphans' Home Cycle*. The lines are very close in Hallie's letter to Foote. In spring 1963, Hallie wrote that "magnolias are in full bloom in Sealy" (a picturesque town that Foote and Lillian loved to visit). She also raved over azaleas and camellias, "which are always beautiful." She added, "I have had Dutch Iris and Louisiana phlox in bloom."

Hallie kept up with Foote's work closely. She asked him several times about *The Traveling Lady*, which became *Baby, the Rain Must Fall*, a popular movie: "How is 'Traveling Lady' coming on?" She quoted Foote's literary agent on that play when Lucy Kroll was in Dallas. "If 'Traveling Lady' is filmed in Wharton," Hallie wrote, "wild horses can't keep me away."

After *To Kill a Mockingbird* was released in 1963, Hallie wrote that "Dad" read of "its opening in the Houston papers." They could hardly wait to see it. Al Foote, like many men, let his wife write the letters. I have not seen a single letter from him to his son, but Hallie referred to Al often in her letters to Foote, and Al talked to his son on the telephone. Hallie reported that, in late 1963, "Dad" talked with Foote "on Tuesday." After this long call, Al "had a big cry," she noted, "He is grateful for two fine sons."

In another letter of the same period, Hallie wrote, "Dad is stepping out tonight. . . . 'Abe' invited him to the brotherhood at the Jewish Community Center." She added that it would be easier to go now than when he attended for the first time last year.

In 1962–1963, Foote's mother wrote constantly to her son, virtually every day. In the newsy letters she mentioned persons that played a central part in Foote's life: his aunts Laura and Rosa Brooks. They inspired many female characters in his plays. The Brooks sons have been recognized, but the daughters have been overlooked.

These aunts were constantly present in Foote's life, and they influenced him as much as their brothers did. Laura, the second daughter, was gentle and shy, like Laura in *Courtship*. She married Oliver Ray and moved to Dallas, pregnant with her first child. Like Laura of the *Cycle,* she had a sweet voice and a scar on her throat from an injury.

The Rays were close friends of Al and Hallie Foote's and saw them often. They lived on the road to "Corpus (Christi)" in Jackson County. Hallie writes Foote that Laura "almost bought a Thunderbird" and a Hammond organ, expecting to strike oil, like the family in *The Oil Well.* Further checks showed no reason "to try for a well." Foote obviously found an idea for the one-act on television here. When the big storm hit the area in 1962, Laura's beach house was damaged but not destroyed. On September 7, 1973, Laura reported going to church with Nan Dean Outlar "almost every Sunday."

Aunt Laura appears as Laura Vaughn in *Courtship*. Laura is as complex in that play as the real Laura was. Foote saw the real Laura's timidity and fearful personality, and thus she is the beginning of the character. Foote makes the character a contrast to Elizabeth and heightens her as pitiable. She does not have as large a part as Elizabeth, but her part is just as interesting. Her personality is melodramatic, near tragic. There is no other character quite like her in Foote's plays. In the film, she is simpering and pretty, but doomed. She is overcome by her fears of disappointing her parents. More deeply, Laura is overcome by life. In the film, she wants direction from Elizabeth and asks questions about her future. Her life remains "open-ended," and no final answer is given, as it should not be in a realistic play.

The third daughter of the Brookses was Rosa, to whom Foote was closest. She was highly educated, having graduated from the University of Texas and received a master's degree from Columbia University. She married Dick Johnston, who was not a good provider and drank. Their first child, a son, was born dead. The second, a girl, was named Daisy Brooks after her grandmother. Rosa left her husband and went to live with her mother in Houston. She eventually became a social worker.

"Rosa" is the niece of Josie the matriarch in *Night Seasons* (1993), a late play. Foote made use of family members very patently, sometimes not even changing the names. This fictitious character is pathetic but still a strong woman. The stage Rosa works in an Austin cafeteria, needs an operation, and is always short of money. In these years Foote repeated the habit of modeling characters in Harrison after his immediate kindred. In the depictions of Laura and Rosa he is still objective but has great compassion for these aunts.

Rosa did not marry in the play. By the time Foote wrote it, she was dead but that did not stop Foote from mourning and portraying her. He was stimulated by her life and loved her. She was the poor relative who really has no home. For him she represented the Victorian woman who was trained for nothing and thus could not find a good-paying job. Evidently this aunt was the model for other characters named Rosa in Foote's plays. If a character reminds this playwright of someone, he often calls him or her by that name.

Foote's aunt Rosa had more "compassion" for her brothers than anybody. She gave her life to them, getting them out of one scrape after another. She was caring for Billy and Speed until the day she died.[2]

The first child of the characters Horace and Elizabeth Robedaux in *1918* died. She was named Rosa. In the play, her mother visited her grave and put flowers on it. This parallels Foote's grandmother Mrs. Brooks, whose name was Rosa and who daily put flowers on her husband's grave. Her generation continued the custom of visiting the cemetery. Foote's mother also visited the grave to see the marker.

In her letters, Hallie spoke of her religious activities as a Christian Scientist. On a Sunday morning she went to "S.S." (Sunday School). The Footes asked "Flo" to attend a Christian Science lecture in Bay City.

Hallie kept up with Foote's work and wrote him whenever she had news. She said the opinion of *Variety* on *To Kill A Mockingbird* was most gratifying. Also, she had read in the *National Observer* (February 17, 1963): "'To Kill a Mockingbird' is nothing short of superb." Hallie quoted proudly: "The major credit should go to Horton Foote, who adapted the novel."

Hallie was a good-natured woman who never scolded. What is more, her writing was always grammatically correct, as was her spelling. Foote followed her example, as in other matters.

Hallie asked about and heard from her grandchildren often. Gladys (the housekeeper while the Footes were away) sent her "a picture of Daisy B." According to Hallie, she was "a little beauty." Hallie could "spy" B. (Barbara) Hallie in the background of one picture. Gladys wrote that the children had had "a wonderful and active summer."

The most important woman in Foote's life was his wife, Lillian Vallish Foote. She was the basis for Rosa Lee in *Tender Mercies* (1983). By this time Foote had had abundant chances to observe her moral strength. She gave him self-confidence, a trait that Foote thinks is indispensable for a man and that he treats in the portrait of Horace Robedaux.

Gerald Wood has this to say about Lillian: "*Tender Mercies* can be seen as a love poem for his wife. Through Rosa Lee in *Tender Mercies* he testifies to his wife as an authentic person. . . . She has her own anxieties and doubts while remaining empathetic and loving."[3]

Lillian Foote was a good businesswoman. She became coproducer with Foote of the *Orphans' Home Cycle* and other productions. On November 20, 1957, she wrote a letter to their lawyer, which showed her knowledge of financial affairs. In this two-page, typed letter she stated that she wanted some of the money Foote made previously to go into this year (1957).

She wrote, "As for the Spiegel money [an advance from Sam Spiegel] for the film of *The Chase* (1966), Horton said he definitely will receive the remaining 10,000 before the end of this year and I told him this was very necessary as this year was a relatively low income year and it was best to get it under the line now." Lillian was a woman of sound judgment, like the Bertie Dees of Foote's one-acts. Lillian handled business matters wisely for her husband.

Foote and his children had admiring words to say about Lillian. Her husband told a reporter in 1985, "It's an extraordinary marriage. We're deeply in love with each other, plus the fact we're best of friends." Foote's daughter Daisy joked, "It's almost nauseating, it's so good. He absolutely adores her."[4]

Barbara Hallie commented on the women in her father's plays: "There's always a woman, gentle but very strong." These women survive with dignity. Rosa Lee "soothes fears," Barbara Hallie reported. "That's how my mother is. She believes so completely in my father and his talent. It's like she has a plan for him." Hallie, speaking of her mother's role in their family, said, "She's the *rock*."[5]

In 1992, Lillian Foote died suddenly. Foote was married to her for forty-seven years and remembers her in his play *Alone*. She gave him love, happiness, and confidence in full measure.

The most entertaining letters Foote received came from his cousin, Nan Dean Outlar, who died in 1990. She was formerly a Bennett and had known Foote a long time in Wharton. Both loved the theatre, and her letters to Foote are a riot, priceless. She is clearly the model for many characters.

Nan Dean is likely the basis for the doctor's wife in the late play *Vernon Early* (1998); for Mary Jo, a socialite from Houston in *Dividing the Estate;* and for composite characters such as Delia Weems in *Night Seasons*. Her letters read like the comic dialogue of middle-aged women in his plays. She was the society columnist for the *Wharton Journal;* her column, "Nan About Town," which she started writing on September 3, 1937, was that newspaper's longest-running column. Nan Dean, as she was always called, and Foote corresponded over a long period of time. She seems to have been about the same age as Foote. He enjoyed her acquaintance because she was vivacious and well traveled. She and her husband obviously had money, and her letters portray a lady with a crowded social life.

She often referred to a snack shop that she helped staff in the hospital as a work of charity. Foote appreciated her sense of humor and used it in his plays. What is more, she was a theatregoer in New York and Houston. She went to movies in Houston if they did not come to Wharton. This woman was clearly a type: a funny southern woman, Texas style. She was very talkative, like Mamie in *Only the Heart,* and always saying something funny.

Nan Dean commented on Foote in her column, and she sent him a copy. Hallie wrote Foote on a Thursday in 1962: "Hope Lillian sends Nan's clipping from the column to you. It is a gem."

Foote's irrepressible cousin enjoyed meeting the star of *Baby, the Rain Must Fall.* On January 7, 1965, she wrote Foote after seeing the play. She got only a "bare glimpse of my glamorous (?) self as I followed the pall bearers and casket down the steps at the old house on Resident St." She "LOVED the picture," although hated to admit that cutting her scene "didn't really hurt the picture." She adored "hobnobbing with Lee Remick, Steve McQueen, Don Murray and the others."

Nan Dean wrote that she hoped to see *The Chase,* which was to open in New York in March 1966: "We can hardly wait to see it. . . . Hope Lillian Hellman didn't wander too far from your original story"—or if so "you were able to get things back on track." Later she wrote, "I'll never forget the opening in N.Y. and how thrilled we were."

Nan Dean always wrote Foote a long Christmas letter. It was this time of the year when she brought Foote up to date. She wrote a long letter on January 1, 1957, to the Footes. Her pet dog "Fritz" had collapsed "about December 22 and we had to put him to sleep—it nearly killed me and completely ruined my holidays," she wrote. "I was so worried those days I wasn't responsible for my actions and hardly conscious of what gifts I did receive."

In a letter of January 9, 1966, she said that she wanted another sketch from Foote for the History Club, where she must have been scheduled to give a talk on her friend: "I can supply all the 'spice' about your 'dark past.'" On February 22, 1967, she sent a drawing of a doctor and a baby with these words around them: "Jingle Bells. Jingle all the way." She wrote, "Just took our Christmas tree down and am completely 'pooped.'" She had invited about 120 people in all to her parties. She complained about not being able to get to New Hampshire: "It's too far from N.Y.— I do get up there every blue moon or so—but New Hampshire!!"

In the same letter, she noted, "The Herman boy married in Galveston. I knew how much Bolton [her husband] wanted to go. It was a horribly cold and wet nite. Though Fritz was dead, I had to 'go on' with activities which involved New Years Day dinner with Myrtis and Sunny [her daughter and son-in-law]—14 adults and 6 children. I appreciated being included of course but was in no mood for family. Actually by the end of the holidays I was fed up with family, food, and football!!"

She continued: "The little Dairy Farm Salt and Pepper shakers are so cute—they'll be just right for our barbecue and informal parties. . . . Myrtis still has not thanked you for the gifts which doesn't set well with Bolton, I can tell you, but she's a 'big girl' now and I can't boss her or Sunny either."

In another letter, dated September 6, 1973, she writes that Bolton's aging parents were coming to live with them. They did soon afterward.

Since Nan Dean wrote for the *Wharton Journal*, Foote called on her when he wrote the script for the Wharton pageant, performed in the summer of 1976. The project combined his love of Wharton and his scriptwriting ability. It is Foote's tribute to his hometown.

Two years before production, he wrote to Nan Dean about helping him, in a letter dated December 30, 1974: "I will need someone who is used to doing historical research to help me (hopefully a native Whartonian). I hope to get down in March but if I can have someone begin at once for me it will be a great help." He said he had a few sourcebooks including the history by Mrs. Annie Lee Williams, but would prefer going to "actual sources" such as courthouse records. "A pageant is a difficult and tricky thing," he wrote. "The first trick is to get something that can be done meaningfully and believably on the budget and resources locally available."

He continued: "What I do know needs rechecking, as so much of my knowledge has been through listening to oral history given by old time friends. . . . where is the pageant to be done? Out of doors? Indoors? Is there a person co-ordinating the whole?"

All was put together in Foote's systematic manner, and Wharton had a pageant for the bicentennial. The script itself is deposited in the Horton Foote Collection. It tells of the first contact with the Indians and is lengthy. Foote wrote to Nan Dean after the successful production of the pageant (August 11, 1976).

Foote kept in close contact with his correspondents. His letters supplement the letters from his mother and the profiles of his aunts on the Brooks side. This correspondence covers thoroughly his life from the 1930s to the 1990s. It names his many friends in New York, Texas, California, and other places.

Throughout, they provide information on his four grown children, as he mentioned and wrote to them. In 1962, Foote told Hallie that he would meet Gregory Peck for the first time. We begin to hear of Barbara Hallie's love of acting. Foote wrote that Barbara Hallie was working at the Loft Studio in Los Angeles, run by Peggy Feury. Later Barbara Hallie married Devon Abner, who appeared with her in *Night Seasons* at the Signature Theater.[6]

On March 10, 1972, Foote reported that he had bought airplane tickets to London for the musical of *Gone with the Wind,* for which he wrote the script. In letters from London to New Hampshire, he wrote to Barbara Hallie and the others. He praised them and said they would spend time together on his return.

In 1972, Horton Junior served in the U.S. Army. He was in the military police in Germany and wrote many letters to his parents in New Boston, New Hampshire. On December 30, 1974, Horton Junior was coming back "for good," Foote wrote to Nan Dean. Foote also told her that his son Walter had gone to Springfield on December 22. He had had a basketball game at night, and "we drove back to N.H." Only Daisy and Walter were at home that Christmas.

On May 20, 1975, Lucy Kroll wrote to Foote that the deal with Universal City Studios concerning an adaptation of *Children of Pride* had been approved. Foote checked *Children of Pride,* a novel about slavery, out of the library on August 9, 1975.

On December 20, 1976, Foote wrote to Valerie Bettis that Daisy would graduate from high school in late spring. Horton Junior was working, and "we see him often." Walter was at the University of Texas and liked it "very much." Daisy had applied to the University of North Carolina and other colleges for admission. Foote described her as "our scholar."

He wrote to Valerie on November 21, 1977, that Carol Hall, a Texas composer of Larry King's musical *The Best Little Whorehouse in Texas,* had written the music for *The Dancers.* In 1978 Foote wrote Valerie that he had done the teleplay adaptation for *Brother to a Dragonfly,* by Will Campbell.

Among Foote's acting friends, Kim Stanley was close. On August 8, 1976, Foote wrote to her, saying that it had been nice visiting with her and Paula, her daughter. Foote wrote to Herbert Berghof on January 11, 1977, that Kim had played the part of the girl in *Flight* (1957). Foote kept up correspondence with Stanley, who had acted in *The Traveling Lady,* Inge's *Bus Stop,* and several other plays by Foote. Her life was sad because of drinking and emotional problems, which she mentioned in her letters to Foote. A native Texan, she lived in California, where Foote visited her.

Stanley was interested in writing a screenplay and asked Foote for assistance. He wrote back on October 15, 1976, and said, "You're on to something and I'm sure will find a way to finally work it all out for yourself." Then he philosophized about writing itself: "Writing is a lonely, personal search and really there is little help we can give each other— just a kind of sympathetic understanding of the need to persevere in our own way." Foote supplied the best support and understanding he could. She was on her own, though. He ended the letter: "I hope to see you and Paula the next time I'm in California."

Joseph Anthony, whom Foote had known in Pasadena, was a close friend. They corresponded and worked together in the theatre. The two also discussed political issues and agreed. In December 1967, Anthony wrote to "Hortie" about the Vietnam War. Foote wrote to Joe on February 2, 1972: "I thought of you during the coal strike—and glad it's over." On May 5, 1963, Roland Wood wrote to Foote about Anthony: "Last Monday we had a cast party [for *The Dragon*] at the Anthony's humble digs" in Ardsley. Joseph Anthony had directed the film *Tomorrow,* Foote wrote to Jane Harris of the Kroll Agency on February 10, 1988.

About events in contemporary times Foote talked with Joseph Anthony. This actor-director had appeared in *Camino Real* as Casanova and had directed plays from the *Orphans' Home Cycle* at Berghof's theatre. Foote discussed life and ideas with Anthony. Both were influenced by Christian Science and knew many of the same theatrical people and members of each other's families.

Foote sent *Christian Science Monitor* clippings to Joseph Anthony. On January 4, 1975, Elli Anthony, daughter of Joseph, asked Foote: "Do you use Science in your creative work?"[7] Several other correspondents also referred to Christian Science. On January 15, 1962, "Miriam" asked if Lillian and Horton were still Christian Scientists and reported that her niece was a soloist at the Christian Science church on Long Island. "She gave me a much needed boost," Miriam confided.

Lillian and Horton wrote to Gladys Beech, of Ridge Manor, Florida, on April 29, 1963, that "we get reports from others in our church about you in Florida." Kitty Gussman of Sarasota, Florida, wrote Foote on May 16, 1963: "During the picture I felt the scientific thought which you must have had when you wrote the film play" of *Mockingbird.*

We get valuable information on Foote's reading in his letters, particularly about Faulkner. After reading the Malcolm Cowley correspondence, Foote wrote, "In 1945, I was still groping for judgments and expressed the first that came to mind." He continued: "I still feel that Faulkner's genius was not primarily novelistic . . . but rather epic or bardic." Foote's purpose in 1945 was to emphasize what others overlooked, "the scope and force and independence of his work as a whole" (February 11, 1974). These words described his own cycle later. His opinion of *As I Lay Dying* was now "much higher than what I expressed in 1945."

On May 9, 1962, Foote wrote to Lucy Kroll's husband, Nathan, about Paul Green and J. Frank Dobie. When a friend stayed in the Foote house in New Hampshire, she noticed books by Chekhov, Hart Crane, and James Agee. Foote renewed the book *The Religious Instruction of the Negro,* by Charles Colcock Jones, until July 17, 1975. At this time Foote was also reading *The Political Economy of Slavery,* by Eugene D. Genovese, for use in writing the script *Children of Pride* (July 1, 1975).

When Foote and Lillian really wanted to enjoy themselves, they visited antique shops. This hobby agreed with their liking for old towns like Sealy and with Foote's grief over the loss of Victorian homes in Wharton (October 10, 1988). On October 10, 1971, he wrote to a correspondent, "I dread to think of all the beautiful antiques that have come and gone."

Foote referred to Harper Lee in some letters. On March 1, 1976, he wrote to Sharon K. Muller that the leisurely time sequence of the novel *To Kill a Mockingbird* had been changed to "the more strict form used in our film." He continued, "I was asked to write the script because the actor, producer, and Miss Lee" were familiar with my writings.

Tennessee Williams was "delighted" that Foote was writing a screen-play for *This Property Is Condemned* (January 19, 1962). When Foote went to the University of Mississippi, he gave lectures entitled "On First Dra-matizing Faulkner" and "'Tomorrow': The Genesis of a Screen Play" (February 17, 1978).

The picture we get of Foote from the many letters in his collection at Southern Methodist University is full and rich. We see him as genial, close to his family, and a diligent worker. Some interests besides the the-atre and family emerge and come into sharper focus, like his love of an-tiques. These details of Foote's personality are valuable for filling in the picture we have received from straight biography and his writings.

Having recognized the persons on whom Foote frequently based his main characters, I will next point out how they represent the themes of his plays. Foote continued to develop these subjects to the end of his career. "Each experience played an important part in his early career and influ-enced all subsequent writings," according to Marian Castleberry.[8] In the story of his great-great-grandfather, the lieutenant governor, Foote dis-covered the need for courage in the face of deprivation and loss. Courage was also the dominant trait of his mother. Foote exemplified it in the char-acter Elizabeth Robedaux, based on Hallie Brooks Foote. Those who lacked that virtue, like her sister Laura, were doomed to ineffectiveness.

The longing for a father became a central issue in the *Orphans' Home Cycle*. Albert Foote hardly found a father but instead found a family when he married Hallie Brooks. His dream had been "to belong to a family."[9] That is why he revered his deceased father. Foote's strongest plays, such as *Courtship,* show the need for a family. In *Courtship,* Horace searches for one and marries Elizabeth. He develops into a caring father. That is the keystone of his arch, Foote seems to say, and without it the arch will fall. Foote's own father, rejected by P. E. Cleveland, wanted a family above all. Albert was attached to Hallie—his security. They were never apart from each other for one complete day in their lives.

The freedom Foote felt as a boy as he raced through the fields and streets of Wharton became a "norm" for all his characters. His Brooks grandmother offered him "security."[10] Foote shows death and mourn-ing in his plays. He sees mourning as a vital part of the healing process: "Now everything is so anonymous."[11]

Foote learned the value of self-reliance and practiced it in his own life. He shows the Emersonian cultivation of that quality, which would be found also in the Christian Science of Mary Baker Eddy, who admired the philosopher Ralph Waldo Emerson.

Foote inherited his town's greatest resource: storytelling. He has an inexhaustible supply of stories and tells them in plays, often one-acts. His father had told him of a convict farm where he had once worked. Out of that story, Foote concocted *Convicts*. There was a severe sibling problem in his father's family with Lily Dale. Foote developed this conflict in many scenes. Lily Dale cannot accept Horace's love of her father in the *Cycle*. She detested him because he drank.

When Foote joined the American Actors, led by Mary Hunter, he learned the group approach to acting, which gave him security. This group led him out of the wilderness of commerce into the land of art. Next, he returned to Wharton as a writer and found his artistic salvation. He wrote *Wharton Dance* and a series of plays about the town. Realizing he was better as a writer than an actor, he chose that vocation.

It was the turning point. He found in the television plays another way of returning home and writing about the people he knew. His first real successes were in the television playhouses. Fred Coe and Paddy Chayefsky liked his one-acts about the small town. He had found his audience, which liked the humor of *The Old Beginning*. Further he used the language he knew, Texan, and not an artificial Broadway-ese.

Foote continued to write the plays that grew out of Wharton. In the *Cycle,* he covered historical eras from 1900 to 1926. He was always returning to the same people, though changes in lifestyles are reflected in *Tender Mercies* and *Dividing the Estate* in the 1980s.

Foote was fascinated by the people around him, who lived and died, loved and lost, prevailed and endured. The dramatic tensions between their inner lives and the appearance of calm made a profound impression on him.

He mined and remined the experiences in Wharton. The past could not be understood truly except in his writings. By articulating them in writing, he began to comprehend.

With *Only the Heart,* "his regional stories are gaining their resonance, the texture that he will return to in the 1950s," Castleberry writes.[12] Ironically, because of Grandfather Brooks's real estate development, the town experienced "erosion of tradition and identity."[13] The death of Papa meant the loss of the total security he had enjoyed. His grandmother's daily mourning taught him that death and grief are the subjects for all time.

Foote moved closer to his father when he worked in the haberdashery. He appreciated the kindness his father showed to others. Foote adopted his speculative nature from his father, asking himself hypothetical questions: If this had happened, what would have followed? A sibling problem also existed among the Foote brothers because Horton intended to remain the favorite grandson.

Not stars but group acting was the proper goal. Uncovering cultural roots led him back home. His first play, *Wharton Dance,* gave him security. He was a small-town Texan and needed it.

Texas Town showed the need for order and stability. He would explore these themes throughout his career. In *Out of My House* he showed the tragic consequences of alcoholism, racism, and greed but also the inevitability of change and the resiliency of the spirit. In *Only the Heart,* work was praised, but extremes of it were not. Affluence left one disconnected from humanity.

It will be helpful at this juncture to take a look both backward and forward to understand clearly the organization of this book. Horton Foote is concerned primarily with moral themes. That is, he deals with what is good and what is bad in human behavior. Because he places great value on religion, he does this naturally. The principal virtue that he admires is courage, and the second is adjustment to change, both seen in the character Mrs. Watts of *The Trip to Bountiful.* Of the exemplary characters, many are women or are men who are guided by women. Foote's choice repeats the great love for his mother and his wife and their influence on his characters and writing. His admiration of Mary Baker Eddy also plays a part.

Through the 1950s Foote showed himself a moralist, since he chose characters who stood for moral values or, by contrast, for undesirable, harmful qualities. Mrs. Watts is his outstanding creation of a woman with the virtues of courage and adjustment to painful change. As Gerald Wood pointed out in discussing the teleplay *The Dancers* (1956), young people admire the courage upheld so cogently by theologian Paul Tillich, who stated that "acts of courage" affirm the "power of being." In the one-act play *The Dancers,* Mary Catherine builds up the self-confidence of her date, Horace. Wood says that the teenage word for courage is "confidence," which is inspired by "moments of deep sharing." [14]

Mrs. Watts shows courage in her perseverance to reach Bountiful. By doing so, she adjusts to change in her life, that is, to living with her son and his selfish wife. Another play that features a major theme is *The Oil Well* (1953). The wife, Loula, whom Foote modeled after his great-aunt Loula Horton, endures her husband's obsession with striking oil. Ensuing characters based on life, as we will see, would continue to embody many of Foote's themes. They are based on individuals Foote knew and will be noted subsequently.

1. Brooks family. Seated (*left to right*): Papa (Foote's maternal grandfather), who is holding Tom Brooks Foote; Daisy Brooks (grandmother); Speed Brooks; Billy Brooks; and Laura Brooks with Horton Foote, Jr. Standing (*left to right*): Tom Harry Brooks, Jr.; Rosa Brooks; Hallie and Horton Foote, Sr.
WITH PERMISSION OF DEGOLYER LIBRARY, SOUTHERN METHODIST UNIVERSITY, HORTON FOOTE COLLECTION #A1992.1810 BOX 108, FOLDER "CHILDHOOD."

2. Foote family. (*Left to right*): Barbara Hallie, Daisy Brooks, Lillian Vallish (wife),
Horton Junior, Walter Vallish, and Horton Foote, Sr.

3. Lillian Gish and Eva Marie Saint in *The Trip to Bountiful*.

4. Gregory Peck in *To Kill a Mockingbird*, with script by Horton Foote.
PHOTO COURTESY OF HORTON FOOTE.

5. Hallie Foote (at back) as Elizabeth Vaughn in *Courtship*, Foote's best one-act play from the *Orphans' Home Cycle*.
WITH PERMISSION OF DEGOLYER LIBRARY, SOUTHERN METHODIST UNIVERSITY, HORTON FOOTE COLLECTION #A1992.1810 BOX 110.

6. Hallie Foote and William Converse-Roberts in *Valentine's Day*, from the *Orphans' Home Cycle*. PHOTO COURTESY OF HORTON FOOTE.

7. Horton Foote in his office in Wharton, Texas.

10

COUNTRY MUSIC

THE TRAVELING LADY, BABY, THE RAIN MUST FALL,

AND TENDER MERCIES

FOOTE has had a recurrent interest in country music, a passion that is endemic in Texas. He turned to this subject matter for three of his most interesting works, beginning with *The Traveling Lady* in 1954. His country music trilogy also includes his original screenplay for that piece, called *Baby, the Rain Must Fall,* which appeared in 1965, and *Tender Mercies,* his climactic treatment of country music in 1983. With these works, Foote used his creative skills more than in his adaptations of the work of others, even *To Kill a Mockingbird* (1963), for which he has received the most popular acclaim. Country music has much to tell us about Foote's artistic development and commentary on Texas life.

Though *The Trip to Bountiful* was not a hit in the theatre, it earned enough critical praise to direct Foote to another attempt on Broadway. It was a thriving era of the theatre, with Tennessee Williams continuing to succeed with plays like *Cat on a Hot Tin Roof* (1955) and *Sweet Bird of Youth* (1959). William Inge, with *Picnic,* and Arthur Miller, with *Death of a Salesman* and *The Crucible,* enjoyed considerable success.

In the spring of 1954, Foote took a leave of absence from television to begin writing *The Traveling Lady.* Robert E. Sherwood, a distinguished playwright and member of the Playwrights' Company, which produced the play, wrote to Foote after seeing a tryout in Princeton. Sherwood showed keen interest in Foote as a young playwright, whom he thought needed some constructive criticism. In a letter dated October 11, 1954, Sherwood made detailed comments, including advice on how the characters should look. Sherwood also noted that his wife, who was from the South, found "points of intimate recognition." On opening night, Sherwood telegraphed Foote, saying, "you are a fine writer and I hope that fact will be recognized tonight." Elmer Rice, another member of the Play-wrights' Company, also wired Foote on opening night. He wished a "big hit" for *Traveling Lady* (HFC). The Playwrights' Company gave the play "a wonderful mounting and a capable cast," according to Walter Kerr in the *New York Herald Tribune* (October 28, 1954).

The Traveling Lady opened at the Playhouse Theatre on West Forty-eighth Street on October 27, 1954. It was directed by Foote's friend and television director Vincent Donehue. Kim Stanley, a rising actress and friend from Texas who had appeared in *The Chase,* played the female lead of Georgette, the long-suffering wife of a disturbed country music singer named Henry Thomas. For her performance she won the Sylvania Award. This play shows the violent, chaotic side of life in Harrison, Texas, much different from the quieter one, seen in television plays like *The Death of the Old Man.*

The Traveling Lady is Foote's last full-length play to be produced on Broadway until *The Young Man from Atlanta* in 1995. After the qualified success of *The Chase* (1952), Foote had directed his creative energies to television for the next two years, 1952–1953. Nevertheless Foote had not achieved success in New York as had his colleagues Tennessee Williams and William Inge. Making a hit on Broadway was the sine qua non of theatrical achievement, a prize that Foote still sought.

The Traveling Lady, with its story of a misdirected orphan who wants to sing with a string band but sadly goes to the penitentiary, resembles movies of the 1950s that portray misunderstood, rootless teenagers who receive no emotional support from insensitive parents. A famous example, *Rebel Without a Cause* (1955), starred James Dean, the personification of the rebellious, angry young man. In *The Traveling Lady,* Foote described a country musician for the first time. A fan of country music bands that later played rhythm and blues as popularized by Elvis Presley, Foote por-trayed the tortured lives of musicians in the films *Baby, the Rain Must Fall* (1965), which was an adaptation of *The Traveling Lady,* and in *Tender Mercies* (1983). In his quest for Broadway success, Foote may have felt that a strongly dramatic work, featuring a tempestuous hero, like Stanley Kowalski, stood the best chance of success on Broadway. Thus *The Traveling Lady,* like *The Chase,* which was partially successful, presents a young man with a tortured past who fights a losing battle against the odds in his life. He is another of Foote's defeated men.

Coming soon after Foote's many television plays, *The Traveling Lady* also supplies social criticism. As in *The Chase,* whipping of the young is attacked as well as temperance, fanaticism, and nosiness—all faults of Texas small towns. The lead, Henry Thomas, the tormented young musician, possesses the free will to face the stark realities of his life, his prison record, and alcoholism. He is not driven by internal neuroses, as would be true in the naturalistic play. Nevertheless, he refuses to face reality. Since this fault is found among others in society, it can be exposed with the hope of reform. Also criticized is the naiveté of young women who marry irresponsible men.

The most compelling character in *The Traveling Lady* is this troubled young man, whose flight from reality is a common theme in the plays of such contemporary playwrights as Williams and Miller. Although other persons contribute to Henry's fall, he shapes his own fate. The play recognizes the harmful effect of society but, in the last analysis, sees the individual's flaws, like the attempt to escape reality, as the cause of his tragic downfall. The former viewpoint is too pessimistic and radical for Foote's thinking.

Henry cannot face the truth of his shattered life and attempts to escape it. He gets out of the penitentiary and returns to Harrison, but he does not inform his wife, Georgette, immediately. After being out for a month, he writes her to come in a week, but he plans to flee with money stolen from his foster mother, Miss Kate, before her arrival. Georgette, however, having lost her job in Tyler, decides to come sooner. Thus when she appears, Henry says, "This sure is a surprise."[1] Next, in quick succession, he gets drunk, steals the silverware of his employer, Mrs. Tillman, and prepares to flee, though he has told Georgette he will see her again in a few hours. Unfortunately, he makes the mistake of going by the cemetery to tear the flowers off the grave of his foster mother, Miss Kate, providing old Mrs. Mavis with the opportunity to abscond with the black bag holding the silverware. Georgette and Slim Murray, a kind neighbor, then confront Henry, who admits he lied about remaining with Georgette. He asks forgiveness and swears he will do right now. But even after his arrest, he tries to escape. At his entrance, Henry sang "True Love Goes On and On," expressing an illusion that his own actions belie. When he is caught and handcuffed by the sheriff, Georgette finally faces the truth about her faithless husband.

Henry Thomas was an orphan, taken in by an unbending, loveless old maid. The only discipline Miss Kate knew how to administer to the misbehaving boy was whipping. She wielded the strap so fiercely that the neighbors complained. After he went to Lovelady, Texas, as a singer with a string band and married, he stabbed a man, for which he was sentenced to six years in the penitentiary.

Out of prison and back in Harrison, Henry encounters another strict mother figure in the person of Mrs. Tillman, a temperance advocate. He goes to work for her as a live-in yardman. She succeeds in obtaining his promise to abstain from alcohol by pouring black coffee into him until he promises never to drink again.

Though Henry expresses regret when his guardian Miss Kate dies, his actions tell a different story. After Miss Kate is buried, the drunken Henry tears the flowers off her grave at night, revealing the hatred that had been repressed during the daylight hours. Stark Young said in his introduction to the play that this harrowing scene was "as dark and hideous as anything in Strindberg" (p. 7), thus implying that Foote dealt with the deep feelings that corroded the human spirit. Henry confesses his submerged resentment after this incident when he says that Miss Kate and Mrs. Tillman gave him no rest: "Don't do that, Henry, don't do this, Henry" (p. 53). Thus he robs Mrs. Tillman of her precious silverware so that he can get away.

What is lacking in Henry's soul is a feeling of self-worth. Miss Kate makes him feel shame by her whipping. Knowing that he lied to his wife about wanting her to join him, he says, "I'm not worth killing" (p. 53). Henry gets the most pleasure and pride from singing with the band. He returned to that passion as soon as he left prison. When the neighbors of Mrs. Tillman ask for a song, he is proud to oblige. In the best and climactic scene of the play, Henry proudly fulfills his daughter's request for a song, which he sang for her mother when they first met. On his way back to the penitentiary for violating his oath not to break the law, he begs the sheriff to remove his handcuffs so that he can touch his daughter, Margaret Rose. She asks to hear her father sing "New San'tonia Rose," but immediately after the sheriff removes his handcuffs, he attempts to escape (p. 63).

The inability of Georgette to face the reality of her husband's lies signals that Foote, like other major playwrights of this era, adopted the truth–illusion theme. He observed it first in *The Glass Menagerie* (1945), in which Amanda retreats to the beautiful past and Laura cannot face the harsh reality of business school. Foote had another very good chance to learn of this theme in *This Property Is Condemned,* Williams's one-act about a young girl's dream of her sister's romantic life, of which he wrote a television adaptation in 1962.[2] During these years, Edward Albee was presenting this subject with great success in *Who's Afraid of Virginia Woolf?* (1964), which was revived again and again throughout the 1970s.

Traveling, in the terms of this play, connotes the search for a happy life by moving to another town, as unrealistic as that hope may be. The ending of this play is ambiguous, but Foote consistently discovers a ray of hope in the future of his surviving personages, who possess endurance that is missing in the nonsurvivors. In the last and best line of the play, Georgette muses, "From Lovelady to Tyler, from Tyler to Harrison, from Harrison to the Valley. Margaret Rose, we sure do get around" (p. 66). Reminiscent of Lena Grove, the innocent traveler of Faulkner's *Light in August,* Georgette also seems destined for a better life as she leaves town with Slim. Foote admits that Faulkner's novel did have some influence on his play.[3]

The comedy of small-town life appears in the hilarious pair of bawdy old Mrs. Mavis and her solemn daughter, Sitter. The humor lies in the juxtaposition of old impropriety and young propriety. Mrs. Mavis runs away from her daughter continually and scandalizes her by childish behavior. Mrs. Mavis is more than a match for her daughter. When Sitter complains that she is exhausted from running after her mother, while Mrs. Mavis is "fresh as a daisy," Sitter asks how her mother can still have all that energy. Mrs. Mavis replies, "From livin' right. I live right, honey. I eat my greens. I get my exercise and I eat cornbread for breakfast every morning of my life" (p. 57). The actress playing this part usually steals the show.

As Foote reached the end of his major effort to succeed on Broadway with *The Traveling Lady,* one could not say that he had reached that goal. On the other hand, after four full-length works (including *The Trip to Bountiful*), he was firmly established as a good, very talented writer for the theatre. He was the first playwright to write seriously about genuine life in Texas, as Katherine Anne Porter had been the first fiction writer to do so.

Both *The Chase* and *The Traveling Lady* focus on a young man who has been spiritually maimed in his youth. Henry Thomas is only slightly less tormented than Bubber Reeves by the conditions of his life. Much time must be expended in defining the emotional states of Georgette and Slim in *The Traveling Lady.* There is not sufficient time left in the play to scrutinize Henry. In the movie adaptation, *Baby, the Rain Must Fall,* this deficiency is corrected by making him the unqualified central figure.

All seven reviews were either mixed or negative. The only consistent praise was for Kim Stanley in the role of Georgette. Brooks Atkinson had several complaints, remarking that Foote was not "a forceful playwright" and that he never made "a statement except in extremis." These objections, however, did not end the appraisal. There were "genuine and very poignant scenes in this play," Atkinson wrote. "Even the bum has his points." Atkinson also wrote that Foote's impulses were "decent enough, but he lacks strength and goes to pieces in crisis." Atkinson called the character of Miss Clara a compassionate lady in the best tradition of the small town, writing that it was a pleasure in a theatre populated by "decadent people who don't understand anything" to watch characters who behaved like "normal human beings." Atkinson said that when the characters managed to say something—as in the final scene—the were "wonderfully honest." Atkinson concluded that the emotional scenes were worth the "languors" in between (*New York Times,* October 28, 1954).

Walter Kerr in the *New York Herald Tribune* (October 28, 1954) said the play lacked "theatrical vitality." Miss Stanley's acting must supply that because the author has given nothing beyond "the feeblest Chekhovian flutterings by way of activity." The critics did not comment on the psychological trouble of the young man, which is the crux of the play. Foote did not develop this aspect sufficiently to attract the attention it warranted.

In the *New York World Telegram,* William Hawkins, who had lauded *The Trip to Bountiful,* called the childish old woman Mrs. Mavis the most interesting character (October 28, 1954). Immediately after publishing this review, he wrote Foote a letter dated October 29, 1954. Hawkins recalled from talking with Foote "a most agreeable sense of built in and permanent compassion and a relaxed sense of humor about yourself and what you do." Hawkins cautioned, however, against an overbalance of compassion, saying that when that spilled over to the portrayal of characters, it was not "diverting" (HFC).

L. Arnold Weissberger, counselor at law in New York, who had given Foote legal advice, wrote Lucy Kroll on December 10, 1954, after seeing *The Traveling Lady.* He had been "thoroughly engrossed by it from beginning to end," he wrote. "It had for me an inner tension that never ceased to be absorbing." Weissberger could usually understand the reaction of the critics even "when I don't agree with them," he said, "but in this case I find them quite puzzling" (HFC).

Likewise, Foote's supporters were disappointed in the play's reception. Lucy Kroll wrote Foote on March 11, 1955, that Kim Stanley wished that the success she had with *Bus Stop* in 1955 had come instead to *The Traveling Lady,* "as Georgette is someone she knows and loves and understands and there is no playwright like Horton Foote" (HFC).

The Playwrights' Company remained loyal. William Fields, its press representative, wrote Foote on November 9, 1954, that the *Christian Science Monitor* review by John Beaufort was the first "sensible" appreciation of *The Traveling Lady* he had seen. The poor critical estimate, he held, had delayed by a year the recognition of Foote as "about the best God damn playwright of the current American theatre." Foote provoked better reactions from laymen than critics, indicating his appeal to the larger public.

Foote later adapted *The Traveling Lady* for television. It was broadcast on *Studio One* the night of April 25, 1957, with Kim Stanley taking the part she had acted in the theatre. According to an article preceding the television broadcast, Foote condensed the play, observing, "I feel the play has been improved. Technically, many problems in the Broadway play have been solved in the adaptation" (*New York Journal American,* April 15, 1957). Saul Levison praised Foote's adaptation highly in " 'Traveling Lady' Rare TV Treat" (*New York World-Telegram and Sun,* April 23, 1957). He wrote, "Last night Studio One presented the finest drama we have yet seen on television. . . . It spoke directly; it drew its characters most precisely; its language rang most clearly with the strong ability of poetry; it had something to say." Levison added that Foote had the ability to throw a net over a large area of Texas life. Both Foote and Kim Stanley agreed this was "the finest review we've read anywhere" (HFC, letters in Kroll correspondence, April 23, 1957).

Baby, the Rain Must Fall (1965) shows the influence of *To Kill a Mockingbird* (1962). This feature film produced by Columbia Pictures, again with Pakula as producer and Mulligan as director, starred Steve McQueen, who had become famous for his working-class, tough-guy roles. He played Henry Thomas, while Lee Remick took the part of Georgette. Filming was done mainly in Wharton, much to the delight of Foote's fellow townspeople.

Although *Baby, the Rain Must Fall* essentially follows the plot of *The Traveling Lady,* there is a clear change, since the film version projects the same passion of social protest as *To Kill a Mockingbird,* shown three years before. Here racial prejudice is not condemned, but rather small-town narrow mindedness, a target in Foote's previous works also. Religious fanaticism and the objection to honky-tonk music are the overwhelming causes of the young man's fall. Here, Henry exerts his free will and consequently is a better, more sympathetic character in the movie. But the misguided actions of narrow-minded persons prevent the accomplishment of these worthy goals.

Baby, the Rain Must Fall, like *Mockingbird*, makes an emotional indictment of society. In the play, the fall of the hero had occurred because of his personal faults, especially his untruthfulness; he lied to Georgette about staying with her. In the movie the cause of Henry's disaster is a corrupt small-town environment, where evil persons crush him and victimize him. Society, represented by Miss Kate, the sheriff, and the judge, wants to send him back to the convict farm. Miss Kate's prejudice against the rock music provokes his rebellion and drinking. Those who block the expression of Henry's musical talent, notably his villainous guardian, are to blame for his downfall. He is a young man deserving of our sympathy. In the movie, when Georgette finds her husband in the town, he embraces her, plays with Margaret Rose, and tries to make the marriage work. No longer is Henry responsible for the unhappy events that occur in his life.

The change in title expresses a different focus: from Georgette (the traveling lady) to Henry (who sings the song from which the title comes). The title refers to the hard experiences that Henry, or anyone, must endure in this cruel, meaningless world. The contemporary Existentialist view of Ionesco, which viewed life as meaningless, makes itself evident. Violence adds to the sense of absurdity. Robert Mulligan, the director, noted the violence in the movie before the filming was finished. The script has "the violence that rests under Foote's characters—and the terror; bold Gothic strokes."[4]

There was some experimenting with the new title before the final one was decided on, which many found unsatisfactory. On May 18, 1964, Alan Pakula wrote Robert Ferguson of Columbia Pictures: "We are still sweating out the title situation" and will report "any further inspirations" (HFC).

Although the title leaves something to be desired, this question must not detract from the change in the central character and his emotional life. Narrow-mindedness is the accurate term to denote the attitude of Miss Kate Dawson, an unadulterated witch if there ever was one, who lets this Hansel into her gingerbread house to devour him. In the play Miss

Kate has a better relationship: she enjoys Henry's singing and never even appears onstage. In the movie, on the other hand, she blames Henry's stabbing of a man on his performing in a honky-tonk and says, "You're not worth killing."[5]

Mockingbird had a strong influence on *Baby* (1964), Terry Barr argues convincingly in his dissertation. In the first film, Foote confronted the "darker human realities."[6] Tom Robinson is found guilty and afterward killed for a crime he did not commit. Bigotry overcomes justice. In *Baby* the dark force is Miss Kate Dawson's hatred of Henry; she is a sadistic old woman. Barr says Foote altered the story because of "his darkening view of society," as expressed in *Mockingbird*.[7] On her deathbed, Miss Kate curses Henry and leaves instructions to the sheriff to rearrest him if he does not go back to school. This dark force, also seen in *Mockingbird*, shatters Henry's life.[8]

In the movie, Henry's passion for rock music is presented more positively, and this aspect shows an interesting side of the film. The tone of Henry's singing, now done to guitar accompaniment, has an angry, defiant sound, quite in keeping with his determination to persevere with his music regardless of Miss Kate's strict prohibition. Her rigidity is not so much religious as social. And Henry confides to his daughter that he will become a star "like Elvis" (p. 37) and live in Hollywood, where he will own a white Cadillac, not "this back-yard Cadillac," his jalopy. Georgette joins him in foreseeing a happy future with a house, around which she will plant "sycamores, oaks . . . flowers," as the admirable Elizabeth will do in *Valentine's Day*.[9]

Evaluations of this movie were not favorable. Bosley Crowther's review (*New York Times,* January 14, 1965) was very negative. A major weakness, he wrote, was Foote's failure to clarify why Henry Thomas is so badly mixed up and why the wife, who seems sensible, does not make a move to straighten him out. Crowthers adds that Foote could have written a stronger script than this one, which is based on *The Traveling Lady,* "from which it considerably departs," and that he might have supplied some insights into the "nervous" fits and starts of the "pathetic but emotionally obscure Mr. McQueen."

Despite negative criticism, the movie was profitable. It was distributed in South Africa, Spain, Australia, and many other countries. On June 7, 1968, Lucy Kroll reported a gross income of $1,245,176.06 (HFC).

Joseph R. Millichap observes that the hero of *Baby, the Rain Must Fall* resembles some of Tennessee Williams's tragic protagonists (like the outsider in the small town, Chance Wayne of *Sweet Bird of Youth*) in his "inarticulate rage at a disordered world." In Foote's screenplay, however, the reason for the tragedy seems more obscure than inevitable, according to Millichap.[10]

This movie also demonstrates the influence that a popular medium like the movies exerts. It shows the stereotyped picture of Texas, with its scenes of fighting in a tough tavern. The movie was successful financially, showing the monetary rewards that would come with a name actor like Steve McQueen. The enticements of Hollywood were hard to resist, but the taint of commercial movies could be unacceptable if taken too far—a fact that Foote next discovered to his regret in the movie of *The Chase*.

Foote's satisfying experience with *Baby* was followed by a most disagreeable one when his play *The Chase* was adapted for the screen in 1966. Foote had similarly bad experiences in Hollywood when he wrote adaptations of two novels, *Hurry, Sundown* (1967) and *The Stalking Moon* (1968). The former is a confused melodrama about racial prejudice set in Georgia after World War II. Issued by Paramount (1967), the movie was badly produced and directed. It received scathing reviews and was a financial failure; Foote wanted no connection with it. He was co-credited for *Hurry, Sundown,* but not a word by him was used.[11] While working on these poorly received motion pictures, Foote had been laying plans to give up writing adaptations for Hollywood. He had moved to New Hampshire with his family in 1966 when he concluded that the arrangement with Hollywood was not working for him. Having reevaluated his career goals, he began to write what "I thought about" and to hope that somebody would eventually watch it.[12]

At the root of Foote's dissatisfaction with the commercialism of Hollywood was the determination to be his own man once again, to write for himself, not for the management of movie corporations. After a rewarding experience composing the adaptation of Faulkner's *Tomorrow* for PBS in 1962, Foote wrote a strong statement defining his goal as a writer for film, which, alas, would have to remain an ideal. Film should be a lot like theatre, he said, adding: "[In the latter] the writer is, of course, very dominant to be quite frank. It's a collaborative effort with the acting team. It should be enormous co-operation with everybody to achieve a final work of art." He noted that that wasn't true in Hollywood, where one was instead "a writer for hire."[13] The last phrase encapsulates Foote's repeated objection to the commercial medium: the artist surrenders his integrity when he signs the movie contract. This statement was Foote's declaration of artistic and intellectual independence.

For a short time in the early 1950s, Foote had turned to the religious play, but he did not develop this interest again until *Tender Mercies* (1983). This successful film shows Foote's admiration of religion to strengthen people's lives.

Tender Mercies had its beginning in a script about country music, "The Summer of the Hot Five," offered to *Playhouse 90* in 1956 but not produced.[14] In the movie the five young musicians are reincarnated as the Slater Mill Boys, a country music band that admires the hero, Mac Sledge, a famous country music singer and composer whose career has plummeted. Foote's brother, John, loved country music, as noted earlier, and Foote followed closely John's son's ambition to become a country music professional. Foote drew on this nephew's life for "The Summer of the Hot Five" and *Tender Mercies*. At first he wrote only of the band of five but was advised to include one older musician. He did, thus giving shape to the story that became *Tender Mercies*. Foote did not know country music stars, but he did know many failed actors whose lives were likewise in a shambles.

This movie demonstrated that Foote did not and could not give up the testimony of Christian faith in his writing. After achieving major success with his screenplay *To Kill a Mockingbird* (1963), he felt more confident in writing for the movies. No doubt this caused him to explore a full-scale religious work. Foote wrote *Tender Mercies* as an original screenplay.[15] By this time he had gained much more independence in filmmaking than he had had in the late sixties. He succeeded in getting the backing of EMI, a British company, and enlisted as the director Bruce Beresford, an Australian whom Foote found very congenial. There were none of the objections to the screenplay that he had encountered from other companies, because Foote and Robert Duvall, for whom the playwright wrote this story, were coproducers.

This treatment of country music makes an illuminating contrast to Foote's play *The Traveling Lady* (1954) and the movie based on it, *Baby, the Rain Must Fall* (1964). Most striking is the absence of small-town narrow-mindedness against country musicians, dancing, and liquor, attitudes that marked Texas of the 1930s and 1940s but not the 1970s. This difference changes the subject entirely, since the country musician's trouble in *Tender Mercies* is caused not by an oppressive society but by his own faults.

Before Foote settle on the final story for *Tender Mercies*, which won an

Oscar for original screenplay, he tried out preliminary plots. On March 8, 1979, Lucy Kroll informed Harry R. Sharman of Marble Arch Productions that Foote was working on an original idea: "The Austin Sound," that is, music coming out of Austin, where Willie Nelson got his start. The idea involved five young musicians, aged twenty to twenty-five, touring honky-tonks and beer joints as a country-and-western band "trying to make it" (HFC). The germ of *Tender Mercies* expanded to include an older singer, the role played by Robert Duvall. The addition of a famous country music singer, now a has-been, distinguished *Tender Mercies* from *Baby, the Rain Must Fall* (1964), which featured a young singer whose personal problems overshadowed his music-making. The movie was made for $4.5 million, a very low sum for a movie at that time. This fact, plus the listing of Foote and Duvall as coproducers, indicated that it was not a typical commercial movie. The author had a much greater say, a privilege that Foote now insisted upon, to the great advantage of the film's quality. He strove to make films that circumvented control by the commercial media.

Despite Foote's efforts, *Tender Mercies* was greatly altered, according to the director's wishes.[16] This information shows that when an original screenplay gets into the hands of movie directors, the results are unpredictable and may alter the author's conception.

The overriding theme of the film is the inability to face reality, seen as a spiritual failing. Mac Sledge cannot accept the truth of his failed marriage with another country music singer, Dixie Lee Scott, from whom he is now divorced. Mac's stubborn illusion finds expression early in the song he composed, "It's Hard to Face Reality" (p. 142). Mac sings other songs that express his inability to confront the truth of his life. They recount his loss of fame and resulting drunkenness.

The truth-versus-illusion theme shows its influence in this film. Foote thereby demonstrates his awareness of this illuminating idea, so strong in modern literature. He uses it intermittently but always seriously in his works. Foote sees the weakness of escaping reality in country music singers, since they live in the world of public entertainment and often suffer shattered lives, which they do not confront effectively. In this film, as in the play *The Traveling Lady* (1954), Foote draws on this subject. Here Mac tries to escape the failure of his marriage to Dixie Lee Scott. With the help of a strong second wife, Rosa Lee, whose attention never wavers from her troubles, Mac overcomes the temptation to elude the realities of his own tortured existence. Foote makes use of the themes of intellectual drama, like the truth-versus-illusion bifurcation, but comes to it later than Williams. When Foote does, he expresses it in familiar formulations that do not alienate a popular audience. Because of this technique, Foote's similarity to leading dramatic artists like Williams, Miller, and Albee is overlooked, but mistakenly so.

The antidote to Mac's spiritual malady is conversion to a strong Christian faith. Mac is guided to this change by his new wife, Rosa Lee, a believer who leads him to a reformed life. Her portrayal reveals the unmistakable influence of a strong wife, one of Foote's favorite character types. Rosa Lee thanks God for his "tender mercies" (a phrase in Psalms 79:8) in sending Mac to her. When her new husband does not return home one night after seeing Dixie and buying liquor, she prays for God's help. As if in answer to her prayer, Mac returns and tells of his near flight to "San Antone" but of his pouring out the liquor and subsequent return home.

This film is more openly religious than any of Foote's writings since he composed *Ludie Brooks* (1951), the television play about renewed faith for the *Religion in Everyday Life* series. In a central scene, Mac is baptized with his foster son at the Baptist church, where Rosa Lee sings in the choir. Here is a big change, since Foote presents the Baptists, including the minister, very favorably, much differently from his satirical portrayals, such as the pretentious Baptist lady of *Lily Dale*. After Mac has been baptized, Sonny, Rosa Lee's son, asks if he feels any different. Mac replies mischievously, "Not yet" (p. 134). In this film, however, Christian faith, without apology, gives the main characters the strength to lead a better life. The title reinforces the religious tones of this work.

In *Tender Mercies,* Foote also writes social criticism. Dixie, Mac's first wife, cares only about making money from songs composed by him. She lives in luxury and buys her daughter by Mac all that money can afford. But great wealth does not bring happiness. The sexual immorality of some country musicians also receives severe reproof in the account given of Dixie's promiscuous life after her divorce from Mac. Dixie drapes her leg across her manager's, showing that she and Harry are living together but not married.

Tender Mercies is first of all a sensitive character study with an affirmative ending. Mac cannot face the reality of his shattered life at first and escapes into drinking and regret for the loss of Dixie. We are made privy to his prolonged spiritual anguish. But this country music singer overcomes his personal flaws. With the indispensable assistance of Christian faith, the unflagging love of a strong wife, and the encouragement of close family ties, seen in the growing affection for his stepson, Sonny, Mac can look forward to a better life in the future. The popularity of this film indicates that Foote is most successful with audiences in both legitimate theatres and movie theatres when he combines insight into character with social criticism.

In this film we see both the bad and the good versions of country music. The former is evident most clearly in the career of Dixie, the singer that Mac boosted to stardom. Dixie appears at the Grapevine Opera House, singing "The Best Bedroom in Town" (p. 105), a salacious number that tells of a singer's moving to this part of the house with her lover.

The Slater Boys also sing songs of moral degradation. Robert belts forth a song about filling up on Canada Dry until his sweetheart returns. But these callow musicians are also subject to a better influence. They admire Mac Sledge, who tells them to sing as they feel and supplies them with his new compositions. Impecunious novices that they are, they make no money on their own songs until they begin to record Mac's, which succeed. The band boys are like small-town people, helping someone in need. They are humorous Texas types who come to Mac's aid. Harry, Dixie's manager, wants to employ Mac by giving him $500 earnest money for the "Ladder Song," but Mac refuses it; he will give his allegiance to the band boys, who have supported him. At the end, we hear on the radio their recording of Mac's tribute to Rosa Lee, "The Ladder Song": "You're the good things I threw away. . . . You are what love means to me" (p. 148). Presumably Mac's positive songs will have a salutary effect on these five young musicians.

The life of the wealthy Dixie stands in marked contrast to Mac's. Sue Anne, her and Mac's daughter, runs off with a drunken country musician who wrecks their honeymoon car, killing her. Dixie can only exclaim to Mac: "Why did God do this to me?" When Sue Anne visited Mac before her death, she asked him to sing the song of how God sends His love "on the wings of a snow-white dove" (p. 128). He says he can't remember it, but after she leaves, he does sing this song while alone, which expresses his love for her. Here again we have a good, caring song of country music. After Sue Anne is killed, Mac remembers "little sister" (p. 143).

This film emphasizes wholesome Christian family life, supporting the other religious elements. Mac becomes a good father to Sonny, who lost his father in the Vietnam War in 1971. This war was still in the background of many movies of the 1980s. When Mac sings the "Ladder Song," which he composed for Rosa Lee at the Plowboys' Club (a contrast to Dixie's venue), children of all ages are present. Sonny talks to another boy, whose mother has brought along her drunken boyfriend. The boy remarks that he does not think much of him. Sonny, however, can speak proudly of his new foster father. Mac has told Sonny not to throw rocks at him after plowing a nearby field, and he does not. Sonny instead throws a football to him, as we hear the song Mac wrote for Sonny's mother on the radio at the end. Sonny changes. He is proud of his stepfather at the end. In this story of a country music singer, a new, united family grows up. Country music singers need not create single-parent families with suffering offspring.

Although Foote presents a positive treatment of country music here, he still sees defects in it. These musicians are prone to flights from reality, to marital infidelity, and to drunkenness. Mac confronts all of these failings but surmounts them, facing steadfastly the truth of what has happened in his life, by the love of a strong woman who believes in him. Foote presents these aspects of a man's restored life with dramatic and credible effectiveness. Several scenes are very moving, like the last one of Mac and Sonny, but they appear without sentimentality. No false or excessive devices are used to excite the audience's emotions—a result of being free of control by the commercial medium.

This film tells a moving story. Though Mac is lost, Rosa Lee loves him and starts his rescue. The band boys also help. They encourage him to compose and sing. He recalls songs but does not sing in public until he puts Dixie behind him.

This is a good film because it deals with a man's emptiness, the loss of his vocation. He forgives his former wife and admits that her talent made his songs successful. One of the best themes is the surrogate father. In this time of fragmented families, surrogate fathers are particularly needed by children who lost young fathers in Vietnam. Mac becomes a father to Sonny, the Slater boys, and Sue Anne once again. They all admire him, and he lives up to their expectations. He acts as a supportive father to Sue Anne by being willing to see her derelict boyfriend.

The reviews of *Tender Mercies* were highly laudatory. Lucy Kroll sent "the lovely review" in *Variety* to Foote on January 5, 1983. On December 29, 1982, this publication had called *Tender Mercies* an "outstanding film," but one that would require "special handling if it is to find its deserved audience." The *Variety* review stated that, in the best sense, this was "an old-fashioned film," adding "There's no sex, no violence." The review noted, "[Rosa Lee is] deeply religious and sings in the church choir; unfashionably, the film accepts this at face value." When she watches her son and new husband being baptized, the review predicted that "all but the most cynical viewer should be touched by her joy." According to the reviewer, Foote was "espousing the old values here, looking to a way of making things simple and direct again." The critic observed that although "some may find this a reflection of the New Right," Bruce Beresford handled the film with such "sensibility and honesty" that the viewer is gradually captivated. The critic concludes: "This may be his best film" (HFC).

Stanley Kaufman, who had followed Foote's career since the 1950s, called *Tender Mercies* "one of the best American screenplays in years." He later denigrated the film *1918* (1985) as "flaccid." According to Kaufman, Foote, who should leave his past alone, "broke loose to write *Tender Mercies*" but then "returned to the past material he had progressed from." Kaufman, in other words, wanted Foote to write about the present more.[17]

The trouble with Kaufman's advice to continue writing more up-to-date works like *Tender Mercies,* and not about the past, was that it went against Foote's fundamental philosophy. He wished to return to the past in the *Orphans' Home Cycle* because he wanted to write about his own people in a traditional and realistic way at that time in his career, and he did. This attitude, to be sure, may have hurt him commercially.

Foote moved away from the commercial media at a time when few chances for noncommercial films existed. This essentially noncommercial film handles emotionally charged scenes with better taste, fewer stereotypes, and less sentimentality than *To Kill a Mockingbird,* made by a commercial producer in 1962. Even representatives of commercial movies extolled it. On May 23, 1983, John Kohn of Twentieth Century Fox wrote to Foote that he was thrilled by the reviews. Kohn predicted that the *Los Angeles Times* would praise it: "I am positive the picture will be greatly admired" (HFC).

Lucy Kroll was overjoyed with the success of *Tender Mercies.* According to her letter dated February 15, 1983, E. J. Dionne in the *New York Times* reported strong sentiment at the Cannes Film Festival to honor Bruce Beresford as best director and Robert Duvall as best actor, but the film had to be eliminated on the technicality of its having been shown already in New Delhi. On March 16, 1983, Kroll wrote to Foote that "we can celebrate the wonderful reception of *Tender Mercies*" (HFC).

As Foote demonstrates by his work in television and the movies, he is interested in American popular culture and has something serious to say about it. His trilogy—*The Traveling Lady; Baby, the Rain Must Fall;* and *Tender Mercies*—focuses on country-and-western music, found most richly in the South and the West, not in the metropolitan East nor on the sophisticated West Coast for that matter. The first play about country music did not attract Broadway interest, but the movie, which was distributed nationwide, did much better. And the final film, *Tender Mercies,* was very successful when the popularity of country-and-western music soared.

The Traveling Lady has demonstrated staying power with regional audiences, which are closer to small-town life and more appreciative of country-and-western music. This play reveals good potential for the Saroyanesque combination of drama and singing seen in *The Time of Your Life.* The singing in this play should be exploited to the fullest before audiences that enjoy country music.

These works make an indirect comment on the Elvis Presley phenomenon, that is, the popular singer of country and rock music. This type of musician makes a protest against strict, Victorian, middle-class society, which has been strong in the South. It is quite evident in the defiant singing of Henry Thomas in both *The Traveling Lady* and *Baby, the Rain Must Fall.* This angry young man, passionately devoted to this style of music, will go on singing no matter how much opposition from society he encounters or how many personal crises beset him. Such musicians lead tormented lives. They take refuge in liquor, outbursts of violence (including mayhem), sexual license, and, last but not least, materialistic consumption, like the desire for the white Cadillac. Often the behavior brings destruction to themselves and others.

Foote suggests, but does not spell out, remedies for the crises of self-indulgent musicians until *Tender Mercies.* Here, in his last look at country music and its purveyors, he includes brave exemplars. Besides religious faith and family support, the words of the songs speak to the lost musicians and to their listeners no less. Mac Sledge gains self-knowledge when he declares, "It's hard to face reality." Finally in the simple, cliché-ridden but heartfelt "Ladder Song," the composer makes a promise that inspires him, "If you'll just hold the ladder, Baby, I'll climb to the top" (p. 122). For those who need sacrificial love, such words, backed by pulsating music, can change their lives.

CHAPTER

11

ADAPTATIONS OF HARPER LEE, FAULKNER,

O'CONNOR, AND STEINBECK

FOOTE'S life as a playwright is extraordinary because in midcareer he withdrew from concentration on original plays and turned to adaptations of others' works.[1] He had made a strenuous attempt to hit the big time on Broadway, like his famous contemporaries, Tennessee Williams, Arthur Miller, and William Inge. But his principal successes, like *The Young Lady of Property,* had been offstage on television in the happy years of its Golden Age. Being a sensible man with good judgment, Foote shifted his energy from the inhospitable, sophisticated theatre of New York to the distant, more receptive embrace of Hollywood. He became the adaptor of various works. From the age of forty-two in 1948 to the age of seventy-six in 1992, he wrote many screenplays for television and movies. This work won him financial success and much more freedom as to what original writing he would do during that time.

As for adaptations, Foote has made plain his dislike of them in several forceful statements. First, he has asserted that he has never enjoyed the process of adaptation, because he felt he had important ideas of his own to express.[2] Foote observes that Hollywood eventually "relegates the writer to the role of adaptor." Though he admires David Mamet for retaining originality, Mamet is a distinct exception. Adapting, Foote says, "is not an atmosphere conducive to creativity." In original work, Foote says, he has the freedom to explore his own imagination ("Lecture," given at Spaulding, Louisville, Kentucky, p. 20). Terry Barr concludes that adaptations do not contain the character types that Foote knows nor the themes that have preoccupied him. After discussing a series of adaptations that Foote wrote in the 1960s, Barr turns gladly to the works of Foote's own *Orphans' Home Cycle,* stating that they are his "most meaningful" plays. Like the work of our best writers, Foote's original plays enable him to get the stories he knows best into the plays of his parentage, such as his mother and father's determination to elope against the opposition of his mother's parents, and the formative events that molded him into the person he is.[3] In his own works, Foote knows the people and his native ground, through and through. In fact the more he dramatizes Harrison, Texas, the richer are his insights into its true life and life in general.

For a lengthy period after *The Traveling Lady* closed in New York, Foote wrote movie adaptations. This change meant that he had to deal with the motion picture industry in Hollywood, where he had to produce screenplays, as Faulkner did on his frequent jaunts there. Foote had many of Faulkner's complaints about the inartistic demands of Hollywood, but Foote devoted more creative energy to screenplays than Faulkner and in fact had greater success. Foote objected strenuously to working for Hollywood commercial filmmakers. While writing for live television, he enjoyed much-cherished freedom and also did so on some films, but not others. From the beginning of his contact with Hollywood, he wanted more freedom, but he did not gain it until suffering many painful experiences over a long period of time. In essence he could not develop his own original material as a writer for the commercial media, which was not surprising, given that the test for commercial movies was always monetary success.

Foote first worked as a staff writer for Warner Brothers, churning out the screenplay for *Storm Fear* (1956), the adaptation of a novel, starring Cornel Wilde. The movie is based on a minor southern novel about a bank robber who retreats to a mountain home, where he is frightened by a storm. It was indifferently received by the critics and the public. This job convinced Foote that a screenwriter does not get sufficient satisfaction from adaptation. He cannot please the author, nor the audience, which has definite ideas about plot and characterization. Furthermore, the screenplay can be brutally altered by the director and his team.[4]

The real test of Foote's willingness to write adaptations came with the offer to write the screenplay for *To Kill a Mockingbird*. At first Foote was reluctant to undertake the project, despite the novel's fame and the enticement of large financial profit. It was a sprawling novel, in the first place, and furthermore Foote wanted to write works that would come from his own imagination, like *The Trip to Bountiful*. He did not wish to be a specialist in movie adaptations. His wife, however, persuaded him to read the novel, which he found moving.[5] Because of his liking for former television colleagues Alan Pakula, the producer, and Robert Mulligan, the director, plus the congenial relationship with Harper Lee, whose memories of a small Alabama town echoed his own of Wharton, he agreed to compose the screenplay. Happily for Foote's contribution, the contract stipulated that Pakula and Mulligan would make the final cut of the film, not Universal Pictures. Foote comments, "Universal did not like the picture very much, and if they had got their hands on it, Gods knows what they would have done, but they couldn't."[6]

Foote received more acclaim and response to the movie *To Kill a Mockingbird* than he had ever before. It made him a household name both in Texas and the nation. The state representative from Wharton sent Foote the congratulatory resolution of the Texas House of Representatives for his screenplay on April 29, 1963. Though Foote's many kindred had followed his theatrical career loyally, they responded with even greater enthusiasm to this popular movie when it was shown in Texas. It gave Foote fame in his home state that he had never known before.

His mother wrote him proudly and repeatedly about the film from 1962 to 1965. On January 1, 1963, his uncle Speed Brooks informed him from Houston ("Bagdad by the Bayou," he called it) that he was going to see the movie. On April 11, 1963, William Jovanovich, president of Harcourt, Brace, and World, Inc., which published *Harrison, Texas,* wrote to congratulate Foote on winning the Oscar for his screenplay. Foote graciously thanked all these correspondents in letters personally signed by him (HFC). He had attained national renown that would remain attached to his name and would undergird his playwriting efforts many times for the rest of his career.

To Kill a Mockingbird is indeed a sprawling novel, being a mélange of children's tale, social protest, and satirical anatomy of a backwater small town, not unlike Foote's Harrison.[7] It was a challenge to Foote's resourcefulness to alter this successful novel and give it his own personal touch. The story is highly melodramatic in its sharp division of characters into heroes and villains, recalling that ur-treatment of the racial issue *Uncle Tom's Cabin.* Admirable blacks contrast with deep-eyed villainous poor whites. Lee satirizes the inanity and racial prejudices of traditional southern ladies unmercifully. The story of the retarded Boo is sentimentalized, though Lee has a good scene in the end when Scout discovers him in the corner.

The most interesting question in a study of Foote is, What will the adapter do with this well-known story? The movie is divided into two plots: the children's life and the racial conflict. The trial of Tom Robinson, accused of raping Mayella Ewing, is the same in both forms. As for a noticeable difference between the two, Foote greatly lessens the satire of the ladies.

Foote reinforces the moral outrage in Lee's novel. Wholeheartedly adopting her protest against racial injustice in the South, the movie reflects the spirit of the civil rights movement. It possesses a power that had not appeared in Foote's works before. Social protest, which permeates the film, empowers Foote's screenplay. In effect, Harper Lee's indignation toward the racial conditions in the South becomes Foote's own, as a long-time southerner who grew up in the part of Texas where blacks were a substantial majority. The result is a film that is equal to the novel in the intensity of its social protest. In Foote's screenplay, there is not merely the mild criticism of his previous writing but also the portrayal of the bigoted, villainous father, Mr. Ewell; the racial prejudice of the small-town residents; and the unjust conviction of an innocent black man. This protest, advocating a social cause, had not appeared before in Foote's works.

Mockingbird the novel provides plentiful plot material, so Foote had only to be selective. The main characters and racial prejudice are all there. Foote is as strong in his condemnation of the injustice done the black man as Harper Lee. His background as a playwright gives the film dramatic concentration. In a play, but not always in a movie, one proceeds by clearly defined scenes. The big scene in this film shows Foote's skill as a playwright. It is the trial. He repeats, without change, telling lines in the novel like "Your father's passin'" by one spectator at the trial after Atticus Finch has finished his defense of Tom Robinson.[8] The movie, like many others, has a compelling plot, but there is not time enough for exposition of thought in words.

The characters in the movie are based on well-known stereotypes. Jim is a "manly" boy who wants his father to do heroic deeds (like shooting the mad dog). Also the tomboy sister who fights becomes obvious in the movie. The good cook; the serious black reverend; the bigoted, abusive po' white father; the abused, lying daughter; and the heroic black husband who is the victim and martyr can be added to the list. The country boy who lathers his meal with syrup is not forgotten. These clichés have sure-fire appeal with audiences. The widowed father, who must be father and mother and is also the upright defender of an innocent black man, is well drawn, but still he is part of the gallery of stereotypes. In *Mockingbird,* Foote appeals to popular taste repeatedly and makes a hit at the box office.

What did Foote do in the screenplay to make *To Kill a Mockingbird* the phenomenal success it was on the screen? He was faithful to the text and tone of Harper Lee's novel and made only a few noticeable changes. Of the old ladies satirized for their idiosyncratic traits and southern foibles, Foote transfers few to the film. He changes Miss Maudie — a widow who is friendly to the children and the possible wife for Uncle Jack Finch, Atticus's brother — into a younger, attractive woman. She mothers the children and draws close to the widower Atticus, hinting stronger ties in the future. Foote eliminates many of the female characters satirized in the novel, like Mrs. Meriwether, who gives a long, tedious speech at the pageant about the founder of the town, Colonel Maycomb, a follower of Andrew Jackson. By eliminating the satire and stressing the noble qualities of the leading characters, he makes the movie more enjoyable for most spectators.

Foote decided skillfully what to omit and what to preserve from the novel. Most significantly, the film retains and enhances the mood of nostalgia. Faulkner's *Intruder in the Dust* (novel, 1948; film, 1949) lacks a nostalgic mood. Faulkner's plot of a black man unjustly accused and defended by a courageous white attorney reveals the similarity of the two novels. Harper Lee and Foote reach deep into the collective unconsciousness of Americans that give *Huck Finn* so much of its emotional appeal and retell the story of childhood — the adventures of preadolescents, the excitement, and the danger. The story has the universal appeal of gripping childhood experience, occurring some thirty years ago. Foote did not tamper with that strain but enriched it by putting into visual form — what the novel could not — the children's view of their mysterious neighbor and their confrontation with life and death in the adult world. Among the reasons that may be enumerated for the success of his film but not the adaptation of Faulkner's novel are the addition of a big-name actor, Gregory Peck, and the timely context of the civil rights movement, from which *Mockingbird* benefited.

By use of Scout's adult voiceover at the beginning, intermittently, and most appropriately at the end, the mood of memory, as in *The Glass Menagerie,* provides a unifying atmosphere that enhances the film. At the end, Foote adds this line spoken by Scout: "I was to think of these days many times; of Jem, and Dill, and Boo Radley, and Tom Robinson . . . and Atticus" (p. 80). Recapitulation of these names recalls the main figures of the story and the magical life of children.

Bosley Crowther's review of this film and screenplay was very favorable, especially as to the ingratiating portrayal of children's lives in a small southern town (*New York Times,* February 15, 1963). Further, Crowther praises the lesson promulgated of justice and humanity toward blacks. But he also speaks of "the conventional line of social crisis in the community," arising from the charge of a Negro's raping a white woman, and the lengthy "melodrama" in the courtroom. The bigoted poor white father and his abused daughter are "almost caricatures." Stereotypes in the film also include the young son and daughter, who are highly conventionalized types, he adds. Because they are made so appealing, their portrayals would verge on sentimentality for some spectators.

This popular adaptation of Harper Lee's novel had a major influence on Foote's subsequent writing. He became a sharper, more committed critic of wrongs in the small town after composing this screenplay. For his adaptation, he was much influenced by R. P. Blackmur's review of the novel. That well-known New Critic said that we should "discover the evil and hypocrisy of the small Southern town" in this famous, highly acclaimed novel, which won the Pulitzer Prize for Literature.[9]

As a result of the denunciation of wrong in *To Kill a Mockingbird,* there was a change of focus from the play to the movie about Henry Thomas, the luckless country musician, of *Baby, the Rain Must Fall* (1965).[10] In it, Foote turns his attention to the evils of the Texas small town and condemns narrow-mindedness and religious bigotry, as he had condemned racial prejudice in small-town Alabama.

Foote is adamant elsewhere in asserting what material he intends to write about. His original plays present "my people and my stories and the plays I want to write." In fact, they are "really the only ones I know how to write" ("Learning," p. 91). We must conclude that even though he felt an affinity with Monroeville, Alabama; Jefferson, Mississippi; and middle Georgia, he misses his own place, Southeast Texas. Foote tells about the South, but it is *his* personal South, a Texas variation, which differs importantly from the South of Williams, Faulkner, and O'Connor, because of its size and its more diverse population.

During this period of adaptations, Foote made notable achievements that elevate his standing in the world of television and movies. Foote underwent the transition to Hollywood when he adapted Faulkner's novelette *Old Man* for *Playhouse 90*. This ninety-minute program, presented on November 20, 1958, and sponsored by CBS offered excellent entertainment. It was praised by the critics and also was popular with viewers. Foote, who had come to be an admirer of Faulkner, was an avid reader of that author in the 1940s and considered himself a student of his works.[11] In an interview on November 11, 1987, Foote claimed Faulkner as his greatest influence.[12]

Old Man was directed by John Frankenheimer and produced by Fred Coe, with Sterling Hayden playing the tall convict and Geraldine Page the young woman.[13] In place of Faulkner's anatomy of complex modern society, Foote concentrated on the tale of a misogynist and the woman he rescues, as they become more attached to each other during the Mississippi River flood of 1927. The convict finds a pregnant woman, helps her have a son, and paddles a small boat with the three aboard until rescued. He returns to prison.

In the adaptation of this novelette, Foote made the relationship of the convict and the woman warmer and more personal. He thus added his contribution to the original. Some romantic feeling comes through between the convict and the woman. Seven years, she says, is not too long to wait on his getting out of prison. She names the baby "Gerard," giving a personal touch to Faulkner's intentional anonymity.

Foote does a good job of plotting this wandering storyline. He makes things much clearer, like the plump convict's desire to escape in contrast to the tall convict's obedience. Foote supplies gentle humor, but little of the sharp tone in Faulkner's text; the tall convict uses no obscenities as in the original. In the novelette, the convict's last comment on the whole affair as he sits in prison is "Women,—!"[14] Rebecca Briley writes that Foote was intrigued by the character of the woman and said, "I never tired thinking [of her]. I made her a talker and gave her a detailed history."[15]

What is lost in the adaptation is the provocative quality of Faulkner's themes: the changing roles of male and female in modern industrial society and the convict's aversion to regimented life. The visual medium would regularly fall short with such complicated subjects when extended disquisitions were needed to explore them. Foote understands the convict well, particularly his intense pride. The convict will not take money from a doctor because he could never repay him. One does not get the feeling of a return to primitive existence, however. The convict's complete inability in the story to function normally with women in complex society is not realized in the film. The television movie adds human appeal and is much easier to follow than the novelette, but Foote necessarily had to popularize and simplify the work. At a later time with a new cast, Foote's adaptation was shown on the *Hallmark Hall of Fame,* winning the Emmy and Humanitas Awards in 1997.

After the first adaptation of *Old Man* (1958), Foote gained distinction by writing other adaptations of works by Faulkner, who was famous by then, having received the Nobel Prize for Literature in 1950. Foote composed a television adaptation of "Tomorrow," a short story by Faulkner, in 1960. It was originally presented on television's *Playhouse 90* on March 7, 1960, and repeated July 18, 1961.[16] Foote later rewrote this play for film in 1972. In 1977 he adapted Flannery O'Connor's "The Displaced Person," in 1980 Faulkner's "Barn Burning" for PBS, and in 1992 Steinbeck's *Of Mice and Men.* For these excellent adaptations, Foote won critical acclaim. He maintained his artistic credentials with these distinguished works, which rescued him from the label of merely churning out commercial movies.

Foote's adaptations of Faulkner's stories reveal the pitfalls of transferring the original writings of an author like Faulkner to film even when the products are not commercial movies. The tendency to develop the easily understandable human relationship and to concentrate all the emotional force on that object distorts and lessens the original concept.

The evolution of "Tomorrow" begins with Faulkner's story, published in the *Saturday Evening Post* (1940).[17] This brief tale tells about the country man Jackson Fentry, but Faulkner's version is more difficult to follow and more complex in its ideas than Foote's. For instance, Faulkner notes that the girl whom Buck falls in love with is clearly an archetype of the disobedient daughter who does not heed her father, and thus the tragic event of her father's killing of Buck is inevitable and universalized. Further, the hero Jackson Fentry is a classic type: proud and stubborn. Like the tall convict, he cares for a woman who is about to have a baby. He comes from those hard country people whom Faulkner admires so much and who have forgotten how to love, because they have to use all their time and energy to get enough to eat and breathe. Fentry is, however, exceptional because of his enduring love.

Foote follows Faulkner's story closely in the television play of *Tomorrow* but shows much more of the development of Buck, a villainous young man who is shot. The television play starred Richard Boone as Fentry and Kim Stanley, who had appeared in *The Traveling Lady,* as Sarah Eubanks, whom Fentry marries. The teleplay was directed by Robert Mulligan, Foote's cousin.

Fentry begins to live with Sarah, whom Foote names and fully characterizes as the frail but pretty mother of Buck, who is shot later by Bookwright. In the television play, edited by David Yellin and Marie Connors, it is made plain that this was made for television, because there are four commercial breaks, making in effect as many act divisions. The lawyer who defends Bookwright is Thornton Douglas (called Gavin Stephens in the story), who is accompanied by the teenage nephew now named Charles Douglas, the average southern boy.

This lawyer cannot understand why one man, Fentry, did not vote to free his client. The lawyer drives out to talk with the Pruitts, who knew Fentry. They tell him all they know about him and his wife, Sarah, and relate how Fentry picked out a homesite for the couple. Then Thornton goes to see Isham Quick, the friendly son of the sawmill owner whom Fentry worked for. He says that Sarah was sick before having the baby and, just after it was born, told Fentry that she would marry him. Preacher Whitehead, a fine, strong man (a repellent reprobate with the early evangelist's name Whitefield in *As I Lay Dying*) is fetched from seven miles away by Fentry. He marries them as she lies abed. She asks what the baby's name will be, but it is not yet chosen. Fentry describes the house site to her, which he does not do in Faulkner's story: "While I was bringing the Preacher here, I went right by the place where our house is going to be. It's going to have three rooms in it—and a porch for us to sit on. And around it I'm going to put some pretty trees" (p. 87). Then the woman he has just married dies.

The next act shows Fentry's raising of his son, named Jackson and Longstreet. After the boy is abducted by his uncles, Fentry is inconsolable and goes to Texas and other points west for eight years. He then returns to his father's house and later observes the boy, now named Buck. The boy does not recognize Fentry and yells, "Get out of here!" (p. 105). After a few days, Pruitt reports, Bookwright kills Buck.

Foote finishes this melodrama quickly. Thornton says that Charles would not have freed Bookwright either, though his nephew said that he would have, because Buck terrorized the community. The lawyer believes that Fentry did not free Bookwright, because of his "memory" of the boy (p. 105). He pronounces the epitaph for Fentry used by Faulkner to the boy in his story: "And you wouldn't have freed him either. Don't ever forget that. Never" (story, p. 52; television play, p. 106). Then Foote adds a line, spoken by Thornton, that is not in Faulkner's story: "The lowly and invincible of the earth—to endure . . . tomorrow and tomorrow and tomorrow" (p. 106).

"Tomorrow" had a long period of development before it finally reached the screen. After publishing the story in 1940, Faulkner collected it in *Knight's Gambit* in 1948. Joseph Blotner called it merely "a detective story."[18] Foote, however, hoped that, after *Old Man,* lightning would strike in the same place with another Faulkner drama on *Playhouse 90* in 1960. Faulkner liked Foote's teleplay very much. He gave him permission to publish it and allowed him to share the copyright. Foote said Faulkner's generosity was "a kind and almost unheard of thing."[19] Adapted for the stage in 1963, the play *Tomorrow* was performed at the Herbert Berghof Studio in 1968, directed by Foote's friend Joseph Anthony. In 1972 the film version was shown in New York, starring Robert Duvall, but it failed financially because the influential Vincent Canby of the *New York Times* panned it. Eleven years later with the Duvall fans behind it, this movie was a box-office hit. Duvall called it "my favorite part" and "my most complete film role."[20] In Yellin and Connors's volume is an essay by Foote called "The Visual Takes Over," in which he says Hollywood failed often because it tried to "improve" Faulkner. Foote stated in this essay: "Faulkner can be dramatized. He can't be improved."[21]

For the screening of *Tomorrow,* Foote invited several friends to come. On October 8, 1971, he asked Lillian Gish, who attended on October 23, 1971. He also invited Fred Coe, Alan Pakula, and Agnes de Mille. Later, on May 17, 1972, he replied to Thomas D. Anderson of Southern Illinois University that the story had been collected in *Knight's Gambit.* The screenplay was not yet available, he said. As with the many congratulations on *To Kill a Mockingbird,* Foote was unfailingly prompt and gracious in answering letters about *Tomorrow* (HFC).

In the film adaptation (1972), Foote delineates fully the developing relationship between the woman and Fentry. Sarah is reminiscent of Faulkner's character Lena Grove in *Light in August* (1931). Like Lena, Sarah is also wandering aimlessly. Her husband has deserted her, but she takes up with a kind man, Fentry (who resembles Byron Bunch, since he works in a sawmill too in Faulkner's novel). Fentry says to her, "I'll never leave you unless you ask me," in a very believable southern accent (p. 139).

Fentry shows her where he plans to build their house; this hope becomes quite evident and is repeated, but not sentimentally. Sarah thinks of the flowers they will plant in the yard, as Foote's young wives often do. Fentry has asked this distraught woman to marry him twice, but like Lena Grove, Sarah declines modestly because she already has a husband. Finally, when she has the baby and realizes that she is near death, she agrees. Fentry fetches a preacher who lives seven miles away. After the son is born, Fentry holds him in a moving scene. He makes a cradle and promises Sarah to care for him. He asserts that she will not die. Sarah, nevertheless, dies.

In this family, Fentry must be mother and father, like Atticus Finch in *To Kill a Mockingbird,* which was published long after this story by Faulkner was written. The midwife, who is particularly authentic with her lean face and sharp features of the plain folk of north Mississippi, tells Fentry he must give the boy goat's milk, except one must milk a goat every two hours, which we see him start to do. Showing the loving education of Jackson and Longstreet, the father and son appear in several scenes together. He and Jackson and Longstreet pick cotton in a sparse field as country music plays in the background, something a film can portray better than the printed page.

This idyllic existence, however, cannot last. The wife's three brothers, with their menacing looks, arrive with a paper from the sheriff. Although Fentry fights desperately, they take the protesting son away. Fentry stays on his father's farm and does not go back to the sawmill.

At the end, we return to the opening scene. We see in flashback the action that precipitated the trial, but it is changed from Faulkner's version. The young son, now called Buck, is presented more positively. The girl has a suitcase and goes willingly with Buck. She has not been persuaded by his "swagger," as Faulkner writes (p. 135). In Foote's version, Bookwright appears with a gun. Buck has a gun also but does not fire before he is shot by the father.

In the final courtroom scene, Fentry is on the jury. He refuses to free the father even though all the other members insist on it. The defense lawyer, played by Foote's cousin Peter Masterson, pronounces the final words, as Gavin Stevens did in Faulkner's story. He states that in reality the promise that Fentry had made was not the reason that he voted as he did. As is illustrated by the images of himself and the boy that pass through his mind in the end, he acted out of love. That is a love that will endure in the heart and soul of Fentry, one of the humble country people. They are "the lowly and invincible of the earth to endure and endure, and then endure. . . . Tomorrow and tomorrow and tomorrow" (pp. 159–160).

The ending is moving and a worthy addition to the more neutral version by Faulkner, who wrote only that Fentry's promise made him take his final stand.

Foote's last adaptation of Faulkner was the short story "Barn Burning." It had been published first in 1931 and reprinted by Vintage Books and in Louis Rubin's well-known anthology in 1977.[22] It was shown on PBS in 1980. An informative article on its filming was published in *Southern Quarterly* (Winter 1983).

In Foote's teleplay, as in the short story, the boy Sarty overcomes his past, enabled by intelligence and inspired by the love of justice. Foote uses the power of the visual medium to intensify these forces and make them moving. In the film, Ab Snopes wakes his son in bed by kicking him and commanding him to harness the horses. This hateful father gives his son a piece of cheese on a knife at the store. Sarty manages a smile, showing his desire to have a good relationship with his father. This scene is completely Foote's addition.[23] Sarty will not help his father in burning his aristocratic employer's mansion. But the boy still feels close to his father. Besides Faulkner's words, "Father, Father,"[24] Foote adds the intimate ones "Daddy, Daddy."[25]

Foote wrote his adaptation of Flannery O'Connor's "The Displaced Person" for PBS in 1977.[26] It was filmed entirely on Andalusia Farm, O'Connor's home, according to the production credit. The television play is well acted, and the main points are the same as in the original story. O'Connor ends by writing that on visits to Mrs. McIntyre the priest brought "a bag of breadcrumbs and, after he had fed them to the peacock, he would come and sit by the bed and explain the doctrines of the church" (p. 251). In the film these words are omitted. The silent gestures of the priest and the blank vacuity of Mrs. McIntyre compose the last scene.

Foote turned once again to film for an adaptation of John Steinbeck's *Of Mice and Men* (novella, 1937; first film, 1939; Foote's film, 1992).[27] Why? Foote has made clear that he would do this if the subject matter appealed to him. The idea of loneliness in Steinbeck's work is one that Foote had treated before, as in *The Traveling Lady*, *Tomorrow*, and *Tender Mercies*. Mistreatment of blacks had also been depicted in *Convicts* (1985). This novella is theatrical, easily divided into acts and scenes. Foote's teleplay about George and Lennie, who were played by Gary Sinise and John Malkovich, was successful and has been shown often on television.

By choosing Steinbeck, Foote showed that he now wished to adapt the master storytellers. The original story is so close to Foote's film that only a few differences may be noted before discussing the adaptation.[28] This is a tale of two migrant workers, the smart George and the retarded Lennie, in California during the Depression. Steinbeck opens with the pair talking by a quiet stream. By contrast, Foote begins in medias res, with the two men jumping into the boxcar of a passing train, chased off their former place of work because Lennie touched a pretty girl.

After the exciting opening scene of Foote's movie, the two "bindlers" (novella, p. 240)—that is, bundlers—go to Tyler's Ranch, very slowly because the thoughtless bus driver leaves them standing on the road. In Foote's adaptation, the boss of the ranch does not sympathize with their vexing delay. Many other workers arrive, neatly divided into the compassionate ones like Slim the skinner, who supervises the horses and mules, and the hostile ones like Carlson, who does not care for the new arrivals, and Jack, who cannot stack the bags as fast as Lennie lifts them on the wagon. Slim gives Lennie a puppy, which he accidentally crushes.

A project is soon articulated by George, giving the plot more philosophical interest. He tells Lennie and an old man named Candy that someday they will get a little place and have cows and even rabbits. Lennie is delighted with this plan and wants such a "place" with rabbits, a stove, and a vegetable patch. Likewise wanting companionship is Crooks, a Negro who is said to stink and therefore must live by himself. Crooks is alienated and has no friends among the white workers. Very bitter, he voices his hatred of whites to Lennie, who doesn't understand.

In another change from the novella, Foote ends the tale more quietly than Steinbeck. In the novella the vengeful posse arrives to lynch Lennie for squeezing a woman to death. Its two leaders do not understand the chagrin of George and Slim. What's "eating them two guys?" they inquire in Hemingway fashion (novella, p. 327). In Foote's ending, George shoots Lennie in the back of the head, just as Candy's old dog was killed. The last scene shows George, now truly alone, sitting by the unmoving Lennie. Then he remembers lifting the bags of barley with his big friend and walking silently away at sundown. Lennie is pressing his hand on George's back, behind him as usual.

Of Mice and Men was produced by Lewis Milestone, with screenplay by Eugene Solow, in 1939 by United Artists. It was issued on DVD (Corinth Films) in 1998. There is more sentimentality in the 1939 film than in Foote's version. In the 1939 version, Candy sobs pitifully when he hands the old dog over to be shot. The background music is highly emotional in the tense scenes. In short, the commercial movie is designed more for entertainment and is dependent on the acting of the stars. Foote is to be commended for his quieter ending and for the acting, which is not so theatrical and is more low-key.

Foote's version makes a good film. By this time, Foote was interested only in writing an adaptation that treated a provocative, congenial theme, like loneliness among migrant workers. He also wanted to be familiar with the character types. George and Lennie, who are in an isolated place and are in need of compassion, resemble the character types in *Convicts*. The two stand together and oppose the owners, who are heartless like Soll Gautier in *Convicts*. Of course the men in *Convicts* are also rural and bigoted.

Foote became skilled at transmuting others' writings. In fact, some of his best works are adaptations, especially *Tomorrow,* which he changed the most. By his creation of Fentry and Sarah, Foote added much of his own to Faulkner's excellent story.

12

THE *ORPHANS' HOME CYCLE,*

PART 1

R EFLECTING the changes in Foote's writing during the period when he started adaptations with *Old Man* were the alterations he made in his place of residence. From New York City, where he worked assiduously from 1935 to 1955, except for an interlude in Washington from 1945 to 1949, Foote moved to Nyack, New York, on the Hudson River in 1956. By this time he had three children and could provide a more spacious abode for his family away from the metropolitan environment, but still be close enough to reach New York easily by train. He built a house in this town, known as a quaint artists' haven. Ten years later in 1966, Foote moved even farther from New York City when he transferred his family, now grown to four children—two boys and two girls—to New Boston, New Hampshire. Evidently, Foote sought a quieter, more congenial atmosphere for thought and composition. Since the home in New Hampshire was located on a country road to which Foote always had to give directions, the family lived in a place of New England charm, even of Thoreauvian character.

Foote's second move in 1966 coincided with the earthshaking change in the New York theatre and American society for that matter. This was the era now labeled "the sixties," the years of the disruptive Vietnam War, the civil rights movement, and the assassinations of Martin Luther King and Robert Kennedy in 1968. The New York theatre and the film industry responded to this turbulent time with political musicals like Megan Terry's *Viet Rock* (1966), civil rights plays like *Purlie Victorious* (1961), and calls for a revolution in sexual behavior. Foote did not join the political activism of the 1960s. He preferred the drama of small-town life, epitomized by his collection of television one-acts entitled *Harrison,*

Texas (1953). That kind of play was Foote's forte. Probably he also realized that such a change would not have been feasible, given his tastes and temperament.

In fact, Foote did not like the political orientation of the theatre. In answer to one interviewer, he replied that he felt "displaced" in the 1960s.[1] He stated further that when he went to New Hampshire he did not care for the direction the theatre was going, nor that in which America was going, for that matter. As for the sensational fashion in the theatre and films, Foote remarked pointedly that though Oedipus blinded himself, he did so offstage.[2] Of course, Foote had to pay the price, so to speak, of marching to his own drummer and not following suit in the theatre during the revolutionary 1960s. He bided his time and at last, at the ripe age of fifty-eight, resumed serious playwriting in 1974. When he began to compose the *Orphans' Home Cycle,* his saga of Harrison, Texas, from 1902 to 1926, he dramatized the life of his hometown and his father's coming of age. It is written in a style and spirit that barely differ from his television plays *The Trip to Bountiful* and *The Traveling Lady.*

After the 1950s, Foote went deeper into his principal themes: courage and adjustment to change. The central play in the *Cycle, Courtship,* features a shining example of courage. Elizabeth is based on Foote's mother, who eloped against her father's wishes. Elizabeth loves Horace and disobeys her father. This step takes every ounce of courage she can muster. She goes to live in a one-room apartment and must endure the shame of her father's rejection. Horace is made a man by Elizabeth; he loved her and married her. Laura, the younger sister, lacks courage. In real life the sister with this name evidently matured and married a man with whom she had a good life.

In Foote's movies he also emphasized a moral theme. *To Kill a Mockingbird* (1963) shows the courage of Atticus Finch. That stalwart lawyer opposes a bigoted town in the South and defends a black man charged with a murder he did not commit. In *Tender Mercies* (1983), Foote gave a full picture of country musician Mac Sledge, who is being ruined by liquor. He meets Rosa Lee, who runs a motel and has a son. This woman, based on Foote's wife, saves Mac from ignoring the reality of his misdeeds. She gives him courage. Mac becomes a Christian along with the son of Rosa, who inspires his songs. With the inspiration of a strong woman, Mac abandons his immoral life and marries her. He becomes the foster father of other country musicians.

In *The Man Who Climbed the Pecan Trees* (1982), Bertie Dee shows courage by disagreeing with her mother-in-law and holds the family together despite the weakness of her husband. A fine example of how working-class people adjust to changing circumstances comes in *Talking Pictures* (1994). Myra, who plays the piano at the silent-movie theatre, marries Willis when their world comes crashing down. They will move, and she will get a different job.

In *Night Seasons* (1993), another Laura is a weak character. She cannot make up her mind about anything—even a simple purchase. This indecisive woman dies without ever buying a house she desired for many years.

In *The Young Man from Atlanta* (1995), Will is the courageous figure but has been a workaholic. He has ignored his son and must live with the consequences. Foote condemns excessive work, as seen in the businessman of *The Old Beginning* (1956).

Foote discussed the *Orphans' Home Cycle* in a long lecture entitled "The Orphans' Home Cycle," given at Texas A&M University on April 14, 1993. This extensive commentary covers seventy-two pages, which I will refer to from time to time in this chapter and Chapter 13.[3] Foote opens this lecture by saying that "it might interest you to know how *I think* it all started" and that he has "reconstructed a history of its beginning that I have come to believe is accurate" ("Lecture," p. 1).

The *Orphans' Home Cycle* had its inception with an idea of Stark Young's. After writing the foreword to the television play *The Night of the Storm* in 1962, Young urged Foote to turn it into a stage play.[4] Eventually this suggestion led to the composition of the nine-play *Cycle*. After his father and mother died, Foote remembered what Stark Young had said. This prompted his rereading of the television play. Recalling the lives of his father and mother in Wharton launched his writing of the *Cycle* in 1974 ("Lecture," p. 11).

When Foote finished the drafts of eight plays, he thought they should be done together, and he says, "Public Television seemed the one place with the will and means to undertake such a formidable task." He sent them to Robert Geller, who produced the *American Short Story Series*. Though Geller liked the plays, he was not able to procure the financing for television, and thus the project became stalled ("Lecture," p. 13).

Foote's mother died in 1974, and his father in 1975; these events released many long-stored memories in their son, which took form in a series he wrote from 1974 to 1977. Only one play of the nine-play sequence, *The Widow Claire,* was written later. After his parents died, Foote started taking notes for the plays. He thought about their lives and the town that had surrounded them from birth to death. When his mother died, Foote spent one week in Wharton, going through letters and meditating on the fifty-nine years that his parents had spent in that house.[5]

Foote's decision to compose a cycle of nine plays in 1974 marks the turning point in his career as a playwright. From then on—a period of more than twenty years—he was committed to playwriting and became a better, more important playwright. Although Foote had written for other genres, expending much creative energy on them, he was ready to return to playwriting. This emphasis, the result of choice and inclination, which had been a long time in coming, gives the work from then on a unity and direction that his writing had lacked before. Foote was happiest when writing for the theatre. In Hollywood he was "a writer for hire" who could not write what he wanted. From this time on, Foote became a playwright in the fullest sense, because his writing was designed strictly for the theatre.

Foote has often spoken of himself as a social and moral historian of his own small piece of Texas soil. He made the following statement about the *Cycle:* "I'm a social writer in the sense that I want to record, but not in the sense of trying to change people's minds."[6] In fact, this is a key statement about Foote's writing in general. Consistent with his avoidance of polemical drama in the preceding 1960s, Foote emphasizes that he is objective. He states repeatedly that he does not try to change the thinking of others.

Comparing Harrison, Texas, to Jefferson, Yoknapatawpha County, is appropriate, given that Foote had written three adaptations of Faulkner. In Samuel Freedman's influential essay on the *Cycle,* he compares Foote's writing about Texas while hunched over a stove in icy New England to Quentin Compson's remembering Mississippi in *Absalom, Absalom!*[7] As will become clear in analyzing the *Cycle,* parallels with Faulkner's saga throw light on Foote's sequence.

These plays of Foote's *Cycle,* like Faulkner's fictional works, trace the decline of the aristocracy and the subsequent rise of the commercial class. Although the plays take place in Texas, they unerringly follow the real fall of the Old South aristocracy and rise of the New South business class, epitomized respectively by *Gone With the Wind* in fiction and *The Little Foxes* in drama. Foote's ambivalence toward the aristocracy should be noted. In his interview with Freedman, Foote discussed the aristocracy through examples from his kindred. His grandfather Brooks, a well-to-do patriarch, took haughty offense when some men came to his property and cut down an ancient pecan tree. This reaction had particular meaning to his grandson. Foote remarked that part of him says he does not believe in aristocracies while another part does. From other comments, it becomes evident that Foote considered Papa Brooks a member of the local aristocracy, although he would not have used that appellation to his face.

In the first two plays of the *Cycle,* Foote records the decline of the landed aristocracy. Like Faulkner, Foote shows that he is very conscious of its status in the past. Besides the Brooks line of his mother, Foote could also distinguish the Horton ancestry; the Hortons owned vast plantations but were cheated out of their patrimony by dishonest relatives. To be sure, this aristocracy lacks the Virginia names and achievement. In decline it even resembles the comic ways of poor whites, captured by Erskine Caldwell and Tennessee Williams. Nevertheless, a genuine aristocracy existed in the collective memory of the Hortons, which Foote inherited just as surely as their physical traits.

The first play of the *Orphans' Home Cycle, Roots in a Parched Ground,* was preceded by an earlier version entitled *The Night of the Storm.* This television play was broadcast by CBS from New York on the *DuPont Show of the Month,* on March 21, 1961. Recounting the time when Horace, the hero, was only a young boy, the screenplay contains no act or scene divisions. It presents essentially the same plot as the later play, which was composed between 1974 and 1977, after the death of Foote's father, the model for Horace. Set in the 1890s, it presents the separation of the boy's mother and father, the antagonism of their two families, and Horace's running away from home during the night of a terrible storm, when his father, Paul Horace Robedaux, dies at the young age of thirty-two. Both families lay claim to an aristocratic past. The mother's kin, the Douglases, look back to the first lieutenant governor of Texas while the father's kin tell stories of a splendid fleet of merchant ships sailing around the world from Galveston.

Stark Young was enchanted by the little boy in *The Night of the Storm,* who was "the gentlest and sweetest child I have ever encountered in a story."[8] The review of the television production in *Variety* (March 29, 1961) was unfavorable. The critic called it a "retrogression" for Foote after *The Trip to Bountiful* and said it was "overstated, weakly constructed." The name performers, who included Julie Harris, E. G. Marshall, and Mildred Dunnock, were "categorically wasted." The reviewer is correct in his dislike of this first play of the *Cycle,* because Foote's plan had not yet taken shape in his mind.

Foote set aside *The Night of the Storm* for a dozen years before he returned to the story, transforming it into *Roots in a Parched Ground.* By that time, Foote's plans for the *Orphans' Home Cycle* had taken final form. The second version of this first play in the *Cycle* was much more successful. Before finishing it, Foote had composed *1918,* to be the seventh in the series. By this time Foote had decided on the setting, the names of the characters, and the times of the various plays. In *Roots in a Parched Ground* the place is Harrison, Texas, and the time 1902–1903. Horace's maternal line, based on the real Hortons, bears the name of Thornton, not Douglas. Julia, the mother of Horace, becomes Corella, who introduces her new husband, Pete Davenport, at the end of the play. He was called Mr. Stewart previously. Her sister, who was named Callie before, is now called Virgie but still disdains "common" people. She is based on Foote's aunt Loula Horton, who was loyal to all with a drop of Horton blood in their veins, as she said many times ("Seeing," p. 10).[9] In the second version, Foote presents the friends of Horace's father as much less solicitous of Horace's welfare than they were in the first. Jim Howard looks after Horace attentively and helps him with arithmetic at the end of the first version. John Howard in *Roots in a Parched Ground* cannot spare any time for the orphan, though he had promised Horace's dying father to care for him. Before exiting in the last scene, John Howard speaks these curt words to Horace, whom he promised to train as a lawyer: "Here's a dime for you. Buy yourself something."[10]

The most interesting theme in *Roots in a Parched Ground* is the decline of the antebellum aristocracy. Here it is in Southeast Texas and in a variation that is novel. We recognize the decadent class of Alabama in *The Little Foxes,* but this time the setting is Texas. The gentry is the Thornton family, whose most illustrious ancestor was the first lieutenant governor of the state. These rural aristocrats were cheated out of their inheritance; they have moved to town, where their finances are much reduced. Virgie Thornton bemoans the hard times suffered "after the war" (p. 53). Corella is separated from her husband, a Robedaux, and now shockingly, according to Virgie, makes men's shirts in Houston to support herself. After her alcoholic husband dies mercifully, she marries a man employed by the railroad, who is only a simple working man, Virgie says.

The Robedaux clan (based on the Footes) does not have an agricultural origin but rather owns a shipping fleet in Galveston. Mrs. Robedaux, the proudest aristocrat in the play, tells how the Robedaux were all lawyers, doctors, and scholars. They were forced to live with people who only liked "the common" (p. 12). Now this family is destitute. The elder son, Paul Horace, reportedly a brilliant lawyer in Harrison, drank himself to death. His brother, Terrence, sold his newspaper and spends his time reading Greek and Latin.

Foote differentiates between the two families through the use of music in this play as well as in subsequent ones. He states: "In the Thornton house music in some form is almost constantly being played or sung, while in the Robedaux house there is the silence of death" ("Lecture," p. 28). This distinction between the carefree, musical Thorntons and the serious Robedaux is discussed in an article on *Roots in a Parched Ground*.[11] These conflicting ways are resolved by Horace, since he sings but also respects his father. Lily Dale, Horace's sister, who is totally attached to the Thorntons, does not reconcile her two legacies. Nor is she an integrated personality, but becomes neurotic.

On the comic side, we see the ridiculous gentry, as in Chekhov's plays. One can say only that they are a special, Texas breed of the fallen aristocracy. Mr. Ritter (meaning "knight" in German) has no means of support, can only wait on a check, and disappears into the river swamps at the end. The Brodler Brothers live on a huge, isolated plantation, which twelve-year-old Horace, the present-day descendant of the aforementioned Thorntons and Robedaux, visits after running away from home. He eluded the Brodler Brothers unscathed, recalling Huck's escape from Pap Finn, but another was not so lucky. As Jim Howard relates, Mr. Comstock stepped into the Brodler domain once and was forced to eat a huge platter of fried chicken. Clarence Brodler pointed a gun at him and said, "Now, you sonofabitch, I want you to eat every piece of that chicken or I'll blow your brains out" (p. 30). Seizing an opportune moment, this visitor jumped out a window and never stopped running until he reached his home in Harrison. The descriptions of the decadent aristocracy, landed and maritime, mark this work as a picture of the formerly well-to-do class before the war.

Horace Robedaux nevertheless survives the hardness of his young life as the offspring of these families. He is abandoned by his mother, snubbed by his selfish sister, Lily Dale, and rejected by his stepfather. In the manner of Huck Finn, he skips school, collects empty whiskey bottles to sell, and chews tobacco. Horace admires his dying father; he forgives him and will honor him later by erecting a tombstone in his memory, as Al Foote did for his father. Furthermore, Horace is determined to become a merchant. Predicting the emergence of a new class of humanitarian businessmen, standard-bearers of the New South, Horace will start a more promising life despite his degenerate family lines.

This play deals mainly with a social theme, the fall of the once ruling class, but it also has several moral themes. The two families not only have undergone financial and social ruin but also suffer from moral decay. The Thorntons and Robedaux squabble constantly; there is much hatred between them, embodied finally in the separation of Paul Horace and Corella Robedaux. Grandmother Robedaux considers the Thorntons frivolous, with their love of dancing. The Thorntons, on the other hand, condemn the other family for their overeducation. Lily Dale, a true Thornton, wants to hear nothing about her father, a Robedaux. He was a cigarette fiend and drank himself to death. Corella cannot bear to be around her in-laws. Minnie Robedaux Curtis hates the Thorntons, blaming them for her uncle's death. And so it goes. Jealousy and vituperation are destroying the two families. This internecine fighting, producing disunion, has as much to do with their downfall as drinking and laziness do. It is in this parched ground that Horace must plant his roots.

For *Convicts,* the second play of the *Orphans' Home Cycle,* Foote drew on stories told by his father about convicts.[12] At the beginning of *Convicts,* the setting is named Floyd's Lane, Texas, and the time 1904 (p. 93). In *Wharton County Pictorial History, 1846–1946* is a photograph of "Floyd's Lane," showing a stark railroad crossing. In 1907 this rural community contained only one store, a blacksmith shop, and fewer than a dozen families.[13]

Convicts gives a full, shocking picture of this moribund society, not in town but in the more familiar plantation setting. Horace, now thirteen, goes to work in a plantation store, thus starting his apprenticeship in the mercantile business. Slaves have been replaced by convicts, who are hired out by the state to the owner of an enormous plantation, owned by one Soll (implying "solitary") Gautier (pronounced "Gaw-teer"). Horace's experience in this hell forms the second installment in Foote's saga of the South.

The central figure of the play is Soll Gautier, the caricature of a southern planter, but one who had a basis in reality. Foote commented that he never knew the model for him personally, but he heard his father tell stories about this man all his life.[14] Soll represents the worst kind of landowner; he is immoral, is against education, works his hired convicts unmercifully, and has, according to his own report, killed four of them.

Soll repeats in extreme form the traits of the so-called aristocracy seen in the Thornton and Robedaux families of the preceding work. In Soll's case, however, the conflict is not between families but rather within his own family. Soll and his brother, Tyre, do not speak to each other. According to the former, Tyre had their brother Melvin poisoned. Tyre has two daughters whom Soll calls "whores" (p. 136). Asa, who will inherit the huge plantations of her father and of childless Uncle Soll (though he claims she never will), remains drunk throughout the play.

Soll is glad to have Horace working in his store, since Soll rarely converses with a white person. There are obstacles to his companionship with the boy, however. Soll has promised to pay the boy the $11.50 owed for working in the store, but he never does. Horace, who obtained the job for room, board, and 50 cents a week, keeps bringing up the amount owed him, and Soll just as often assures him that he will receive it. The boy also learns that the old man despised his father, Paul Horace Robedaux, though Ben Johnson, a black employee at the store, says Paul was a good lawyer. Paul was Tyre's lawyer but helped cheat Soll. This information, furnished by Soll, threatens his acquaintance with Horace, but later Soll promises to leave him "a thousand dollars" (p. 161).

The most bizarre motif of the play concerns Soll's fear of being killed by a convict. According to his made-up story, a prisoner named Tucker tried to run away but fell into a bear trap, which crippled him. According to this fictitious story, this convict, seeking revenge against Soll for setting the trap, hid in a closet of Soll's house. Convinced that the convict is hiding in the closet, Soll shouts, "Come out of there. You hear me, you sonofabitch." When no one answers, he threatens, "I'll give you one more chance to come out of there" and then shoots many times (p. 144). The casual cursing on this plantation is authentic. Soll's life, the consequence of his violence and hatred, has made him the victim of his fears, a fitting punishment.

Completing the image of the hateful aristocrat is Soll's final identification as a Confederate soldier. He becomes a foreboding avatar of the Old South regime. When he was in the Confederate Army, Soll says, he fought in every battle they would let him. As he nears death, with the convict-made wooden coffin beside him, he tells Horace to read from a preserved newspaper, dated 1865. This issue reports that Texas cannot reenter the union. Similarly Soll, who carries on the worst ways of the unreconstructed South, has never adopted a different outlook; he still treats his laborers as if they were his property. At the end, Soll dies while asking Horace to read the old newspaper to him. Symbolically, Soll retains a viselikelike grip on Horace's arm until Soll's hand is removed by Ben Johnson, who has taken Horace under his wing. This boy has heard the dying gasp of the Old South—Texas style.

Horace has another story to tell about the Brodler Brothers, whom he visited on their isolated plantation in *The Night of the Storm*. Talking to a convict named Leroy Kendricks, Horace remembers visiting these old bachelors when he ran away from home during the big storm. Afterward Clarence and Murray Brodler got into a fight in Dowdy's Saloon. Jessie Shather killed Murray and wounded Clarence, who fled to Tennessee, where he had originated, but Clarence returned to Harrison, where he entered the same saloon and shot Jessie with a pistol. Next, Clarence was killed in a fight with William Jenkins. "The Brodler brothers were terrors," Horace pronounces (p. 100).

Participating also in the violence of the older time are the black members of this society. The convict Leroy, from La Place, Louisiana, where *Convicts* was later filmed for television, was given a sentence because he "cut" a man in Texas, and he was sent to a prison plantation on the coast (p. 101). Transferred here, he has killed a man who was "bothering" him (p. 103). The sheriff, who comes to arrest Leroy, reports that the convict tried to "overpower" him (p. 111), forcing the sheriff to kill him.

Horace also has a learning experience with Martha and Ben Johnson, who are not convicts. They work in the plantation store with him, and when it gets cold, they sleep by him next to the stove. Because the question has been preying on his mind, Horace asks Martha who his mother will be married to in heaven, since she has remarried after his father died. Martha advises, "Read the Bible . . . everything's in the Bible" (p. 118). "I hope so," Horace responds. Ben speaks wisely after Soll has died, while Horace listens. In the last lines, Ben says that soon the cane will cover everything, the cemeteries of the whites, the blacks, and the convicts: "Cane land they called it once, cane land it will be again. The house will go, the store will go, the graves will go, those with tombstones and those without" (p. 163). From Ben's viewpoint, death is the great equalizer.

Of all Foote's plays, *Convicts* has the greatest affinity with Faulkner's Yoknapatawpha saga. Foote must have discovered aspects of the plantation society that reminded him of his father's experiences in the *Cycle*. Not only does *Convicts* have Faulknerian resonance because it takes place on a plantation near the turn of the century like *The Bear*, but it also includes memories of the Civil War and dark Reconstruction times. In this play, familiar characters reappear, requiring us to draw on previous information. Uncle Albert Thornton, who entered as Horace's kinsman in *Roots in a Parched Ground*, promising him a job in a plantation store, is mentioned several times by Horace in that play. He did get Horace employment in *Convicts* when the crops were coming in and business was brisk at the store. However, he left his nephew to fend for himself when he returned to gambling in the county seat, the equivalent of Jefferson in Faulkner's mythical geography. Albert is reminiscent of Ike's gambling relatives in *The Bear*. In *Convicts,* Horace also mentions "Mr. Ritter," who had a small speaking part in *Roots*. This doddering, courtly old fellow had wandered into the river swamps and was not heard from again. In *Convicts*, Horace notes that, according to some, Mr. Ritter did not drown in the Colorado River but is still alive. He may return to life like Nancy Mannigo, the heroine of "That Evening Sun," who was thought killed by her revengeful husband but turned up again as Temple Drake's servant in *Requiem for a Nun*.

The most interesting parallel between *Convicts* and Faulkner's saga is its closeness to the maturation of Ike McCaslin in *The Bear*. Foote shows extensive contact between blacks and whites in this play, which records a unique black world. Horace listens to the fatherly Ben Johnson, as Ike heeds Sam Fathers. Ben (who bears the same name as "old Ben," the ursine mentor of the hunter Ike) speaks the last words of the play when he wisely pronounces the end of the moribund plantation system, saying all the fields will go. As the hunting grounds disappear with the coming of the modern age in *The Bear*, the plantation economy will be superseded by the commercial. Horace, like Ike, will see this change and survive into a later time. But one element of Faulkner's work is lacking in Foote's play. There is no comparable commentary on the historical change that we follow in the dialogue of Ike with his cousin Cass Edmonds in the commissary. Ike has been taught to admire freedom by Sam Fathers and announces to his cousin that "Sam Fathers set me free" before he flees the curse of slavery by relinquishing the tainted plantation.[15] In *Convicts*, Ben Johnson, a similar mentor of Horace, proves by his concern for Horace that blacks and whites can converse and form friendships based on respect and human feeling. But in the play, the searching discussion provided by the novelist is absent. Foote's insight into the distinct plantation culture of Texas must be largely inferred by the reader.

Convicts, filmed in 1989 and released in 1991, is now available in some video stores. The films was directed by Peter Masterson, who directed *Bountiful* in 1983, and starred Robert Duvall as Soll Gautier. Foote stated in a feature for the *New York Times* that he created this part with Duvall in mind. He and the well-known actor tried for twelve years to bring the film to life. Duvall remarks that this play lacks "the sweetness" of Foote's other plays, since this one has brutality in it. Duvall adds that, in this play, Horace comes to realize that a convict is a human being like himself.

In this newspaper article, Foote commented on the challenge to production presented by the *Cycle.* He did not know then how this long series could be produced. "I thought of the theatre at first, but that's impossible." Regarding film production, however, he wished the plays to be done out of sequence because he did not want "a mini-series or something like that." He wanted each "to stand on its own." [16] Productions of the *Cycle* would indeed prove a challenge and a call for all the resourcefulness Foote could muster. Ultimately, he would have to undertake independent film production.

Convicts was released as a film by the Sterling Van Wagener Entertainment Company. It received a mostly unfavorable review in *Variety* (December 2, 1991). The critic wrote that Robert Duvall added another memorable character to his reputation, but this was "a static uncinematic play." Others noted in the cast were James Earl Jones, who gave "a quite understated" portrayal of Ben Johnson, and Carlin Glynn as the dissolute Asa Vaughn. The reviewer predicted that the picture of this "decadent society" would not please southerners but was vividly realized "in microcosm." The reviewer also noted "a powerfully modern, almost militant turn" given by Calvin Levels, who plays Leroy, the convict in chains.

The third play of the *Cycle, Lily Dale,* takes place in Houston.[17] There are only a few references to the fallen aristocracy. Corella, Horace's mother, who has now remarried, mentions "Papa's plantation" (p. 190), which they were cheated out of. Horace briefly recalls that Grandmother Robedaux was so wealthy before the war that she never even had to tie her own shoes. Afterward, she had to learn to work when she opened a boardinghouse in Harrison. We begin to get a glimpse of the new commercial age. Will Kidder, Lily Dale's suitor, is a gregarious man, as his name implies. He is going to work for a coffee company, which will sell "the cup of Southern hospitality" (p. 221). Kidder seems destined to join the rising business class in Houston.

This play focuses more on personal development than on social commentary. Like *The Trip to Bountiful,* it analyzes the personality of the central character, who in this play is again Horace Robedaux, the "orphan" and hero of the *Cycle.* The year is 1910, seven years after *Convicts.* Horace is now twenty, well past adolescence, and a young man setting out on his adult life. But he has not passed through his youthful crisis of becoming independent after his father's death. He must become his own man and compensate for the actual loss of his father and the symbolic loss of his mother, who has remarried and must bow to her new husband's rejection of her son.

Horace began searching for a father in *Roots* without success. In this play he becomes estranged from his stepfather, the cold workaholic Pete Davenport. When Horace arrives in Houston, he soon encounters the harsh treatment of Mr. Davenport, who insults Horace to his face, saying that he would never ask anyone for a job—he has too much pride to do that. Davenport speaks curtly to Horace and is happy to see him leave soon after his unexpected return from Atlanta. When Lily Dale keeps talking about her stepfather, whom she idolizes, Horace pulls a quilt over his head as he lies on a sickbed. He has come down with a high fever, which is certainly psychosomatic, caused by his hatred of Pete and his exclusion from his mother's house, where he had hoped to find support. The best and most dramatic scene of the play comes when Horace wakes from a bad dream about his stepfather and stares the man in the face. Horace blurts out his true feelings three times: "I despise him" (p. 218). In this play, one sees Horace truly as an "orphan," since he is ostracized by his stepfather and his mother, who, though she loves him, cannot give him a home.

The cycle is called the *Orphans' Home Cycle,* owing to the epigraph from Marianne Moore's "In Distrust of Merits": "The world's an orphans' home."[18] The title, with a double meaning, implies also one orphan, Horace. He is having to face the designation most painfully in this play, and though he is overcoming the stigma of "orphan," wherever he lives he will continue to bear that name.

The play has a positive theme of rebirth. In this phase of Horace's life, he becomes sick and endures fever but is revived by his own determination. When he resolves to leave, he gets stronger. In the television play, Corella visibly helps him take the first steps after he has been lying in bed helpless for two weeks. Horace completes the cycle of his trip by his return to Harrison. During Horace's visit in *Lily Dale,* Foote "used all the past anger and rage I sensed from my father" whenever the name of his stepfather was spoken. Al Foote had identical feelings. Horace always addresses his stepfather as "Mr." ("Lecture," p. 31), but he will gradually overcome his resentment toward his inhospitable hosts and forgive them, thus saving himself from the anguish of revenge.

Lily Dale's portrayal is the second outstanding feature of this eponymous play. The conflict between sister and brother compounds that between son and stepfather. Horace and Lily Dale have differences that can poison such a relationship. Lily Dale, two years younger than her brother, is as much adored by her stepfather as Horace is hated. Pete always wanted a daughter. A typically Victorian male, he cannot bear to hear a woman cry and grants Lily Dale's every request. Pete is the only one who will listen to Lily Dale's piano playing, which she imposes on anyone present. She cannot tolerate Horace's distaste for Pete and complains bitterly when Horace reveals how much he dislikes his stepfather. In *Lily Dale* the familial conflict between Thorntons and Robedaux continues. Lily Dale is close to her mother, a Thornton, and hates to hear of her father, a Robedaux. She cannot abide Minnie Robedaux Curtis, who she thinks is spiteful, like all the rest. Horace does not join this ancestral fight. He tells his sister honestly that he does not resent his stepfather's favoritism toward her. Horace admires his father, a Robedaux, and will live with his aunt Loula, a Thornton, and her husband when he returns to Harrison. He will not perpetuate the hatred between the two families.

Adding to the extreme tension in this household is the jarring intrusion of Lily Dale's piano playing. In the television play, Corella remarks, "Lily Dale, can't we have quiet for once!" Counterpointing the incessant piano playing are the soothing songs rendered by Horace, like "Mother Macree" and "Go Tell Aunt Rhodie," Corella's nursery song to quiet him when he lies ill.

Resolution of the conflict between brother and sister brings relief in the end. Lily Dale declares that she loved her papa and regrets the mean things she has said. Finally she asks "forgiveness" for the cruel words (p. 233).

Lily Dale is a self-centered girl. She is a neurotic, in the tradition of Tennessee Williams's abnormal women like Alma of *Summer and Smoke.* Lily Dale reflects the Victorian influence of the time, especially with regard to sex and marriage. She brings up the subject of sexual passion with her mother after she thinks of marrying her robust suitor, Will Kidder, because of fear that her husband will hurt her. Mortally afraid of dying in childbirth, she extracts a promise from Will that they will not have children. Foote used the name of a deceased aunt, Lily Dale, because "I wanted to use in the play the song 'Lily Dale' a sentimental favorite from the Civil War" ("Lecture," pp. 32–33). The lyrics, which we hear twice, describe the death of a young girl of this name, and Lily Dale herself is afraid of death. The song epitomizes her dislike of the sorrowful past; she only wants to think of the future.

Part of the Victorian outlook is also that no one must argue (see also *The Old Beginning*); all must appear happy living with each other, whether they are or not. Victorian women in Texas do not look at past or present conditions realistically. Not willing to discuss embarrassing subjects, like having babies, they are tormented by their fears. Horace provides an antidote. In the style of Ibsen, he admits his feelings about his stepfather honestly and moves toward mastery of them.

In the television version of this play especially, a universal drama finds expression: the division within a family that can bring unhappiness to its members. The stepfather, in the classic pattern, rejects and torments the stepson. This state of affairs creates an unbearable tension when Horace arrives in Houston, hoping to learn management of a clothing store. The strained atmosphere in the Houston household is palpable in the television play and is one of its best achievements.

As Foote foresaw, theatrical production of the *Orphans' Home Cycle* would be a difficult undertaking. *Lily Dale,* a well-constructed work, fared better than the two preceding parts. It was published in *Best Plays of 1986–87* after playing at the small Samuel Beckett Theatre off Broadway (ninety seats) from November 20, 1986, to February 15, 1987. The cast included the popular new actress Molly Ringwald as Lily Dale, whose appearance was featured in the headlines, and Julie Heberlein as Corella. On February 8, 1987, Lucy Kroll praised the subsequent change from Ringwald to Mary Stuart Masterson as Lily Dale during the stage run, stating that Horace's journey to find his family now came across "with greater emotional impact" (HFC).

Of nine reviews in the New York press, seven were favorable; they noted the literary qualities of the work. Clive Barnes in the *New York Post* (November 21, 1986) recognized Foote as a sensitive writer and able craftsman and noted that, like many southern writers, his writing was "redolent" of that heritage. Barnes wrote that Horace, through his experience, had seen "the final dream of a vanished past." What was distinctive about the play, according to Barnes, was "the manner in which its atmosphere, texture, and construction are merged into one dramatic artifact—an artifact almost pictorial in its effect." Barnes concluded: "The play is one to remember." A scene from *Lily Dale* was included in *Great Scenes for Young Actors* (1991).

Allan Wallach in *New York Newsday* (November 21, 1986) wrote that it would be a treat to see all nine installments of the *Cycle* on successive nights, but *Lily Dale* had "a generous sampling of the penetrating insights into character and the sepia-toned nostalgia we've come to associate with Foote." Wallach noted that the play showed a family album but "keeps revealing people of unexpected complexity." This review, like the others, lacked the previous condescension found in the evaluations of Foote's plays in the 1940s and 1950s. These expressed an appreciation of Foote's merits, showing a growing esteem for him as a playwright.

Lily Dale is one of the *Cycle* plays that has been filmed. It appeared as a television play on Showtime on June 9, 1996, sponsored by Hallmark Entertainment. Hallie Foote was the coproducer with her father. The cast featured Mary Stuart Masterson again as Lily Dale, and well-known playwright Sam Shepard as Pete Davenport. Stockard Channing played a young-looking Corella. Jean Stapleton, of *All in the Family* fame, gave an accomplished interpretation of Mrs. Coons, the Baptist woman who converses with Horace on the train. This television version is faithful to the original and enhances some themes, especially the family conflict, by means of the visual medium. The cold, withdrawn stepfather is shown retreating to his garden. The setting of a fine house in Houston, however, is inconsistent with the working clothes of Pete, a railroad employee.

The television production of *Lily Dale* was reviewed in *Variety* (June 3–9, 1996) by Tony Scott, whose appraisal is generally reliable. Although one evaluation cannot justify calling the play a hit, it argues strongly for a worthy achievement. This critic wrote that although "not a great play, it's absorbing, uninterrupted theatre." Scott stated that Foote's dialogue occasionally stalled the action but offered "an engrossing video play." Calling the production "serious engaging television," Scott noted that the film reflected "Foote's sensitive observations on human frailties as well as strengths" and never faltered in "the sad view of how people can hurt and be hurt." This reviewer believed that there was plenty of room on television for such plays. Whether other pieces from the *Cycle* would reach television was problematic, according to Scott, but he predicted that this one would have a long run. The play's extended life in the medium should always be counted when judging Foote's achievement as a playwright.

The fourth play of the *Cycle* is *The Widow Claire*, which was written last even though chronologically it falls in the middle of the series.[19] It takes place in 1912 after Horace's return to Harrison. One may assume that the author perceived a gap between *Lily Dale* and *Courtship*, when Horace finds his future wife. In *The Widow Claire* we see Horace going courting for the first time; thus it forms a bridge between his youthful activities and the prelude to marriage in *Courtship*. This play was produced in the same month as *Lily Dale*. *The Widow Claire* opened on December 17, 1986, at the Circle in the Square Theatre and closed on April 26, 1987. It featured the talented actor Matthew Broderick as Horace and Hallie Foote as Claire. Both actors have come to be associated with Foote's plays by their definitive interpretations.

This play depicts a distinct era in the social history of Foote's community. It takes place during the age of saloons, reckless social life, and active social organizations. According to the *Wharton County Pictorial History,* saloons were numerous in the early 1900s. Church women opposed liquor and prostitution, but burning saloons did not stop the sale of liquor. Many social clubs gave dances and parties where liquor was available. Al Foote, father of the playwright, belonged to the "South Texas Raggers." [20] Popular songs heard in *The Widow Claire,* such as "Waltz Me Around Again, Willie," contribute to the period atmosphere.

Among the many carousers who form a backdrop to Horace's personal development, we see a colorful array at his boardinghouse. Spence is a gambler; Ed goes with prostitutes and calls aloud for "Roberta" in his dream; Archie has no ambition except to marry a rich wife. These young men avoid regular work. Though Horace has joined their life for a while by gambling and drinking, he now declines to play poker and drink. Further, he aims to become the manager of a dry goods store, for which he will prepare himself by attending business school in Houston. He will not stay with his mother and stepfather but will obtain lodging with his aunt Minnie Robedaux Curtis. According to Foote, Horace's friends had little ambition "and in some ways were victims of a very difficult time of social adjustment for young white males" ("Lecture," p. 34).

If the young men who come and go throughout this work show no respect for women, Horace does admirably. He is a gentleman in his conduct toward the attractive Widow Claire, who daringly smokes and dates several men at once. Horace likes her and takes a fatherly interest in her young son and daughter. Claire often shows her trust in him by asking if she is making the right decision, even about marriage. Horace defies a violent suitor, who beats Claire. After this belligerent visitor knocks Horace out, Claire turns away Val, an objectionable suitor. She eventually decides to marry Uncle Ned, a well-to-do salesman from Galveston, whom her children adore. Horace parts from Claire amicably as he catches the train for Houston.

The story in *The Widow Claire* is "wholly imagined," Foote states, but his father did go with a widow who had two children. In later years, Foote used to see her walking past his father's store and would exchange pleasantries with her. She had a tragic life: "It was her son that Lewis Higgins in 'Cousins' tells of killing," Foote says ("Lecture," p. 34).

This play fittingly ends the first part of the *Cycle,* since it records the coup de grace to the antebellum aristocracy. Uncle Albert Thornton loses the farm he inherited from his grandfather's estate in an evening of gambling. Horace, recalling how his grandfather Robedaux made a fortune shipping cotton for the Confederacy, is left with only recollections of the aristocracy. Horace will be a self-made man.

Frank Rich showed his literary knowledge in an appreciative review of *The Widow Claire* entitled "Texas Survivors" (*New York Times,* December 18, 1986). Calling the intermissionless play a ninety-five-minute "anecdote" in one act, Rich wrote that it had the "buried poignancy of a naturalistic American short story" from the era in which it is set. Among the observers of small-town life, Rich stated, Foote "lacks the exotic Gothic humors of Eudora Welty and Beth Henley, or the debunking anger of Sinclair Lewis or Edgar Lee Masters." Nor were his "plain characters" to be confused with "the more extravagant and tragic souls of Faulkner and Williams," wrote Rich. "Mr. Foote is a chronicler of the quotidian." Rich praised the performances of Matthew Broderick as Horace and Hallie Foote as the Widow Claire. This play earned inclusion in *The Best Plays of 1986–87* but did not reach television, as *Lily Dale* did.

Looking back at the first four plays of the *Cycle* confirms that Foote succeeds better when he writes original plays of his own place than when he adapts the works of others. Foote's original works, including the first four of the *Cycle,* set forth his richest meanings, which are anchored in his native setting. They illuminate the society and moral acts of characters whom he knows, who live and die in Southeast Texas. They come alive, thanks to their creator's original conceptions, not those of other artists.

As for the challenge of producing the plays of the *Cycle* raised by Foote himself, it must be concluded that for theatrical performance, each play must stand on its own. Each play must indeed make its own way, though producing a series on television offers another possibility, as seen in the next three plays of the *Cycle, The Story of a Marriage.*

CHAPTER

13

THE *ORPHANS' HOME CYCLE,*

PART 2

NOT only did Horton Foote face a challenge in presenting the *Orphans' Home Cycle,* but he was also returning to the theatre after detours in the movies and television for twenty years. How was he to accomplish this ambitious task when he had been absent from the legitimate theatre for so long? He was very fortunate in meeting a remarkable devotee of the theatre, Herbert Berghof, who believed in Foote as a playwright.

This founder of the Herbert Berghof (HB) Studio supplied the direction and faith that Foote sorely needed at this time in his career. Foote often talked with Berghof during their long friendship, usually by phone.[1] Berghof and Foote shared the same worthy goal: the advancement of superior theatre in America. Both their thematic and acting standards were high and they would settle for nothing less than the best in the realm of theatre. The tradition of Ibsen, Shaw, Beckett, O'Neill, and Williams, the leaders of modern drama, were their guiding lights.

Berghof and Foote expressed high regard for each other. As early as 1962, when Berghof asked to read an early draft of *The Habitation of Dragons,* he wanted to be associated "with you as you are a major artist."[2] This desire flourished eventually, since Berghof produced at his studio several works of the *Cycle,* including *Courtship* (1978), *1918* (1979), and *Valentine's Day* (1980). The first, performed July 5–16, 1978, was directed by the playwright, as were the other two. Foote was equally pleased with this ongoing partnership. He wrote to a correspondent on December 22, 1977, that some of his "early and later plays" would be done at the HB Studio. "It is a wonderful place to work," he declared (HFC). Most importantly, Berghof restored Foote's faith in theatre, a faith that had flickered during Foote's long years of writing commercial screenplays. In a tribute delivered after Berghof's death in 1990, Foote remarked: "He gave me a theater home and rekindled my faith in theater." Foote closed the address with a personal recollection that expressed how much this symbiotic relationship had meant. Herbert Berghof was a loyal, sympathetic friend. "I loved and admired Herbert," Foote said, and was "indebted to him for many things" (HFC).

Herbert Berghof (1909–1990) was a longtime director and teacher of acting in New York. He came first to Broadway in 1940 and staged the first American production of *Waiting for Godot* in 1956, a play that Foote always esteemed. After studying with Lee Strasberg, Berghof taught acting at the Neighborhood Playhouse and in 1945 founded the Herbert Berghof Studio, which he directed with his wife, Uta Hagen, a well-known actress and another friend of Foote's. Beginning in 1947, Hagen taught at the HB Studio. In 1946, Berghof established the Herbert Berghof Playwrights Foundation to promote the efforts of deserving artists. Its first season began in 1964. Famous actors who performed at the HB Studio included Robert Duvall, Sandy Dennis, Celeste Holm, E. G. Marshall, and Uta Hagen. Foote and Berghof worked most closely together from the late 1970s to the mid-1980s. Many of Foote's new works were given tryouts and premieres during these years. It is hard to imagine how Foote would have made his comeback in the theatre without Berghof's encouragement and production of the many plays that Foote composed during this time. Berghof furnished Foote with the indispensable resources of his studio at a time when staging serious plays on the New York commercial stage had virtually vanished.

Foote himself deserves much credit for the superior plays he composed for the *Cycle* when serious dramatic writing in the United States had reached a low ebb. It was a period of the doldrums, when mediocre plays took the place of genuine artistic works.[3] By his loyalty to the distinguished tradition that had been previously built, Foote contributed to the strengthening of off-Broadway, holding better promise for the American theatre, which had to compete with mindless movies, the wasteland of TV, and Broadway sensations that out-of-town millionaires financed from their overloaded accounts.

Berghof began staging Foote's plays modestly. According to the Lucy Kroll Agency (February 10, 1988), after *Tomorrow* was produced on *Playhouse 90,* Berghof staged it as a play in 1968 with Robert Duvall and Olga Bellin. Though it had only a limited run, it was "a great success," Kroll said (HFC). In 1976, Berghof mounted *A Young Lady of Property* at his studio theatre.

Starting in 1977, with the close cooperation of Berghof, Foote saw a steady stream of his new work produced in the small but sufficient HB Studio on Banks Street. In 1977, *Night Seasons* was given its first performance in the fall. *The Midnight Caller* and *The Dancers* were also performed. Foote sent Berghof a copy of his one-act *Flight* (televised in 1957), which presents the elopement theme of *Courtship*. It was performed on October 11, 1977. On November 21, 1977, Foote wrote to Berghof that he was moved by a play he directed, "and the whole evening was a real antidote to all the sterile theater literature we are surrounded by." In this letter, Foote informed his friend that he had taken an apartment from January through March 1977 in New York "so I can come and go there with more ease" (HFC). This news was significant, because it indicated Foote's return to the center of theatrical life after being literally and figuratively estranged in New Hampshire.

In 1977 the HB Studio had performed *Convicts,* its first selection from the *Cycle*. On August 23, 1977, Foote sent Berghof a new ending for this play. Foote had also enclosed the new ending to Robert Duvall, who would act in the performance, and was delighted that he liked it. Foote called Berghof to report Duvall's reaction and to tell him that Duvall wanted to perform it in the studio. Foote thought that Berghof's nomination of Pat Quinn for Asa was "a wonderful suggestion," because he regarded her talent highly (HFC). In the 1979–1980 season, Sandy Dennis delivered Foote's dramatic monologue *In a Coffin in Egypt,* which was directed by the author and Berghof.

After the three central plays were performed at the HB Studio, another play from the *Cycle* was presented for the first time. A staged reading of *The Widow Claire* was given in 1982, four years before its theatrical opening in New York. A series of one-acts was started also, which preceded many others that were performed off-Broadway in the 1980s. *The Dearest of Friends* and *The Road to the Graveyard* were offered in 1985 at the HB Studio. According to a 1985 playbill, "HB Playwrights Foundation invites you to Harrison, Texas." The following one-acts would be performed without charge for admission July 9–21, 1985, under the direction of Herbert Berghof: *The One-Armed Man, The Prisoner's Song,* and *Blind Date*. In all, Berghof directed four plays and produced many others by Foote at his theatre. The *Cycle* advanced to the stage and television primarily because of the support of Herbert Berghof. A successful return to the theatre is rare, but here we see how Foote did it. The difficulty of such a feat can be observed in the career of Tennessee Williams.

The plays that begin Part 2 form a clear trilogy and fall squarely at the center of the sequence: *Courtship, Valentine's Day,* and *1918.*[4] For this segment of Horace Robedaux's life, Foote used the life of the Brooks family, who are called the Vaughns in the plays.

The Vaughn family of the *Cycle* is closely based on the Brookses, both in real personages and in personality types. They typify the respectable, upper-middle class, who lived according to the strict Victorian standards then prevalent in the South. The father, Tom Brooks (Mr. Vaughn in the play), attempted to rule his family with the stern authority of a patriarch.

In the first play, *Courtship,* the Victorian way of life appears in Southeast Texas, with all its abnormalities and flaws. Within this proper, traditional family, the elder daughter, Elizabeth, stands out as the courageous rebel against patriarchal authority. She is modeled after Foote's mother, admired by her son especially for her courage in marrying the husband she chose against her father's prohibition. Foote uses stories of unhappy marriages, like Aunt Lucy's, throughout *Courtship* "to help us understand what a complex and serious thing it was in that day for a young man to make a decision about marriage." Marriage was then "so final and women were so dependent on their husbands," Foote notes. "It was not easy to defy parents and marry someone they did not approve of" ("Lecture," pp. 37–38).

In place of the hero Horace, a woman now takes center stage in the *Cycle;* she confirms Foote's talent, like Tennessee Williams's, for imaginatively comprehending the female psyche. The scrutiny of a typical household in the South of 1915 gives *Courtship* historical value as an authentic transcription of southern Victorianism. Furnishing an insight into Texas society that is unique, it provides a solid and true corrective to the inaccurate generalization of crude Texas, which has distorted the national understanding of that state, with all its diversity.

The time is 1915, when the Victorian order was coming under attack. In the next decade it would break. The Vaughn household, led by an autocratic patriarch, exhibits all the traits of Victorian propriety. The father, mother, two daughters, and visiting aunts show the traits that mark them unmistakably, as they reveal the virtues that define American Victorians, both male and female. The Vaughns are self-controlled, orderly, hardworking, conscientious, and sober, postponing immediate gratification for long-term goals. Further, they are pious toward a usually friendly

God, believers in the truth of the Bible, oriented strongly toward the home and family, anxious for self-improvement, and patriotic.[5] In accord with the Victorian insistence on social order, Henry Vaughn does not tolerate drinking, gambling, or dancing in his family. He advocates hard work and churchgoing and deplores wild social life, which he perceives in Horace Robedaux. Henry Vaughn argues with his daughter. After Elizabeth says that Horace is an Episcopalian, Mr. Vaughn counters: "Not that any of his family attend much." (Pause) "I hear Horace Robedaux is very dissipated, Elizabeth." When Elizabeth disagrees that "he had whiskey on his breath tonight," her father reminds her, "I could smell it. I have a very keen nose" (pp. 27–28).

Here we have the solid Victorian family with all its force. The father monitors the courtship of his elder daughter, Elizabeth, for any infractions and countermands her requests to spend time with Horace. She keeps asking to go to the drugstore for ice cream. Elizabeth is a level-headed girl and respects her parents, but she rebels against the restrictions on her social life. Although rebellious, she is demure; Elizabeth does not think her boyfriend is "all that wild" (p. 5) and looks ahead to a long, happily married life. She is a rebel, but a moderate one who will eventually become a conscientious wife and mother, fully within the Victorian parameters.

The darkest side of Victorian culture appears in one young woman who becomes a casualty of its strictness. Sybil Thomas, Elizabeth's friend, has become pregnant before marriage. Corseted literally and figuratively, she was able to hide her pregnancy, but after a shotgun wedding ordered by her father, she goes into premature labor and dies in childbirth. The Victorian strictness she underwent drove her to sexual rebellion and now to death.

The plight of the emotional casualties in this play reminds us of young Victorian women in the plays of Tennessee Williams, like Alma of *Summer and Smoke,* daughter of an Episcopal rector in Mississippi, from the turn of the century through 1916. Williams, however, is more aware of the Victorian framework in which his neurotic women live, and for that reason he analyzes them more incisively. Foote recognizes that the characters in *Courtship* are living at a time when the strict, old-fashioned ways and prohibition have become outdated and are the cause of much human anguish. He does not, however, dissect this culture as clearly Victorian, as is seen explicitly in Williams's sets as Victorian houses, which are as meaningful as Faulkner's Gothic house in "A Rose for Emily."

In this long one-act, we see the compelling portrait of the Rebellious Daughter in the Victorian House. The capitals are justified because the play adheres so closely to the typical father, who is fittingly addressed as "Papa," and the supposedly dutiful daughter, who in fact carries out a full-scale rebellion against the master of the family. The household, the house itself, and the standards promulgated express exactly the Victorian rules recognized by social historians and advice manuals of the time. The Victorian age in the United States, all scholars agree, ended with World War I, which announced the end of that social order. By World War I, the ideal of "character," had been superseded by the expression of "personality."[6] The drive for women's suffrage and better working conditions announced the end of the powerful social order that had brought comfort and pain to British and American families during the long reign of that most influential queen, Victoria. For the decade during which her son, Edward VII, continued his mother's tone in social life, this social order ruled the affective lives of father, mother, and children.

Henry Vaughn fits the image of the Victorian father perfectly. Foote has stated: "My maternal grandfather for some unexplained reason wanted none of his girls to get married" ("Lecture," p. 36). Though inexplicable finally, this trait provides some insight into Mr. Vaughn's stubbornness.

If Mr. Vaughn conforms to the image of the Victorian patriarch, his daughter resembles the conventional Victorian daughter until she begins to violate the pattern shockingly in the course of the play. That rebellion, of course, produces the drama and gives the work a tension, a meaning, and a climax that turn it into a forceful play. The young woman's courage to defy paternal authority and choose her own life is a theme that has enough relevance to absorb the interest of a contemporary audience.

To finish this picture of a Victorian family, it only remains to distinguish the younger daughter, Laura Vaughn, based on Laura Brooks. Foote is most original in noticing her contrasting personality, which is unlike Elizabeth's. Laura does not rebel against the Victorian model. Like other girls of her age and class, she has been to boarding school, but unlike Elizabeth, she is going farther off to a finishing school in Virginia. She also has developed her musical talent, but when she sings "Nellie Gray" for her aunts, she becomes so emotional over the sad words that she cannot continue. She lacks the emotional stamina of Elizabeth.

Like Elizabeth, Laura and her friend Annie have also slipped out with boys, which Laura confesses to her sister. But this acknowledgment gained by her mother from Laura does not lead to brave statements about what she will do in her life. When her mother forbids her spending the next night away, Laura meekly replies only "Yes, Ma'am" (p. 36). She is continually anxious about becoming an old maid. In the succeeding conversation with Elizabeth, Laura complains piteously about the oppression of their father. Why can't they go to dances and see boys and not have to slip around?

The prohibition against dancing makes the play distinctively southern because this rule was not prevalent in the North, nor in England. Laura, moreover, is fearful of getting pregnant and dying like Sybil Thomas. In short, she is being incapacitated by her fears. Further, Laura is afraid of God's punishment if she goes against her father's wishes. Her father and mother would never forgive her if she eloped, as Elizabeth boldly said that she herself would. Laura suppresses her rebellious instincts; she is troubled within and is on the way to becoming an emotional casualty of the Victorian order. Because she lacks Elizabeth's pluck, the outlook for this pathetic second daughter is poor.

Much of the artistic success of *Courtship* is owing to its one-act form, with no scene divisions. Of all the plays in the *Cycle,* this one corresponds most closely to the one-act television plays that Foote succeeded so well with in the Golden Age of Television. An admirer of the unities in drama, as in *Oedipus Rex,* Foote adheres closely to the unities of time, setting, and action in *Courtship.* This concentration gives the play a cohesion that is missing in other works of the *Cycle.* The plot encapsulates the climax of Horace's courtship. We see the crisis and anticipate its next phase: elopement.

Courtship treats a familiar crisis in one family: the debate between father and daughter over a husband. The subject is one that every audience can relate to; the situation is familiar in contemporary times also, but the historical period provides a fresh angle as to how the dilemma may be resolved. The characterizations are sharp, provocative, and engrossing. One thinks of the portrayal of the Victorian father, the courageous, determined daughter, and the contrasting, timorous younger daughter. These vitalized types make this one-act the best, most unified, and strongest artistic achievement of the whole *Cycle.* Its presentation in the television trilogy is a worthy addition to Foote's achievement for television.

This play, the centerpiece of the *Cycle,* seals Foote's standing as a Texas playwright. He emphasizes the moralism, including the opposition to dancing as well as patriarchal autocracy. In all of his plays, in fact, we must take into account turn-of-the-century society, which is Victorian in its origin, in Foote's social analysis of Texas. In the principals, we view a true Texas quartet. Both the negative qualities of Victorian Texas, and its positive qualities, place *Courtship* at the vital center of Foote's insight into Texas society.

The television performance, shown on *American Playhouse,* featured Michael Higgins as Mr. Vaughn, William Converse-Roberts as Horace, and Horton Foote, Jr., as his friend. It is faithful to the spirit of Foote's text, though the dialogue is rearranged and shortened considerably. It was filmed in Brookhaven, Mississippi. The tension between the father, who always speaks with an edge in his voice, and the daughter is palpable and well projected. The aunts are finely distinguished; Aunt Sarah comes across as a narrow-minded spinster who insists on bringing up embarrassing subjects, like a young man's being committed to the asylum; the gentle, tolerant Aunt Lucy attempts unsuccessfully to soften Sarah's cutting observations. The aunts serve as an amusing obbligato to continuous disagreements between unflappable daughter and irascible father. Foote succeeds well with the comedy of manners in Southeast Texas, 1915.

The performance record of *Courtship* has been limited. It was acted first by a professional company at the Louisville Actors Theatre of Louisville, March 29, 1984. The play was well enough received to go further. After being filmed by an independent company, *Courtship,* along with *Valentine's Day* and *1918,* was seen in the *American Playhouse* production. Presented May 13, 1987, in a ninety-minute show as the first part of *The Story of a Marriage,* it received a very favorable review from "Tone" in *Public TV Reviews* (May 13, 1987). The critic called it an admirable achievement that noncommercial television occasionally produces. He labeled it a preface to the two subsequent episodes. In *Courtship,* everything is against the daughters except Elizabeth's inner resources, he wrote. Elizabeth's strengths are natural, since the strong-willed father and mother—ironically, he might have added—have passed their steel along to her. The reviewer noted that Elizabeth, played splendidly by Hallie Foote, has to put up with "absurdly strict" parents, who oppose any man for her. The girls have "snuck out" at least once apiece, which unfolds as "shameful counterpoint" to the death of a girl they know, the reviewer reported. The critic added that the dance scenes provide a look at the outside world as the play moves shrewdly through Elizabeth's resignation to her final determination. *TV Guide* (1987) considered *The Story of a Marriage* excellent, much better than what one usually sees on television. John Leonard in *New York Magazine* (1987) praised the whole series.

In rereading the plays of the *Cycle,* Foote has been struck by stories told by characters that have been used in other plays. These echoes give his plays a Faulknerian interconnectedness. Foote notes that the story of Aunt Lucy's love (based on a true family anecdote) is related by Elizabeth to Laura in *Courtship.* Their grandmother would not let Lucy and Jim Murray get married because they were first cousins. Mrs. Watts tells a similar story of frustrated love as part of her personal history in *The Trip to Bountiful* ("Lecture," pp. 22–23). These are examples Foote cites of lasting regret that darken the memories of men and women.

Valentine's Day, number six of the *Cycle,* was filmed in 1986 and televised in 1987 as the second part of *The Story of a Marriage.* In that television program the play covered "After the Elopement," Part 2, and "Reconciliation," Part 3. The time is Christmas Eve, 1916 (erroneously given as 1917 in the published text) after Horace and Elizabeth have eloped and married on Valentine's Day of that year. They have moved into one large room of a Victorian house in Harrison that has seen better days. Scene 3 is correctly given as taking place in January 1917 (p. 84).

This play forms a neat pair with *Courtship* because it gives another intimate and illuminating picture of Victorian life in Southeast Texas. Although the order of moral strictness was under siege by this time, it still dominated polite society. The father was an authoritarian patriarch, and the mother was mistress of the home. Revered for her love and goodness, the mother was idealized as "The Angel in the House," according to the title of Coventry Patmore's famous poem. The two holidays that were most joyfully celebrated by the Victorians were Christmas, the festival of the home, and Valentine's Day, the celebration of love, which meant matrimonial bliss. *Valentine's Day* is a faithful rendition of Victorian home life, combining its ideal pleasures with its characteristic problems.

For Victorians the center of life was "the Home," along with "God" and "Work," the most honored words in their vocabulary. The home was the main locus for the transmission of ideals. Here children learned the virtues of duty to parents. In *Valentine's Day,* "home" has a novel meaning for Elizabeth and Horace because they first move into a single room, not a whole house. When Mr. Vaughn first visits the couple, he is shocked by their living quarters, which he cannot call "a home." When Mrs. Vaughn says they now have "a home," her husband replies, "But it's still a rented room. A home is something you own, that belongs to you" (p. 80).

The couple makes progress toward a home. However, when Mr. Vaughn gives them the money to build a house—directly behind his, it should be noted—Horace insists that the house be in his wife's name. Reluctantly Elizabeth accedes to his request, "but it will be your home," she says. "I hope you'll always be able to think of it as your home" (p. 88). Horace agrees graciously, "I'm sure I will. But I want everyone to understand who the gift was for." Before Mr. Vaughn leaves his daughter and son-in-law, with whom he has become reconciled, he says, "There's peace in this room and contentment. That's why I like to come here" (p. 103).

In the new dwelling, Elizabeth will undertake her mission of providing a loving home, a refuge from Horace's world of competitive business, where he must work for a hard-earned living. At the end of the play, she foresees planting "all kinds of roses"—the symbols of love—"Red roses, yellow roses, pink roses, sweetheart roses, and climbing roses" (p. 107). From being a rebel against the domestic order of Victorian life, Elizabeth is fast becoming a model mother as her husband is a model father, who provides for the family, having put aside his former habits of drinking and gambling. The Robedaux home will be a place of future happiness, unlike the nonexistent home of the orphan Horace.

Like those famous Victorians, Robert and Elizabeth Browning, Horace and Elizabeth have founded their home on lasting love. The love of husband and wife was extolled by Elizabeth Browning, wife of Robert. After Mr. Vaughn makes his first visit of reconciliation, Horace declares eloquently to Elizabeth that though her father is a powerful man of the town, he did not stop their marriage. "You did marry me," Horace says, "and I tell you I've begun to know happiness for the first time in my life. I adore you. I worship you . . . and I thank you for marrying me" (p. 83). Even in this rented room Horace's wife is manifestly "the angel in the house." Nor did Elizabeth marry for security, as her Aunt Sarah did unhappily in the preceding play. Even though her father was unalterably opposed, Elizabeth married Horace out of love and believes they will lead a happy life together.

How parental interference can spoil a marriage appears pointedly in the boardinghouse where Horace and Elizabeth have begun their married life. A drunken resident, Little Bobby Pate, loved his wife but lost her. He claims that she deserted him because of the town's rainy climate, but Bobby's disapproving mother reveals the real reason, her rejection of the wife. She explains that "being born common is like a curse, you can't do nothing about it." Bobby's wife left him because his mother considered her common. He now says, "Well, common or not . . . I loved her" (p. 59). Longing for her return, he feels guilty and drinks to forget her loss. In the most violent scenes of this play, Horace, a doctor, and others grapple little Bobby to the floor in order to quiet him with a hypodermic.

Another boardinghouse resident, the kind spinster Ruth Amos, is more helpful, as her name implies, since "Ruth" means pity and Amos is the name of an Old Testament prophet. She is one of Foote's unselfish and indispensable members of the community. Hearing Bobby Pate's drunken yells, she calls on Horace for help. Miss Ruth sings the tuneful songs of the day, adding a musical background with pertinent titles of significance. This spinster sings regretfully "After the Ball Is Over" at the soldiers' benefit performance, where she is announced as "the songbird of the South" (p. 101). At the end she remembers singing "Oh, Promise Me" at Elizabeth's wedding. The two women venerate the sacredness of married love by singing this song at the end of the play.

If Elizabeth and Horace are the successes of the Victorian family, Brother Vaughn is the failure—a male casualty as Laura was a female one. He is modeled after the pathetic Brooks brothers. Foote is no sentimentalist about the pitfalls facing youth in Victorian America. He states frankly that Brother was "a composite of my own uncles I knew and observed growing up" ("Lecture," p. 41). According to Foote, Brother was "like so many men I've known in the South, and all over America, who had successful fathers and felt constant failures" ("Lecture," p. 42). Fitting the role perfectly, Matthew Broderick, the bad boy with shining eyes, makes this character the most striking and engaging one in the television saga *The Story of a Marriage,* as the reviewers recognized.

Brother is the rebellious son of the Victorian family, and he does not transform to domestic virtue, as did Elizabeth and Horace. He clashes time and again with his autocratic father. Mr. Vaughn has sent Brother to prep school and now to Texas A&M, where, unlike his father, who was an outstanding student, Brother is failing. Papa wants Brother to study law, but Brother tells his father that he only wants to make "a lot of money, like you have." When the Vaughns arrive on their visit to the modest household of the newlyweds, Brother recounts his most recent misstep. After Mr. Galbreath killed Mr. Mason and came to trial, Brother says that he bet $2 that Galbreath would be convicted of murder and sent to "the pen" (p. 74). When his father is outraged that he has not "learned his lesson about gambling," Brother insists, "I have, Papa, I swore to you I wouldn't gamble and I won't. I won't ever go near dice or cards." Mr. Vaughn counters that one can gamble without "the use of dice or cards" (p. 75). Later we learn that Brother bet Bobby Pate $40, not $2, and lost, since Galbreath received "a suspended sentence" (p. 86). Mr. Vaughn, saying that his son has no money, pays the debt, for which he is reproved by Elizabeth.

Brother continues to get into trouble. What is the cause of his irresponsible behavior? Here we surely see the adverse effect of an authoritarian figure. The son is made to feel inferior. His inclinations burst the prohibitions placed on him. The workaholic father spends no time with his obstreperous son, and no communication goes on, as none occurred between Big Daddy and Brick in *Cat on a Hot Tin Roof*. Mr. Vaughn tells Elizabeth defensively in *Valentine's Day*, "I'm not a very sociable man. It isn't just with Horace. I don't have an easy time talking with my own son" (pp. 94–95). Foote's answer to this impasse is to show a kind father listening to his son, defending him, and appreciating his sentiments, as Horace does with his own son, based on the playwright, in *The Death of Papa*.

Another father-son conflict is remembered by Bobby Pate at the end of *Valentine's Day*, which seems irrelevant to the main action but serves as a parallel to the clash between Mr. Vaughn and Brother. As Elizabeth describes her wedding day, Bobby Pate recalls "Mr. Billy Lee's sissy son" (p. 104). Because Edgar Lee cross-dressed, his father whipped him in front of all the neighbors. Bobby Pate's mother said "he beat him until she thought he would kill him" (p. 106). This case was anticipated by the whipping of Bubber Reeves in *The Chase*. Neither whipping changed the son's behavior. The tale of Edgar Lee contrasts with Elizabeth's happy memory of her wedding on Valentine's Day.

The critical reception of *Valentine's Day* was favorable but, like that of *Courtship*, very limited. In fact the whole published evaluation of the play is too small to draw any conclusion. Vincent Canby wrote a highly favorable review of the film in the *New York Times* (April 11, 1986). One may note, however, that it received less attention than *Courtship*, which is a better work, taken solely by itself.

The seventh play of the *Cycle, 1918*, carries Foote's saga to the end of World War I and dramatizes the flu epidemic that had as large an impact on the citizens of Harrison as the international crisis. The play-wright shows again his continual interest in Katherine Anne Porter. Her novelette, *Pale Horse, Pale Rider,* convinced him that the flu scourge of 1918, which devastated his hometown, extended to the whole nation and took an appalling number of lives. Porter's autobiographical story of how her lover fell victim set Foote to meditating on the Negro spiritual "Pale horse, pale rider, don't take my lover away from me." These words could have been echoed by Elizabeth, since her husband almost dies from influenza.

Others in Harrison, however, succumb to the flu, like Elizabeth's baby daughter. T. Abell, Horace's uncle who is only thirty-five years old, dies, leaving two sons and his wife, Inez (based on Foote's great-aunt Lida Horton Abell, who in fact married T. Abell). The wave of death is coun-tered by new life. Elizabeth at the end gives birth to a son, Horace Junior. This play has a characteristically hopeful ending. Here Foote especially resembles Thornton Wilder, who sees new life following death and war in *The Skin of Our Teeth.* Mr. Antrobus's daughter gives birth to a child after the destruction of life in that play. Like Wilder, Foote celebrates the eternal cycle of death and birth, showing his fundamental optimism.

1918 is an antiwar play, like the film *Tender Mercies* (1983), which re-counts the emotional damage done to American families by the Vietnam War. *1918* combines indictment and satire of Americans during World War I, especially Texans. "Jingoism" (the term for militant nationalism during the Victorian age) is rampant. Brother, like many, is stridently anti-German, ironically so, since the state of Texas has a large popula-tion of Germans. This young patriot blames the Germans for everything, saying that their use of germ warfare has caused the influenza deaths. He accuses Mr. Dietrick of backing the Kaiser because Dietrick hangs the Kaiser's portrait in every room of his house. Brother longs to go "over there" to fight the "dirty" Germans. Once he arrives in Europe, he boasts, nothing will stop him. He has visions of meeting General Pershing and the French military leaders, whom he admires next to the Americans.

In fact, Brother is motivated to fight in the war as an escape from chronic differences with his father. Not only academically disgraced, Brother has gotten a girl pregnant, he confides to Elizabeth. Eventually his father gets wind of this scandal and rescues him with money as he did before. After the Armistice, Brother departs for Galveston to work on a cotton boat, much to his father's relief.

On the antiwar side of this play is Horace, who is embarrassed by Mr. Vaughn's offer to move into his home and care for his wife and daughter so he can enlist. Horace admits that he does not want to fight, telling Elizabeth, "What is your father talking about? I don't want to leave you and the baby" (p. 127). Horace uses $4,000 to buy Liberty Bonds, delighting his father-in-law, chairman of the bond campaign in town. Mr. Vaughn declares that we would have won the war by now if everybody had bought Liberty Bonds like Horace.

More of Horace's commendable character after marriage emerges in the responsibility he takes for erecting a tombstone over his father's grave. On two visits to the unmarked grave of his father and two uncles, Horace decides which is his father's grave. After erecting a tombstone, however, Mrs. Boone, who attended the funeral of Horace's father, tells him that he made a mistake in identifying the grave. Elizabeth later reminds Horace that Mrs. Boone could be wrong. Foote has often remarked that human memory is unreliable, a sign that disputes over truth in the past are inevitable.

More antiwar sentiment is expressed in the portrayal of Elizabeth's confused neighbor. Bessie Stillman hates what the war has done to vulnerable men. Horace must walk her home when she passes by a pitiful victim of shell shock, a tragic aftermath of artillery bombardments in World War I. Bessie, the product of an unhappy family, is based on a young neighbor who visited Foote's mother every day. She was not "so much retarded, as she is sometimes played, as eccentric," Foote notes ("Lecture," p. 41).

The duel between pro- and antiwar parties is reflected in the medley of songs heard throughout this play. When the Armistice is announced at the end of the play, the town erupts with patriotic and popular southern songs. In counterpoint, Ruth Amos sings "Peace Be to This Congregation." Mrs. Vaughn loves this hymn and sings along with her. Mr. Vaughn murmurs, "No more wars, no more bad habits" (p. 177). Elizabeth joins Miss Ruth also in singing the words of the hymn: "Oh, the peace of God be near us" (p. 177). The last sound heard, nevertheless, is a battle song rendered by the band. Even though this has been "the war to end all wars," the last music reminds us of the endlessness of wars.

Unable to produce the whole Cycle on television, Foote decided that the three central plays, *Courtship, Valentine's Day,* and *1918* would most likely find "a receptive theater home." Next he was faced with the challenge of casting the major role of Elizabeth. He had worked before with such talented actresses as Kim Stanley, Geraldine Page, and Joanne Woodward, but they were now in their forties and fifties, too old to play Elizabeth ("Lecture," p. 14). After seeing his daughter, Hallie Foote, act in *A Young Lady of Property* under Peggy Feury's direction in California, however, he called his wife to say, "I have found my Elizabeth" ("Lecture," p. 15).

Hallie corralled a group of friends who read *1918* for Foote. He remarked, "It was moving to hear the play read for the first time." He decided to do the plays out of sequence to stress "the fact that they were complete to themselves" ("Lecture," p. 15). He himself wanted to direct this trilogy at the HB Studio. In 1978 he scheduled the opening of *Courtship* for July 4 of that year. Matthew Broderick played his first theatrical role, as Brother in *Valentine's Day*. Next fall, Foote directed *1918*.

Having filmed *Tender Mercies* in 1983, Foote thought of making the trilogy into movies. He and his wife secured the money for *1918*, which was directed by Ken Harrison, a young Dallas filmmaker. Lindsey Law of *American Playhouse* liked it and financed *Valentine's Day* and *Courtship*. They were shot and released in theaters out of sequence, though *American Playhouse* retained the chronological order under the title *The Story of a Marriage* when the movies were shown on television in 1987 ("Lecture," p. 17). For the films, Foote cast William Converse-Roberts as Horace and Amanda Plummer as Laura (p. 19).

The production history of *1918* is tortuous. It was filmed in 1984. The movie was evaluated favorably by Nina Darnton in "Horton Foote Celebrates a Bygone America in '1918'" (*New York Times,* April 21, 1985). Vincent Canby also reviewed it favorably in the *New York Times* (April 4, 1986). After this film was included as the last part of *The Story of a Marriage* on *American Playhouse,* it was noticed in *TV Guide* (May 13, 1987). *1918* came under the headings "Shadows of War" (1917) and "Renewal" (1918). The broadcast was sponsored by Public Television Stations, the Corporation for Public Broadcasting, and the National Endowment for the Humanities.

In the performance seen on television, I believe the best acting was done by Matthew Broderick and the actor who played a poker-faced but comically disgruntled Mr. Vaughn. Brother's remarks are unfailingly amusing and alone make the film worth watching. The same cannot be said for the whole movie. The last scenes about the birth of the new baby, with their sparse dialogue, are glacial.

Cousins, the eighth play of the *Cycle,* takes place seven years after *1918,* in 1925.[7] Peggy Feury read all nine plays of the *Cycle* and had the students at her school, who were professional actors, do scenes from them. Foote went to see their work and reported that "it was most illuminating for me." Later Feury gave a full production of *Cousins* at her theatre in California ("Lecture," p. 19). As with *Convicts,* this play surveys a class of people, but in this case middle-class white southerners. Still showing the decline of the old social order, it satirizes reputedly close kinship in the South. By 1925 the ties are disintegrating in the grotesque lives of Horace's many Harrison cousins and others who have made the move to Houston. Here Foote focuses on social history and earns a place in the comedy of manners. As with Jane Austen, the founder of that school in English fiction, Foote identifies two contradictory strains: selfishness and concern for others' welfare. Among the many cousins of this play, close and distant, which ones still practice the noble virtues of love, kindness, and forgiveness? Not many, sad to say, though a saving remnant preserves the best qualities of kinship and thus some hope for the future.

The most objectionable cousin in this play comes from the line that reportedly stole the ancestral inheritance from Horace's relatives, the illustrious Thorntons (that is, Hortons). A native of Harrison, Lewis Higgins invades Horace's dry goods store, the setting for half the scenes. Lewis is clearly based on Foote's memory of the actual entry of a man like Higgins into his father's store ("Seeing," pp. 11–12). In the play, the fictional cousin's entrance line to all present is "Don't give me any shit" (p. 9). The intoxicated intruder ignores Horace, his third cousin, but says that he admires Brother Vaughn because he knows how to drink. While visiting a tavern with him in Richmond, Texas, his cousin Jamie Dale had the effrontery to insult two women of low morals. Lewis, a defender of ladies, regardless of their morality, killed his cousin on the spot with a knife. Pleading self-defense, Lewis was given "a suspended sentence," according to the local custom, which seems habitual in Foote's plays. A vicious, though ludicrous individual, revealing some of the same inhumaneness that Soll Gautier displayed in *Convicts,* Lewis returns to the store in the end, after breaking a glass case, and his equally disreputable brother, Lester, tries to cash a worthless check. Helping himself to a plate of fried chicken sent by Horace's Aunt Inez, Lewis politely offers some pieces to Horace and Elizabeth. When he leaves, he calls Horace "Cousin" for the first time. Then he asks, "Which cousin are you?" and exits (p. 99). He makes no reappearance in the *Cycle*. Lewis can never re-member whether or not someone is his cousin.

Lewis Higgins has the final word on cousins. Reminding Horace that a lot of their cousins are dead now, he observes philosophically. "The graveyard is full of cousins. . . . We'll be in that graveyard someday. . . . Why the graveyard will be full of cousins" (p. 99). By implication, the close ties of kinships are headed for the grave.

Balancing the malicious, backbiting cousins are those who preserve the virtues of family. Gordon Kirby, son of Aunt Inez, whom we met in the preceding play as Inez Abell, is a friendly first cousin of Horace's who has been hired to work in the dry goods store. Gordon is based on the real Robert Abell (*Memoir*, p. 179). Horace, out of kindness and support of kindred, wants to help Gordon earn money to pay for his education, even though he falls asleep on the job. Gordon is a generous cousin who invites Lily Dale and her husband as well as Monty and Lola to partake of his mother's fried chicken, despite the objection of his surly brother, Leonard, who will appear later in *The Habitation of Dragons*. Gordon even invites Minnie Curtis, whose mother was a Robedaux.

Minnie undergoes a change of heart toward Horace's Thornton rela-tives. When she met Corella in Houston, they got into a shouting match. Now, however, Minnie tells Horace that she regrets her feud with the Thorntons. Though she considered them frivolous, she wishes they had been friends because secretly she liked them. She now realizes that she is alone: "A family is a remarkable thing isn't it? You belong but it passes you by unless you start one of your own." Since she did not start one of her own, she no longer has a family, "only cousins who don't want to fool with me" (p. 92). When Gordon politely asks Minnie home for fried chicken, she declines but lets him drive her to the railroad station. Gor-don and Minnie finally practice the best virtues of cousins: kindness and forgiveness.

The ninth and last play of the *Cycle* is *The Death of Papa*, performed February 8 through March 2, 1997, with Matthew Broderick and Hallie Foote at the Paul Green Theatre, Chapel Hill, North Carolina. Set in 1925, the play begins with the death of the patriarch, Henry Vaughn ("Papa"), civic leader and wealthy citizen, based on Foote's grandfather Brooks.

Despite the title, the focus in this play is on Papa's son, Brother Vaughn. We have come to know him as the failed son, whose bad traits include drinking, gambling, and philandering. In this last play of the

Cycle, we get a final picture of this black sheep. Brother is still the archetype of the misbehaving son, who clashed with his dictatorial Victorian father. Here, though, we understand Brother better as a representative figure. He is the tail end of the landed, ruling class. Brother Vaughn fails to follow in the footsteps of his father. It is Brother's future that maintains suspense. What will he do after his father's sudden death? Will he change his ways that we have seen so far?

To begin with, we observe the repeated failures of Brother to take the place of his successful father. Mrs. Vaughn shows her trust by giving him one of his father's farms and turning over management of all the others to him. But Brother is not up to the task. He cannot get along with the tenants, who complain that he does not come out to the farms. Hatching new schemes, Brother goes into pecan harvesting, but more than half the trees die. When such setbacks occur, Brother has "reason to be drunk" (p. 156). We see him taking one "swig" after another (pp. 118, 138); Elizabeth and his mother smell liquor on his breath, and one time he is seriously drunk when encountering Elizabeth. Another project is to enter the cattle business, which he goes into with a man he considers a close friend of the family. Mr. Borden is the Snopes figure in this contest between inherited money and unprincipled modern business. He cheats Brother out of his investment in cattle. Add to his failed ventures Brother's taking out a mortgage on a farm to secure money, which he spends quickly, plus a ruinous loan at 25 percent interest, and it comes as no surprise that Brother finally agrees that his mother's money should be managed by a Houston trust company.

The climax to this chain of unfortunate events has not yet occurred, however. Leaving for Galveston to board a boat bound for Germany, Brother gets drunk and stabs a man. His mother and Horace rush to his rescue, hire an expensive lawyer, and win him another notorious suspended sentence.

These are the melodramatic events that mark Brother's precipitous fall. But is there an explanation? Do we learn more of the cause of Brother's downfall? Yes, Foote goes more deeply into an older Brother's flaws. In this play the cause of Brother's fate becomes clearer as he expresses his own pain for what occurs. Another casualty of the Victorian order, like Sybil Thomas in *Courtship,* Brother suffers from the demands made on him by his father. Saying that "the ghost of Papa is heavy on me" (p. 155), he confesses his true feelings toward his father, for which his mother immediately chastises him, increasing his guilt and causing him to recant abjectly. He was "scared as hell" of his father (p. 157), by which he means afraid of that powerful figure's censure of his failures, which he heard again and again. The explanation in this play for Brother's record of set-backs does not go deeper than this, because Foote evidently thinks this is sufficient clarification. Like Faulkner, Shakespeare, and others, Foote uses his intuition about human nature to understand personality disorders as best he can. He does not apply psychological theory like O'Neill, for instance, but what he says about Brother is convincing and is backed up by the above statements about resentment toward his father. Brother recognizes an inferiority complex, because he calls himself dumb before Elizabeth: "I'm dumb. I'm stupid. I've no judgment" (p. 195). These speeches offer rich material for an actor's interpretation.

The last line of this play is spoken by Brother, indicating correctly that this is his play. Talking with Horace before leaving Harrison, which he now includes along with bad associates as a reason for his failures, Brother sees nothing in the future but "wandering" (p. 194). He and his mother are moving to Houston, but he won't stay there, he states with uncommon assurance. When Horace says that he himself now has a home and will not occupy the Vaughns' big house, Brother remarks, "Don't be too sure about anything big Horace. Not about anything in this world" (p. 194). This cynical remark is the last line in the play.

Horace Robedaux, now called "Horace, Sr.," denies Brother's prediction that he will move into the Vaughn house, as "this is my home" (p. 194). The former homeless boy practices love, as unselfish consideration for his children, and is confident that it will last. Even now Horace's business is poor, but he decides firmly not to be rescued financially by Mr. Vaughn. How did he overcome his vices? Mrs. Vaughn wants to know. Horace replies, "I don't know. I just did. I loved Elizabeth and I did" (p. 191). Elizabeth wishes that Brother could marry a strong wife. That might straighten out his life. Indeed, a fortifying wife strengthens many stumbling men in Foote's plays, like Rosa Lee of *Tender Mercies*. They are based on Foote's own wife, Lillian Vallish Foote.

The new son in this play, Horace Junior, is based on Horton Foote himself. Foote observes, "I have used myself in my writing consciously twice": first in the early play *Wharton Dance,* which was uncomfortably "literal"; second, more imaginatively in *The Death of Papa*" ("Lecture," p. 63).

The arrival in this play of Horace Junior, based on the playwright himself, again brings up anti-intellectualism in Texas. The bias against intel-

lectual activity was also strong in Victorian times, as seen in the admiration of practical virtues and the objection to religious speculation, provoked by Darwin's theory of evolution. Horace's mother, Corella, continues her diatribes against education, reading, and books when she
observes her grandson with his nose in a book. Reflecting the Thornton
prejudice against learning in contrast to the Robedaux love of reading,
she remembers Terence Robedaux, brother of Corella's husband, who
could read Latin and Greek but was never able to earn a living. Corella's
attack on reading and education provokes Horace Senior to defend his
son's reading. He has known men who had no use for reading and "are
not worth much today" (p. 189).[8]

Foote proves himself to be a perceptive social historian by his imposing cycle of nine plays. The truth of his social history has particular
application to Texas. In the *Orphans' Home Cycle,* we have noted a prolonged influence of the Old South, such as the lasting prejudice against
learning, which lasted longer in Texas. With the Orphans' Home Cycle,
Foote finished his most impressive single achievement: a saga of nine
plays, unprecedented in American dramaturgy.

By the 1980s it is possible to list the distinctive qualities of "a Foote
play." Recognition of these qualities can guide our understanding of his
plays both before and after the *Orphans' Home Cycle*. Along with the television plays of the early 1950s, the *Cycle* plays help us recognize these
identifying qualities.

What are these qualities? First, Foote's characters are ordinary and familiar, like Carrie Watts and her son, Ludie. But these persons have particular problems that we have not experienced exactly. Who has been
a country music singer whose life is in a shambles, like Mac Sledge in
Tender Mercies? Always we are interested to know if the character will
overcome the problem. Perhaps many young women have argued and
lost to domineering fathers. But how does Elizabeth get out of this dead
end? She does so by courage and lives a happy life.

Another distinctive element is original female characters. Religion,
with its emphasis on healing, has a feminine quality. Foote's best characters are women: from the quiet, serious ones like Mrs. Watts to the zany,
hilarious ones like Jessie Mae, and, yet to come, Mabel Votaugh, a Hous-
tonian from Harrison, plus Lily Dale when she is older.

These characters bring to mind an omnipresent humorous phraseol-
ogy, not only of women but also of men. Soll, though repugnant, jokes
about former convicts; he browbeats everyone, saying his nieces are

"whores," and directs the making of his coffin, like Addie Bundren. C. W. Row is a riot in *The One-Armed Man* with his gallows humor. Why are Foote's plays "character driven"—by Henry Thomas, Mr. Vaughn, Stanley Campbell in *The Man Who Climbed the Pecan Trees,* Leonard Tolliver in *The Habitation of Dragons,* and Will Kidder in *The Young Man from Atlanta?* The list goes on. Foote is always fascinated by people: in *Tomorrow* it is Sarah Eubanks, whom he never tired thinking of. Characterization is his forte, and he makes the most of it in his low-key plots. Another example not yet covered is Mary Jo, the Houston socialite, in *Dividing the Estate* (first produced in 1989). Foote shows these personages' traits knowingly. Foote's characters are what stand out in his plays, not the undramatic plots.

14

ONE-ACTS OF THE 1980s

DISINTEGRATING HOMES AND DISPLACED PERSONS

AFTER composing the *Orphans' Home Cycle* in the 1970s, Foote was ready for a change in his writing and his life. From an epic of nine plays, he made a radical shift back to a favorite dramatic form: the one-act. During the 1980s he concentrated on them and composed nine in all. Again there were changes in Foote's personal and professional life. His children had grown up and now required less attention from their parents. He again took up residence in New York City, signaling an active participation in the theatre by having his plays produced there after an absence of more than twenty years. He obtained a residence in Greenwich Village, placing him in close contact with the world of actors, directors, and audiences. Now he would endeavor to resume a vital place in the theatrical world he had left. He has kept an apartment in New York up to the present date.[1]

Foote had stepped aside from the active legitimate theatre in the 1960s and 1970s. He had felt himself "a displaced person" during those decades, a designation used by Flannery O'Connor in her short story, which Foote adapted for television in 1977.[2] The violence and acrimonious political climate of the theatre caused the rift, combined with a feeling that American theatre had declined.[3] The great age of Broadway had ended in the 1950s. Gerald M. Berkowitz, in his book about twentieth-century American drama, entitles the chapter on the years from 1945 to 1960 "The Zenith of the Broadway Theatre."[4] No longer did Williams and Miller sustain the quality of American theatre. Only Edward Albee's plays, such as *Who's Afraid of Virginia Woolf?* (1964), and Amiri Baraka's *Dutchman* (1964) maintained the high level of dramatic excellence in the

1960s. The only plays that reached the big theatres did so because of their box-office appeal. It is no wonder that Foote wrote short plays for off-Broadway theatres, not attempting to compete with the current Broadway fare.[5]

Foote deals with real contemporary problems of American life, what Miller meant by the family and the job. His pieces are a breath of fresh air. Some playwrights still show similarities of subject matter. Miller reviews the decade of the Depression in *The American Clock* (1980), recording a Jewish family's decline into genteel poverty. August Wilson writes a saga of black social life in his series of plays about decades of the past, like *Two Trains Running* (1990), recalling the 1930s.

Among other playwrights of the 1980s, Romulus Linney, whose works Foote likes, provides the most productive comparison. Linney describes the life of a regional culture, analyzes the family, discusses religion, and cultivates the one-act form. Linney's plays, like Foote's, have been produced at the Herbert Berghof Studio and the Ensemble Studio Theatre. A native of North Carolina and an acquaintance of Paul Green's, Linney admires two of Foote's favorite writers, Katherine Anne Porter and Flannery O'Connor. Linney looks back to his forebears in *The Captivity of Pixie Steadman* (1981) and takes a wry view. Like Foote, Linney has mined southern tales and oral storytelling in humorous one-acts such as the three one-acts in *Laughing Stock* (1984) and *When the Lord Come to Sand Mountain* (1985).[6]

Foote had good reasons to concentrate on one-acts as he attempted to stage his work in New York theatres once again. Off-Broadway became vigorous in the 1980s and was receptive to the short form, since it could be performed on a low budget in very small theatres. Foote, also, had long expressed his fondness for the one-act. Having shown his skill for television, he liked the discipline of brevity and observance of the dramatic unities, which he felt required the dramatic artist to work effectively within a condensed framework.

In this second series of one-acts, Houston is often the locale, showing the increased importance of that metropolis for Harrisonians. These plays show the unmistakable influence of the preceding *Orphans' Home Cycle*. In the *Cycle,* Foote wrote an epic of Harrison from 1902 to 1926. This recollection of past times, especially of his father's life, forms the background for the later one-acts. A continuing sense of deterioration gives them a gloomy atmosphere. Families that held high positions in society have gone to seed, reaching near extinction. Foote's later one-acts show a dramatist with more historical sense. He is interested in how such fundamental structures as the home change. He draws much more heavily on his own family than he does in the first group, because he has followed their lives firsthand for a longer time.

Foote's one-acts of the 1980s began auspiciously with a trilogy, *The Roads to Home*, performed May 25, 1982, at the Manhattan Punch Line Theatre, 260 West Forty-first Street, off-Broadway. This sequence of one-acts, given as a three-act play, continues the pattern of sequential action, which was also seen in the *Orphans' Home Cycle*. The trilogy in fact prolongs the previous saga, carrying it further into the 1920s. Beginning in 1925, it comes before *Cousins* and *The Death of Papa*, which take place in 1925 and 1926, respectively, but ends in 1928, after the termination of the *Cycle*. The production featured Hallie Foote in the lead role of the demented Annie Gayle, a friend of Laura Vaughn's in *Courtship*. There are close links of characters and events between the *Cycle* and this trilogy of one-acts.

These three plays discuss conditions of the 1920s, American society was transforming when after World War I, a period that was also examined critically by F. Scott Fitzgerald, an expatriate. We meet Texans who have been displaced, who no longer inhabit their former homes. On September 26, 1975, Foote had sent the first draft of an adaptation of O'Connor's "The Displaced Person" to Calvin Skaggs, who directed it for PBS in 1977 (HFC). From adapting O'Connor's story, Foote had become very familiar with the concept of uprooted modern individuals. The fact that the author was speaking of a Polish immigrant on a farm in middle Georgia did not negate application of the analysis to Americans. In O'Connor's "The Displaced Person," native Georgians on the farm, like Mrs. McIntyre and the Shortleys, are "displaced."

What distinguishes the lives of displaced persons in Foote's second series of one-acts? Above all, it is the loss of their home, especially women's homes, that is upsetting. The overall title, *The Roads to Home,* is bitterly ironic. The women of these plays, epitomized by the demented Annie, seek to return home but cannot. "Home" had been one of the dominant words of Victorian life. Others were "mother," "love," and "duty." These concepts were idealized by the Victorians of Southeast Texas, just as relentlessly as those of the dowager queen's England. The plays carry further the deterioration of Victorian standards seen in *Courtship*. There the patriarchal father ruled the household, provoking one daughter to revolt. When another did not, but timidly submitted, the consequence was shattering, as it is in this trilogy. When the women of these plays try fran-tically to return home, they discover that they cannot. In the worse case, this experience can lead to madness. Not the ideal home, nor even the normal home, is possible, but only the anti-home, refuge of the de-ranged, who no longer inhabit the real world.

The first one-act of *The Roads to Home, A Nightingale,* names the cen-tral character, who sings the sad refrain of the homesick. Annie Gayle Long, who was born in Harrison, married and now lives in Houston. She returns home vicariously by constantly visiting Mabel Votaugh, with whom she can recall her hometown, so much so that Jack Votaugh, Mabel's husband, calls her "crazy."[7] Annie's parents originally moved from the North; her father became wealthy in his adopted town but was shot on the main street of Harrison in front of his daughter, like Boggs in chapter 21 of *Huckleberry Finn.* Annie has never recovered from this trau-matic experience and interrupts conversations at Mabel's by shaping a re-volver with her fist and pronouncing, "Pow!" (p. 298). Her mother never liked Harrison, and she returned north every chance she had after her husband's murder. Despite the violent incident in Harrison, Annie cher-ishes her girlhood there and wants to visit her close friend Laura Vaughn, who has married and moved to Dallas, like the real Laura Vaughn. By conversing with Laura, Annie could imaginatively return home. Annie's obsession with her former home leads to madness. She talks of Harrison incessantly and ignores her husband and two children to visit Mabel. Annie's husband, come to retrieve his wandering wife, who cannot re-member where her children are now, remarks that it may be necessary for her to be committed to the asylum in Austin, a "home" that would mean irrevocable separation from any real home. Annie sings "My Old Kentucky Home" with a weepy voice before disappearing for good.

Mabel and Vonnie Hayhurst, both staunch Baptists, advise prayer to cure Annie's emotional problems. When she talks out of her head, they counsel her to repeat the Lord's Prayer. Annie replies that she is rather in need of mercy and tenderness, to which Foote evidently assents. The Baptists often come in for a drubbing in this play.

Annie's dear friends Vonnie and Mabel have milder, but still marked, cases of homesickness. Vonnie, pining for Monroe, Louisiana, complains to Mabel that big-city women do not entertain as they do in small towns. Vonnie returns home as often as possible, where she enjoys picture show parties, even though "Sister" reads the titles out loud.

Another theme that strikes the note of the Roaring Twenties is marital infidelity, destined to become ubiquitous in Foote's plays of post-Victorian times, like *The Habitation of Dragons*. Annie's lady friends gossip constantly of straying husbands and wives. Mabel reports that Lorena, the organist at her Baptist church, and a deacon named Mr. Lopez are engaged in an adulterous affair. Vonnie reports that a Monroe wife is cheating on her husband. She wishes that a morals enforcement group, like the Texas Ku Klux Klan in the 1920s, would punish the adulterous husbands. Marital discord is evident among Annie's own friends. Mabel and Jack Votaugh hold "Quaker meetings" (p. 315), while Vonnie has refused to give Eddie a divorce. In the next plays more will be heard of this subject, adding to the sense of moral and social decline in the 1920s and 1930s.

The second one-act, *The Dearest of Friends,* takes place in the fall of 1924, half a year after the first play. Annie is no longer in Houston, much to the relief of Jack Votaugh. His wife comments more euphemistically that she has gone to "her new home" (p. 329). All is not calm back in Houston. Marital infidelity has entered the picture, owing to the wives' never-ending desire to return home. A train excursion is planned by Vonnie to visit Mabel's hometown, Harrison, about which she has heard such glowing descriptions. Vonnie raves about "the lovely old homes" they see (p. 330). All is not the same, however, in the town that Mabel still considers home. She reports that the Baptist preacher has run off with a man, and Mr. Lewis at the bank has been cheating on his wife.

Unfortunately, on Vonnie's visit, Eddie falls for an attractive woman on the return trip to Houston. She is Rachel Gibson, who bears the ironic name of the faithful damsel that Jacob met on his journey in the Old Testament. Vonnie bemoans this turn of events to her dear friend Mabel, who consoles her with the remark: "Over here you are among friends." Vonnie replies, "Dear, dear friends. I think friends are the most precious things on earth" (pp. 327–328). The mutually reassuring dialogue of these close friends is decidedly Weltyesque, like those in "Lily Daw and the Three Ladies." This support system is not working in the big city of Houston. Despite Vonnie's sharing her trouble with Mabel, Eddie keeps on seeing the beguiling Rachel. He insists on a divorce. Mabel condemns the behavior of Eddie on the train and his insistence on a divorce. If Jack went with another woman, Mabel says, she would kill him.

The third one-act of *The Roads to Home, Spring Dance,* takes place four years later in 1928. It is the bleakest picture of life in the 1920s, since the only place the characters can call "home" is the asylum. Annie has been there four years. She gets letters from her mother and her divorced husband but complains that they know nothing of what is happening in Harrison, such as the death of Henry Vaughn. Annie turns down partners at the spring dance because to accept would expose the reality of her divorce from Mr. Long.

In this one-act, more uprooted persons appear on the scene. Two young men from Harrison known to Annie are Greene Hamilton and Dave Dushon, both from leading families. Greene admits he did not make his way in life as his three brothers have, one of whom is a successful lawyer. "I'm the nervous one," he says (p. 352). When he returns home for a visit, he merely sits on the porch rocking, but even there he gets "upset" and must return to the asylum. His plans of returning home after the dance are dashed when he get "nervous" on the dance floor, continuing to dance after the music stops (p. 358).

The other young Harrisonian represents an extreme stage in the flight from reality. Dave Dushon went away to college but, on his return home, did not speak. He has been at his substitute "home" for ten years, having reached the age of twenty-eight by now. Unlike Greene, who still shows an interest in life by dancing, Dave sits mute and immobile.

All of the persons in this one-act, except the severely withdrawn Dave Dushon, retain hopes of returning home, a sign of life. Annie says she must get well for the sake of her loved ones. It has become pathetically clear, however, that these individuals are no longer welcome at home. Instead of longing for her lost home in Harrison and living there in her imagination, Annie needs to make a new home for herself. She has not found a true home to replace her childhood home. Nor are any of the other mad characters able to build a home for themselves.

Since *The Roads to Home* was performed in different years, reviews in New York cover two productions. The *New York Times* (March 28, 1982) noted that *The Roads to Home* opened Thursday, March 25, and would run through April 12, 1982. It was described as "a comic drama by Horton Foote about gentle Southern folk living in Houston in the 1920s." John Corey reviewed the three parts favorably in the *New York Times* (April 12, 1982). Writing under the heading "Southern Gothic," he preferred the second one-act, *The Dearest of Friends,* a comedy of manners. He also found the last one-act "charming." He wrote that here Foote was on "tricky" ground since there's not much new a playwright can do with lunacy "down South."

Lucy Kroll, Foote's literary agent, enclosed a flyer for *The Roads to Home* at the Manhattan Punch Line Theatre, March 18–April 12, 1982, to Cathy Wyler, Public Broadcasting System. Kroll added that this is "a lovely company of actors and fine director" (HFC, letter, March 8, 1982). Kroll also sent reviews of *The Roads to Home* to several others. She believed that the one-acts would be perfect for the *American Playhouse,* but they were not given on that series.

The Roads to Home enjoyed success in Texas. On July 27, 1984, Kroll informed Foote that six performances of *The Dearest of Friends,* were given at the Texas Playwrights Festival. Carla Webbles, who directed stage performances, had sent Kroll a program, adding that it was "a lovely production." Working on this was "pure delight," she wrote. "We seem to be living in an age of overwrought melodrama and the subtlety, simplicity, and strength of Mr. Foote's work is a tonic." Actors and audience found "affectionate wit, delicate touch, and profound faith refreshing and challenging," according to Webbles. On October 18, 1984, the literary manager for plays of the Texas Sesquicentennial wrote Kroll that Foote's plays would be considered strong possibilities for production (HFC).

When *The Roads to Home* was performed at Lamb's Little Theatre of New York in September 1992, it received nine reviews. Four were favorable, three were not, and two were mixed but appreciative. Frank Rich, a knowledgeable critic of Foote's work, praised the performances of Hallie Foote as Annie and Jean Stapleton as Mabel Votaugh (*New York Times,* September 18, 1992). Noting that the humorous talk overshadowed the heartbreak, he said he liked the third one-act best, with its "absurdist humor." Rich called the work "modest Foote, but echt Foote."

Clive Barnes (*New York Post,* September 18, 1992) believed the work showed "grace under pressure." It reminded him of Dos Passos's saying that poetry was like throwing rose petals down the Grand Canyon. *Roads* was "a light play not to be taken lightly," he wrote. These women, far from their emotional home, coped with lives gone awry—very much the world of Foote, who was interested in "behavior rather than action, in nuance rather than narrative," he noted.

John Simon wrote a condescending review in *New York* (September 28, 1992). He represents a common opinion of Foote's genteel plays, which has hurt Foote's reputation. Is Foote too nice and normal to be an effective playwright in our present world? Simon asks. Simon had no desire to visit Harrison and wrote that, in most of his plays, Foote was "laboring to become the Balzac or Faulkner of Harrison." That is to say, I would demur, Foote presents insightfully a cross section of ordinary people in a distinct society.

In a mixed, but interesting review, Jan Stuart (*New York Newsday,* September 18, 1992) said that Foote wrote about the life that many who came to New York wanted to escape. In Stuart's opinion, the last one-act, with Hallie Foote, was best.

The Prisoner's Song, produced at the HB Studio in July 1985, was directed by Herbert Berghof. Along with *The One-Armed Man* and *Blind Date,* it composed a series of three one-acts entitled *Harrison, Texas.* Foote himself presented a dramatic reading of *The Prisoner's Song* at the Writers Workshop, Birmingham-Southern College, Birmingham, Alabama, on March 21, 1998. Appropriately the play is set in 1927. During the 1920s, joblessness and transiency belied the much touted economic boom, and the economic contradictions of that decade recurred in the mixed prosperity of the United States during the 1980s, when the play was relevantly presented.

Among Foote's one-acts of the 1980s are two set in the 1930s, the decade of the Depression. Here Foote looks at the decline of the old, formerly well-to-do families in this period of financial loss. Those who formerly possessed status as well as money are losing ground, signs of large-scale decline among the leading families of Harrison. Foote scrutinizes the disintegration of the family, which was rampant in the 1980s, when the plays were performed.

The Man Who Climbed the Pecan Trees was the first one-act composed by Foote in almost three decades after he wrote a large number for the early television anthologies during the 1950s. It premiered at the Loft Studio of Los Angeles in 1982 but was not performed in New York at the Ensemble Studio Theatre until July 1988. The time of the play is 1938. The Campbell family resembles Foote's maternal line, the Brookses, who are central to the end of the *Orphans' Home Cycle.* Mrs. Campbell remarks that those were happy times when "Daddy" was alive (p. 270). Foote has indicated the connection with the Brooks line by noting that the origin of this play goes back to 1930, five years after the death of his grandfather.[8] The three brothers of the Campbell family have much in common with the three Brooks sons, whose troubled lives Foote has often utilized dramatically.

Brother, Davis, and Stanley Campbell reflect the deteriorating state of their family. Brother, like his namesake in *The Death of Papa,* has lost $75,000 of his mother's money in oil speculation. Still consumed with oil fever, Brother has appointed himself president of a fraudulent company. Davis, the youngest, has been through a tragic divorce. It falls to him to pick up Stanley when he becomes drunk on the square and to drive him around at night.

The title character, Stanley, also involved in Brother's oil deal, works at the newspaper, but his wife must write his editorials for him when he is drunk. This husband has no real "home." Stanley is locked out of his home by his wife because of chronic drinking. Since Bertie Dee does not allow him to see his son, he resorts to peeping in the window, which "Son" reports to his mother. Stanley must go to his mother's house next door for the night, the time of day when, significantly, all the play's action takes place. Escape into the night is reflected in words from his favorite song, "In the gloamin', Oh my darlin'," which he sings when painful reality becomes too much for him (p. 272).

Stanley teeters on the verge of madness, showing the severity of his emotional breakdown. He wishes that he and his brothers and sisters could all start over and live in Harrison. He regresses to childhood by climbing the pecan trees on the square at night. Mrs. Campbell remembers that as a child, he always wanted to climb trees. What is more, Stanley hallucinates that his brother-in-law Wesley Cox enters his house to have an affair with the conscientious, hardworking Bertie Dee. Brother Campbell reminds Stanley that Wesley lives ninety miles away in Port Cleveland.

In place of a stabilizing wife, Stanley depends on a destabilizing woman, his mother. When Mrs. Campbell hears the rancor of her sons over their lost money, she has only clichés to offer: "We have our troubles certainly. Everybody does. But if we try to look on the bright side as much as possible . . ." (p. 286). She argues petulantly with Bertie Dee: "Please ask him not to drink" (p. 269). The relationship of Mrs. Campbell and Stanley is oedipal. She babies him now as she always has. In the end, Stanley asks, "Where are we, Mama?" and recalls his fear of falling as a child, giving a cry of "pain and terror." Mrs. Campbell comforts her grown son as she did when he was a child: "I'm holding you, honey" (p. 289).

This one-act, presented as one of four plays in Marathon '88 at the Ensemble Studio Theatre, was reviewed by Walter Goodman in the *New York*

Times under the title "Texas Gothic" (July 14, 1988). The critic felt that the piece was mainly notable for Mrs. Campbell and her reminiscences about Stanley's climbing pecan trees. To Goodman, Foote's down-home dialogue established a place and time.

The Road to the Graveyard was first performed in May 1985 at the Ensemble Studio Theatre. Set in 1939, it is a companion piece to *The Man Who Climbed the Pecan Trees,* with both plays showing old families that are disintegrating in the late 1930s, on the eve of World War II. In these one-acts the old, genteel Harrisonians hit bottom. This is arguably Foote's most Gothic play, with its dark house and macabre characters. The house is located on the road to the graveyard, where the father Mr. Hall notes two funerals pass per day. The daughter, India, believes that her mother's ills would go away if they did not live at this morbid location. Her complaint recalls how Anse Bundren in Faulkner's *As I Lay Dying* blames all his troubles on living by that "durn" road from which bothersome intruders come at any time.[9] The mother of the Hall family, Miss Lillie, compares the present times with the past, when lady friends come to "the tea party" in the afternoon (p. 440).

Here is another play that records the loss of a real home. Lydia, a close friend of Miss Lillie's, cannot bear staying in her own "home" because the kindred there are "fighting just terribly," she screams (p. 433). Going to ride at night like a witch, she spies Stanley Campbell climbing pecan trees on the square. Worry and resentment keep her from eating, a psychosomatic illness she adds to those of the Hall family. India, unlike Lydia, never leaves home. She has been loyal to her aged parents, remaining to care for them, but is angry and bitter. What will she do when they die? She (like Rosa Brooks) has not been trained to do anything, she complains to her mother. "Why didn't you drive us out of the house?" she exclaims (p. 438). Three of the five children have left home, earning the lasting disapproval of their mother, who recalls in Amanda Wingfield fashion being "the belle of many a ball" (p. 460).

The most pathetic member of this family is Sonny Hall, who is small, gentle, and in his late forties. To his credit, he is trying to face reality and improve his lot in the ongoing battle between truth and illusion that marks Foote's plays, as in Lorraine Hansberry's *A Raisin in the Sun.* In the latter, Walter Younger dreams of investing nonexistent sums, as the rich in Chicago do. Sonny, a film operator at "The Gem," plans to buy a minuscule 6 percent interest in the theatre but is opposed by his father, who considers the venture too risky. Most touchingly, Sonny dates a Cajun woman, wishes to bring her home, and then marry her. Miss Lillie, India, and Lydia, adding her strident objection, will have none of this "common woman." Sonny is intimidated by Miss Lillie's remark that when that woman comes, "out I go" (p. 450).

On the evening that Bertie Dee is supposed to visit the family, she does not appear, provoking Sonny to throw up his supper. Lillie insists on her son's snatching an invisible rabbit out of the air as she does. Submissively, he hands a rabbit to his mother: "Here you are Lillie, dear" (p. 460). The picture of this grotesque home, an excellent representation of the absurd, presents for our final consideration the disintegrated family in America of the 1930s. It seems based on the Brookses' home, condensing the three sons into one—Sonny.

Frank Rich wrote a laudatory review of this "overpowering" play in the *New York Times* (November 27, 1985), stating, "On the surface it seems like vintage *Saturday Evening Post,* but beneath there is an unbearable turbulence." Rich notes that the only peace is the "discordant peace of the graveyard" and that a family is dying, as is the social order before World War II. For Foote, who has been writing about changing Texas for decades, this "may be among the finest distillations of his concerns," Rich says. "He looks back at a world whose idyllic glow belies all manner of unacknowledged neuroses and sexual and economic injustices." Further, Rich says, "pain keeps seeping through," as seen in mama's boy Sonny, who politely excuses himself to take care of his stomach, "where his unexpressed bitterness resides." Reviewing the theatrical year 1985, Rich singles out Foote in stating that the theatre is in good shape, concluding that the Faulknerian *Graveyard* created "a magnetic field of anxiety almost suffocating in its intensity" (*New York Times,* December 29, 1985).

Foote's last one-act of the 1980s is *The Land of the Astronauts.* An attempt to film this play was unsuccessful. On May 19, 1983, Lucy Kroll sent two copies to Scott Zeigler and Alan Shayne in Los Angeles. On June 10, 1983, Warner Brothers returned the play. Kroll wrote in reply on the same day that she understood their requirements of "physical action, life and death events, and a need for a feeling of jeopardy." Warner Brothers had said they did not want to compromise Foot's integrity for these "prerequisites which the networks require." Still preserving hope for a film, Kroll wrote Foote on June 10, 1983, that the story is "so lovely it could expand into a feature film" and asked, "Why not show it to Alan Pakula, who wants to do a project with you?" (HFC).

The Land of the Astronauts was first performed at the Ensemble Studio Theatre in May 1988. Foote delivered it as a dramatic reading in the summer of 1993 at the Sewanee Writers' Workshop. Unlike all of Foote's preceding one-acts of the decade, this one takes place in the present, 1983. It is interesting because in this play, which resumes the cyclical view of history, Foote examines the recurring plight of displaced persons and disintegrated homes. The saga of Harrison is carried forward to post-modern times. The home is still fractured, confined to one room in a motel, the Colonial Inn.

Though it is the only one-act to take place in the present, we find many of the same conditions seen in the plays that take place in the past. The personages are displaced once more. The title notifies us that it is the space age; the National Space Center has been located in Houston, thanks to the support of President Lyndon Baines Johnson, of Texas. Phil Massey, a Harrisonian, has gone to Houston to be near the space center. His fondest dream is to become an astronaut, for which he has prepared himself by getting a high school degree at night school and then attending junior college. He boasts that he has seen Alan Shepard, his favorite astronaut, who said "Hi" to him once (p. 468). Significantly, Phil, now displaced and wandering in Houston, has sent his wife, Lorena, a postcard signed only "Guess Who" (p. 473). With no identity, not having become an astronaut, he is one of those lost souls living a life of quiet desperation in the era of the astronauts. He is thirty-five years old, he reminds his wife, when he returns to Harrison, and he wants something "to happen" to him (p. 497).

Lorena is one of Foote's stabilizing women. She works in a fruit store, conscientiously raises her young daughter, Mabel Sue; cuts off the television because it prevents communication; and humors her impractical husband's hopes of becoming an astronaut.

In 1983 the home is once again under siege. For those in this play, "home" is the Colonial Inn of Harrison, which shelters a disparate and troubled crew. This "hotel" (p. 469) is owned by the Taylor family, who have moved from Houston. Their extended family inherited the property from a rich aunt. "Daddy" Taylor dips his hand in the cashbox so freely that he has driven Son Taylor to bed with a psychosomatic backache. The one fortifying force among the Taylors is Son's wife, Bertie Dee, the third bearer of that name to appear in Foote's one-acts. It is a name with excellent connotations. The Bertie Dee of this play is the desk clerk, who attempts to make a profit by keeping Daddy Taylor's fingers out of the till. Furthermore, Bertie Dee is a neighborly woman, a tower of strength in this tottering home. She looks after Mabel Sue when her mother must leave, wants to attend the girl's tap dance recital, disbelieves in fortune-tellers consulted by her in-laws, and recognizes deadbeats unerringly. Miss Sitter Taylor, forty-five years old, wants to marry Mr. Henry, a middle-aged Harvard graduate, who eyes the stock market and promises to pay Bertie Dee the room bill the minute his expected check arrives.

A visitor to the motel is kind to one of the displaced unfortunates. Buster Duncan, whose boss at the police station is a female sheriff, Loula, kindly chauffeurs Lorena to Baytown to pick up her husband, Phil. Lorena hums the hymn she heard on Buster's radio. "They're catchy. I can't get this one out of my head," she tells Phil (p. 506). Buster practices small-town friendliness to a displaced person, which Foote also showed memorably in *The Traveling Lady* (1954).

When Phil finally comes "home," he returns to a motel room furnished with a double bed, a single bed, a table, and two chairs. One is reminded of Mr. Vaughn's disparagement of Horace and Elizabeth's first home—one room—but also of his later remark that he felt a contentment, a peace, there. The "homes" where Annie Gayle, the Campbells, and the Halls live enjoy no contentment or peace. The residents show only lives of despair and madness.

The outlook for the Masseys is better. When reunited, Phil and Lorena begin to talk honestly about their lives. Lorena reminds her husband that even if he left Earth, "you would have to come back down sometimes, or you would die" (p. 497). At the end, Phil still dreams of flying away to the land of the astronauts, where there are "no cares and no worries" (p. 506). He tells Mabel Sue that if he and her mother do not go there, your children will "certainly." Lorena brings the talk back to Earth: "I wonder which of the astronauts will come here to the bank" to be a director (p. 507). In this original picture of life in the space age, Foote has captured the longing of average people who dream of escaping the real world for an imaginary one. This desire represents the emptiness of their lives. Once again, this one-act illustrates Foote's truth-versus-illusion theme.

The predominant mood of Foote's retrospective on the 1920s and 1930s is a dark sense of social and moral decline, symbolized most strongly in the forbidding abode of the Hall family on the road to the graveyard. Little differs in the prevailing atmosphere seen in plays about these two decades. Pathetic women like Annie Gayle never make a successful transition to a new place. Most serious is that the family is disintegrating. Foote is prophetic in this observation. Some of the culprits are familiar: the vacuum left by the death of an autocratic father, like the deceased Mr. Campbell of *The Man Who Climbed the Pecan Trees*. We also recognize the frightened Victorian daughter, such as Annie Gayle, whose loss of her original home is irreplaceable. The rigid, powerful father is replaced by the ineffectual father, like Mr. Hall, who cannot lead and succumbs to the tyranny of his wife and daughter in *The Road to the Graveyard*.

Taking the place of the autocratic father is the possessive mother, like Mrs. Campbell. Foote reinforces Philip Wylie's notorious indictment of "Mom" in *Generation of Vipers* (1942).[10] Both Ernest Hemingway and Tennessee Williams blame possessive mothers for neurotic sons, as Foote does in *The Man Who Climbed the Pecan Trees*.

Coming in for much criticism in these decades is the church, especially the Baptist church, in Foote's one-acts about Texas, where reportedly "there are more Baptists than people." Religious faith takes the form of meaningless prayers in *The Roads to Home*. Ministers are powerless to prevent widespread marital infidelity in that trilogy. Besides true religion, the general moral quality of society has fallen.

If this were the whole story of Foote's one-acts coming after the affirmative ones of the 1950s, the sense of pessimism would be overpowering. In the play set in 1983, however, when one might expect an even lower mood, there is an upsurge of faith in human beings. All is not lost, for the uprooted residents of a motel can form their own caring community in *The Land of the Astronauts*. With strong wives like Bertie Dee and Lorena to lift up sinking families, hope revives. The family has been through harrowing times during the 1920s and 1930s but springs back with human goodness in the 1980s.

Among writers of one-acts, I would place Foote in the first rank. No other American playwright has devoted as much creative effort to them. O'Neill with *Bound East for Cardiff,* Tennessee Williams with *This Property Is Condemned,* and Amiri Baraka with *Dutchman* have composed excellent one-act plays, but they did not continue their efforts after the first successes. Foote, on the other hand, started with one-acts and wrote them over a much longer period of time. He began with the four acts of *Out of My House* in 1942. Then he wrote a superior series for television, including *A Young Lady of Property* and *The Trip to Bountiful,* which he expanded into a full-length play but which retained characteristics of the one-act. *Courtship,* in the *Cycle,* makes a finely realized one-act with its unities.

In fact, the one-acts exhibit the virtues of the short story, a form with which Foote reveals a close affinity. Along with the superior plot, the accurate and superbly humorous dialogue makes his one-acts the equal of Welty's best short stories. Foote likewise shows his skill with the short form by his highly regarded adaptations of Faulkner's "Tomorrow" and O'Connor's "The Displaced Person" for television.

In the second series of one-acts we may single out for praise *The Road to the Graveyard,* which rivals the absurdist accumulation of Ionesco's *The Chairs* by filling the stage with invisible rabbits. Who can name a slyer, more whimsical peek at the space age than *The Land of the Astronauts,* which humanizes unbelievable journeys better than *Star Trek?*

Why are Foote's one-acts so good? Most of all, it is the fascinating characters whom he introduces and we get to know in a very short time. For example, Miss Lillie, one of the decadent Halls in *The Road to the Graveyard,* is grotesque; she must keep Sonny at home with her and opposes his marriage to a Cajun woman. A neighbor Lyda Darst says for the third time: "Sonny will never marry a common girl. Not in this world" (p. 459). In a fantastic scene, Lillie tells Sonny, "Catch me a rabbit, Son" (p. 460). The relationship between mother and son never changes, though Sonny's attempt at liberation provides suspense. The pitiful pair adds to the morbidity of the title. All the people in this one-act are headed toward a sad death. This play could not last for three acts but is just right for one. Then there is Stanley Campbell, another pitiful man who has never broken away from his hovering mother. When he must face the reality of not living with his wife and son, he either climbs a pecan tree or sings mournfully.

15

GREEK TRAGEDY AND FULL-LENGTH

PLAYS ACROSS THE HUDSON

FROM the 1960s and the 1970s on, the expanding network of off-Broadway, off-off Broadway, and regional theatres defined the true scope of American theatre.[1] Increasing dissatisfaction with Broadway and a desire for serious theatre changed the situation. With the arrival of the Absurd, Americans were more willing to attend new theatre. In recent American drama, ancient and modern dislocations appeared. A revival of *Lysistrata* presented sex humorously. In Foote's *Habitation of Dragons* (1988), the structure derived from Greek tragedy. Foote used the play to condemn marital infidelity and to outline its terrible consequences: two sons drown in the river, and the surviving brothers fight each other over the land.

Foote did not dramatize the threat of nuclear war, as Lanford Wilson and Edward Albee did, but many dramatists were sensitive to it in this period. In the 1960s the integration of public schools became an issue, which Foote portrayed in *Dividing the Estate* (1989). The off-off-Broadway movement presaged a formative decade. The Peace Corps was organized, and the Great Society changed the American scene in the '60s. Marginalized people, that is, feminists and gays, became visible.

In the 1970s, David Mamet dramatized the corrupt influence of small-time thieves in *American Buffalo* (1975). Foote likewise showed this element in *The Death of Papa* (1978). The corrupt characters in that play illustrated the breakdown of business ethics that started in the 1920s. Brother, the feckless son, is victimized by dishonest businessmen, though he deserves it. Although this play is set in the 1920s, it has application to the 1970s, when it was composed.

Wendy Wasserstein transferred an excluded group to central status in *Uncommon Women and Others* (1977). Foote also presented the nonconformist woman of the 1900s. In *The Widow Claire* (performed in 1988), the protagonist broke courting customs. Dramatists continued to oppose a culture that seemed at odds with its theatre. In *Texas Trilogy* (1973 – 1974), Preston Jones struggled for a new identity for the single women.

Beth Henley's *Crimes of the Heart* (1978), with its eccentric figures, opened at the Actors Theatre of Louisville in 1978 and won the Pulitzer Prize in 1981. In the play, three sisters unite to gain more freedom. With a related theme, Foote's *Courtship,* which describes a daughter's rebellion against her father in 1915, premiered at the Louisville theater in 1984.

In *The Hot l Baltimore* (1973), Lanford Wilson writes about the fragmentation of families, as does Foote in *Land of the Astronauts* (1988). Both show "the impermanence" of our society.[2] Its human corollaries are retired waitresses in Wilson's play and clerks in Foote's. Hard-earned resiliency balances impermanence in both plays. In the hotel, Susy says, "I need God," not derision.[3] The desolation will destroy the structure of community, but a sense of charity ensures the ability to laugh in both plays. These plays come to terms with family schisms in the United States.

Sam Shepard wrote *True West* (1980), the third in a family trilogy. The internecine fighting is similar to that in Foote's *Cousins,* composed in the 1970s. In the latter, the scion of those who stole the family plantation is a foul-mouthed man.

In short, the playwright of the 1960s and 1970s shows the corruption of individuals and breakdown of families. Foote is becoming gloomier. The sad condition of society is developed ludicrously in his plays. He and other playwrights satirize the disintegration of families in America.

Foote was skilled at writing short plays, but to be a playwright in the full sense of the term, he knew that he must compose longer works. After making a comeback in the 1980s with one-acts performed to critical praise, Foote moved ahead aggressively with full-length plays, starting in the late 1980s and extending well into the 1990s. He did not, however, produce these large-scale works in New York, much less on profit-mad Broadway, but rather way off-Broadway, in regional theatres of New Jersey, Pennsylvania, Ohio, and Florida. When a play like *The Trip to Bountiful* got its first hearing on the road in Connecticut, he repeated the practice of the 1950s of staging tryouts.

In three plays, *The Habitation of Dragons* (1988), *Dividing the Estate* (1989), and *Talking Pictures* (1990), Foote resumed themes he had previously developed in his one-acts, but this time at greater depth and length. Once more, Foote examined the stimulating subjects of marital infidelity in *The Habitation of Dragons*, family disunity in the satiric comedy *Dividing the Estate*, and economic dislocation in *Talking Pictures*. In the first two plays, well-to-do families of Harrison who are in shocking decline resemble those observed in plays set in the 1930s, like *The Road to the Graveyard*. Foote has a gloomy view of the fate of leading families in Harrison. Like the formerly imposing Victorian Gothic houses, the families too are disintegrating to the point of extinction. Of the three plays named, the first is a tragedy, whereas the next two are comedies, like *The Land of the Astronauts*.

With his last large-scale works, Foote returned decisively to the theatre. Among this astonishing series of plays, *The Young Man from Atlanta* (1995) garnered the Pulitzer Prize.[4] Of comparable distinction is *The Habitation of Dragons*, which premiered in 1988 and appeared as a television film on Turner Network Television (TNT) on September 8, 1992. In this major play, which Foote began in 1959 and published first in the collection *Four New Plays* (1993),[5] he composed a work that invites comparison with classic Greek tragedy in the tradition of Eugene O'Neill's *Mourning Becomes Electra*, Jean-Paul Sartre's *The Flies*, and Jean Anouilh's *Antigone*.[6]

The Habitation of Dragons underwent an extended evolution before reaching stage production in 1988. Its long gestation demonstrates the amount of thought that went into this dense play, packed with varied plot material and numerous characters. An early form of the play about the young members of a string band in Texas was entitled *The Summer of the Hot Five* (1956). Two characters named Leonard and George are similar in their conflict to those with the same names in *The Habitation of Dragons*. NBC informed Lucy Kroll on March 15, 1956, that it had drawn contracts for *The Summer of the Hot Five*. It was to be an hour and a half show on *Playhouse 90*, but there is no record of its broadcast. The first script entitled *The Habitation of Dragons* is dated August 1959. After much revision, Foote labeled the script dated July 30, 1962, as "Final," but this was by no means the last version. On October 17, 1962, "Herbert" [Berghof] wanted to read *Habitation*, Kroll wrote Foote. At the end of 1963 there was an exchange of letters between Foote and the New York producer Mary Frank about mounting this play, but nothing came of it (HFC).

Foote resumed his effort to stage *The Habitation of Dragons* in November 1986, when a workshop production was given in New York. Lucy Kroll diligently promoted a full-scale production there. On March 13, 1987, she was awaiting a call from David Putnam as to the interest of Columbia Pictures in a film and theatre piece. She suggested Elizabeth McCann as the best general manager. On September 25, 1987, Dramatists Play Service was considering publication of *Habitation* for "a hefty sum" if we have "a successful production," Kroll informed Foote. Highly enthusiastic about this play, she wrote him, "*Habitation* is your crown of glory and I'm glad I can share in this event" (HFC).

On June 26, 1987, Kroll wrote to William Gardner about producing the play, which Gardner did at the Pittsburgh Public Theatre, with Foote as director. It opened on September 20, 1988, and Kroll saw a performance there on October 8, 1988. Horton Foote, Jr., took the part of George Tolliver, while Hallie Foote played the hero's wife, Margaret. The play ran September through October 1988. Afterward, a revision dated August 4, 1989, was made. The final shooting for television is dated April 17, 1991, after which it received a showing on TNT. The television movie, starring Frederick Forest as Leonard Tolliver and Jean Stapleton as his mother, showed on TNT the evening of September 8, 1992. Like the three central plays of the *Orphans' Home Cycle* televised as *The Story of a Marriage,* this play did not succeed on the stage and ended its acting life as a television movie. Despite this inconclusive record, *The Habitation of Dragons* is an important work in terms of plays in general and Foote's in particular.

Although no commentators have explicitly discussed the parallel with Greek tragedy, some have emphasized the tragic quality of *The Habitation of Dragons*. George Anderson, who reviewed the premiere at the Pittsburgh Public Theatre, felt that this was an ambitious effort at tragedy. Foote himself has remarked that he stands "in awe" of Leonard's endurance of "the senseless tragedy." These illuminating comments correctly characterize the play as a full-fledged tragedy. What they do not add is that this work follows closely the classic structure in order to explore a particular form of American tragedy in its marital and social manifestations. By attempting this challenging subject, Foote goes beyond his well-known realistic works like *The Trip to Bountiful* and demands comparison with such playwrights as O'Neill and Miller.

The Habitation of Dragons does not imitate Greek tragedy by updating one of the classic myths, as O'Neill does in *Mourning Becomes Electra,* where he follows the crimes of Orestes. No, what places Foote's tragedy in the Greek tradition is the plot, named by Aristotle as the most important element of tragedy because all human happiness or misery takes the form of action that is the end of tragedy.[7] With respect to plot, this play features most notably the peripeteia of the tragic hero simultaneously with anagnorisis, in this case when he learns of his wife's infidelity.

Among the essential elements that identify this modern tragedy are the following: the tragic hero, the pity and terror provoked by the catastrophe, and the Furies, famous for their pursuit of the murderer Orestes. They torment the tragic characters of this play, making "dragons" in the title very apt. After seeing Laurence Olivier in *Oedipus Rex*, Foote called that play "the greatest and most profound use of the classic one-act form."[8]

The tragic hero of *The Habitation of Dragons* is Leonard Tolliver, a man of elevated stature in Harrison, Texas. Unlike Miller's Willy Loman, an average man with an overpowering dream, Foote's hero is already powerful and successful in his self-contained world. He conforms to Aristotle's definition that the hero must be highly renowned, like Oedipus.[9] By giving Leonard important status, Foote elevates the importance of the hero and makes us attach greater significance to his life. At the beginning, Leonard has amassed land, wealth, and power, the indisputable tokens of success that set him above his unsuccessful brother, George. In addition to being a leading lawyer, Leonard has added more farms to his inheritance and now forces George, in need of funds, to sell his birthright of land to Leonard for a pittance. George protests to his greedy brother that not only is Leonard's landholding reaching new heights, but his bank account has also kept pace. Leonard, like the land-greedy Cabots of O'Neill's *Desire under the Elms*, possesses a purpose that drives his actions.

Not missing from Leonard's ambition is the desire for political power, a requisite for full success in this Texas community of 1935. Leonard is running his brother-in-law, Billy Dawson, for county attorney, even though his brother, George, is also campaigning for the important office. At the end of act 1, scene 2, the report comes that Leonard's candidate has been elected, further raising his standing and lowering George's in the world of Harrison. We now recognize that Leonard is characterized by the tragic flaw of ambition. He seeks wealth and power ruthlessly, and at this point he seems to have gained them.

Accentuating Leonard's ambition by contrast is George Tolliver, the foil and moral counterpoint to his compulsive brother. *Habitation* resembles a well-made Ibsen melodrama in this way. An unassuming younger man, who gains our sympathy by his painful political defeat, George complains bitterly to his black friend Lonnie that Leonard always gets what he wants. George had to give up his plans for further education because of Leonard's financial need. He confesses to Lonnie, who comforts him, that he feels great bitterness toward Leonard. In a long, impassioned outcry to his confidant, George recalls visiting the former house of his mother's aristocratic family on the Gulf, a wasteland now overrun by weeds. In overheated rhetoric, which reviewer Walter Goodman disliked (*New York Times*, September 8, 1992), George declares: "Here lies power. Here lies ambition. Let Leonard have them" (p. 27). Melodramatic as these words may be, George has exorcized his bitterness toward his brother and put to rest this Fury tormenting him, with the moral support of Lonnie.

Besides the classic elements of ambition and greed, this modern tragedy includes marital infidelity. By this subject Foote supplies social commentary that corresponds to O'Neill's criticism of New England Puritanism and Miller's indictment of American capitalism. Marital infidelity, of course, is not absent from famous tragedies, like the liaison of Clytemnestra and Aegisthus in the Oresteia and of Claudius and Gertrude in *Hamlet,* but its incidence in Southeast Texas calls for special examination. It symbolizes division of the community and is surely based on Foote's personal knowledge. We hear of it in other of his plays of the 1930s, like *The Chase.* This is the stuff of raw realism, which anchors Foote's tragedy in real life—crude, powerful, and true—not in some imagined place of Puritan New England.

The central case of marital unfaithfulness involves Leonard's wife, Margaret, and his farm foreman, the violent Wally Smith. When Margaret learns that Leonard plans to rent one thousand more acres and that his candidate has been elected, she complains that now she will see even less of him than before. The next scene reveals Margaret and Wally secretly kissing, a tryst spied upon by the reappearing Lester Whyte, a townsman who killed his wife's lover, Jim Sparks, but was given a suspended sentence, embittering Evelyn Sparks, mother of the slain man. Lester is still consumed by revenge and walks the streets.

After being beaten up by Wally for peeping, Lester informs Leonard by anonymous letter of the infidelity of his wife, who at first denies but then admits the truth to her husband and asks for a divorce. The rampant infidelity in the town becomes known as we learn that Margaret's father, Mr. Dawson, had an affair with Agnes Thomas before his death. Because of this adultery, Billy Dawson out of bitterness never spoke to his father again. Marital infidelity and the violence it provokes are ubiquitous events in Foote's plays, like *The Chase, The Dearest of Friends,* and his most recent, *Laura Dennis.*[10] Foote sees marital infidelity as the cause of lasting violence in the community.

In *The Habitation of Dragons,* Margaret's affair with Wally follows neglect by her husband, a workaholic. Foote consistently condemns a husband's obsession with making money in business to the detriment of his family. In *Habitation,* Foote singles out the husband as the cause of his wife's infidelity.

Marital infidelity touches the lives of unrelated members of the community, showing how conflict within the family extends beyond, as it does in Greek tragedy when Thebes suffers for the crime of Oedipus. Unfaithfulness arouses the fury of other parties, thus increasing the number of dragons, or hostilities, ravaging the larger community. Evelyn Sparks, mother of the murdered Jim Sparks, holds a grudge toward many in the town for excusing Lester Whyte for killing her son. She attempts to blackmail Leonard into paying her for the love letters Margaret wrote to Wally Smith, with whom she used to get drunk. She comes surreptitiously to Leonard's house, offering to keep quiet and not reveal the letters if he will pay her. She recalls that when her son was shot, a lot of money had to be spent to save the guilty. Menacingly, she asks Leonard and George, "Do I get my share, boys?" (p. 38). She does not, but Harry Brighton does, by stealing the letters and demanding a large sum from Leonard. The widening repercussions of marital infidelity involve a larger and larger circle.

The fury of revenge, unless overcome by forgiveness, spreads like an epidemic. Here, Foote makes by implication the strongest argument for forgiveness in the community. If forgiveness is lacking, vengeance will continue its destructive rampage. Charlie Taylor reports that the trial of Lester Whyte "almost tore this town apart" (p. 21). Whenever Evelyn Sparks met anyone who spoke as a character witness for Lester Whyte, she would threaten to kill him. Charlie speaks self-righteously, but he himself has not forgiven his brother for allegedly stealing his inheritance and never mentions his name.

The reversal of fortune falls on the hapless Leonard. George informs him that his two young sons have drowned in the Colorado River, announced by a fire siren. Leonard exclaims in front of Margaret: "It's for her sins my boys were killed. Their death is her punishment" (p. 31). Beside himself, Leonard screams: "Her whorish will is to blame . . . for the death of my boys" (p. 44). Hearing this, Billy, Margaret's brother, seizes Leonard by the throat and, after being torn loose from Leonard, chases Wally down and shoots him in his apartment.

The catastrophe of the little boys' death raises the question of why such senseless events occur. Ultimately the Greeks attributed human disasters to the decree of the gods, which does not really explain the event for modern audiences. The answer given in *The Habitation of Dragons* is different.

In Harrison, Texas, a stronghold of Christian fundamentalism, disaster is God's punishment for sin, a belief traceable to the Old Testament. Job's comforters say that he is suffering because God is punishing him for his sins. On this question the answer of the play is clear and expresses a consistent stand in Foote's plays. Unlike in Greek tragedy, the cause of catastrophe in *The Habitation of Dragons* is not God, though He is widely considered to be, but human choice.

Lenora Tolliver raises the same question when she asks her son about the deaths of the two little boys, as well as the deaths of her suicidal husband and Wally Smith: "Have we committed some terrible sin?" (p. 48). After Leonard blames Margaret for their sons' death, she asks Bernice, George's bride-to-be and a more impartial judge, if the drownings were her punishment. Bernice replies, "Now, they weren't killed for that." Margaret persists, "Then why were they killed?" The agnostic Bernice replies simply but with force, "I don't know" (p. 33). This is Foote's reply to the powerful belief that when an untimely death occurs, it is God's punishment for sin. Foote differs from other tragedians in that he refuses to answer the question of why. However, *how* the survivors cope with the tragedy receives an unequivocal answer.

Margaret is tormented to the point of madness because of the guilt she feels for her sons' death. She repeatedly asks Leonard to forgive her, but he refuses again and again. Because her emotions break under the strain, she undergoes psychotherapy in a Galveston hospital.

The Furies, however, do besiege not merely Margaret but her husband as well. Leonard's bitterness toward his wife makes his house a habitation of dragons. The title of this play describes a place of anger and revenge, a fitting description of the house of Tolliver. The dragons of the title may be justly compared to the Furies, since both mythical creatures produce unbearable anguish. Those who have wronged others will suffer the torments of hell on this earth, which becomes a habitation of dragons for them. They will waste away from revenge and guilt. What will happen if the Furies are not pacified can be seen in the lives of persons who now suffer unremitting torment. For example, Evelyn Sparks burns inwardly for Lester Whyte's unpunished killing of her son.

Revealing a different attitude, Lonnie surmounts the resentment against his white father, who rejected him. Lonnie tells George that once he felt "great bitterness," not because his father was white but because "he never really did anything for me" (p. 16). Lonnie has, nevertheless, overcome his bitterness toward his father and become a kindly surrogate father for George, who was a semiorphan after his father, Horace, committed suicide.

Providing the moral foil in this play, Leonard's brother, George, renounces the bitterness he feels toward his brother. The emotional rewards enjoyed by George and Lonnie become clear as we learn that neither of their marriages suffer from infidelity and both will have offspring. These happy outcomes reflect the nature of real life, where some individuals do not act immorally and are able to achieve happiness.

A particularly destructive Fury in Horton Foote's works is the refusal to forgive the wrongdoing of another. Throughout the *Orphans' Home Cycle,* Horace hears of the vengefulness of his relatives for the robbery of the ancestral plantation. They refuse to forgive the other line for this wrong. But in *Cousins,* Horace tells his son that he does not hold resentment, as he speaks courteously to a cousin who inherited that stolen birthright.

Joining the tragic Tollivers at their home is Uncle Virgil Tolliver, a befuddled old man who speaks cryptically, like Tiresias, the blind seer of *Oedipus Rex.* Not without significance, this doddering old gentleman provides the indispensable comic relief in the tense tragedy; he bears the name of the visionary Latin poet who prophesied that Rome was divinely appointed to civilize the world under Augustus. The Virgil of this play is also a visionary who relates a dream. Like the other Tollivers noted above, Virgil suffers the torments of the Furies because of the guilt that besets him. He was wealthy but refused to lend his brother, Leonard's father, money when asked; he believes that he is thus to blame for the suicide of Leonard's father. What is more, Virgil promised his sister to raise a tombstone over her grave in Mississippi but has not fulfilled his promise. Virgil's spacey personality and constant misnaming of characters (calling George "Leonard" and vice versa) beset him because of the emotional torment he undergoes. Virgil too is pursued by Furies. His mind wanders amusingly when he tells Leonard that he has not seen his family for a long time because the Gypsies kidnapped him when he was a child, recalling Oedipus's experience. In this tragedy, Virgil enacts the fool to Leonard's Lear, as well as Tiresias to Leonard's Oedipus.

Ironically, the seemingly ineffectual Virgil furnishes the healing balm to the pain of revenge. In the last scene he tells Leonard of a dream that he had as a boy. He was in a room all alone except for a preacher, who kept repeating "Forgiveness." Virgil kept crying, and the preacher kept saying, "Forgiveness." He asks, "But who was there to forgive, except myself? Nobody." In the last lines of the play, the daffy old dreamer asks Leonard if his heart is broken. His interlocutor replies that he himself broke his heart, but it will mend: "I hope. In time" (p. 61).

Foote wrote for the program of the original production: "I am in awe of Leonard" for how he accepts "what has happened to him."[11] Leonard's most insightful speech comes after his tragedy. When he went to Billy's trial day after day, watching the lawyers fight, he realized that because "a man's life can change in a week, an hour, a second," he wanted to cry out "have compassion" because your lives "can be destroyed overnight" (p. 43).

Leonard's recovery from the tragedy that befalls his family gives this play a hopeful spirit. He has not been able to forgive his father for "leaving us all alone" (p. 39). Though both his mother and Virgil believed Horace's death to be a suicide, Leonard did not confirm their belief but burned the note left behind in which Horace begged forgiveness. His son could not forgive him and instead preserved bitterness in his heart. Leonard was so ashamed of his father that he could not bear to hear him mentioned, but he adds that, lately, "I've felt such compassion for him" (p. 39). Having started the process of forgiving his father, Leonard next proceeds to forgive his wife and ultimately himself.

Tragic events provoke terror and pity, a purgation of the emotions, according to Aristotle. At the end of this play, the leading characters experience these powerful emotions and presumably the spectators share them, realizing that such events could happen to them. Margaret confesses to Leonard after their reconciliation that, in the psychiatric hospital, she became distraught while listening to the dreams of a young woman "in terror" (p. 58). Her worst fear is that she will die alone, as her father did. Continuing to expurgate her terror, she tells Leonard that

she keeps having the same bad dream. Horace and Leonard, Jr., are calling her from the river, but she cannot get to them. Soon after having this
dream, she threatens to shoot herself but is prevented.

Leonard's mother also is overcome by terror. Lenora Tolliver, fright-
ened by the deaths that have occurred all around her, appeals to her sons:
"I am in desperate terror. Help me, Leonard" (p. 48). At this point,
Leonard says, he cannot help himself.

After having refused Margaret's repeated entreaties, Leonard forgives
her. He pays for her hospital treatment, gives up his plan of escape to
Canada, and comforts his exhausted wife. Insisting on sleep, she sings the
words of the bedtime song she heard as a child: "Go tell Aunt Rhodie"
(p. 59). Leonard forgives his wife and stays beside her until she drops
off to sleep. Finally the other half of the play's epigraph prevails: "In the
habitation of dragons, where each lay, shall be grass with reeds and
rushes" (Isaiah 35:7).[12]

George Anderson wrote a provocative review of this play entitled
"Ambitious *Dragons* Opens PPT Season" (*Pittsburgh Post Gazette*, September 29, 1988). Anderson recognized it as an effort to create "a genuinely American tragedy" that presents "a disintegrating family against
the backdrop of a crumbling society." Sequences in the play arise "to extraordinary emotional power," according to Anderson, who also wrote
that although the plot sounds like "daytime drama," in Foote's measured
prose it is never "maudlin or mundane." Anderson stated that *Habitation*
is clearly an attempt at "a major American play." The reviewer added
that it would make "an exceptionally strong film since Texans seem to
demand the landscape the stage cannot afford them."

Habitation did not proceed to a performance in New York, but like the
Orphans' Home Cycle, it reached the television screen. Michael Brandman of Brandman Productions was the executive producer. Foote noted
that the scenes took place in front of "a perfect house" of Victorian style,
which Lillian Foote discovered in Sealy, Texas.[13] Walter Goodman wrote
a damning review entitled "A West [that is, East] Texas Family with
Troubles A Plenty" (*New York Times,* September 8, 1992). The actors and
director went down "in the heavy emotional weather," Goodman wrote.
"Only Jean Stapleton might save them but she is too busy saving herself
from lines like 'Have we committed some terrible sin? Are we being
punished?'" Goodman editorialized, "Fraid so, ma'am."

A fairer criticism was contributed by Tony Scott in *Variety* (September 7, 1992). He praised Foote and called Hallie Foote's performance as

Margaret "a stunning and definitive study." Scott wrote that the loosely structured work hovered between "high drama and overwrought melodrama," and that the argument between George and Leonard, like other emotional excursions, "just fades away." Foote's dialogue was as crisp as ever, according to Scott, but could clog the action. Scott added that the direction and camera work created "an impressive sense of live TV."

As for the large cast, making production difficult, additional comments are in order. Tony Scott called Brad Davis's last part before his death, as George Tolliver, "a tight, well-thought-out portrayal." After viewing the video, I would add that Frederick Forest as a perspiring, simian-like Leonard muddled the stature of the hero. Pat Hingle, however, as Virgil, who provided the only comic relief, gave a memorable interpretation.

Foote's next play also traces the decline of a Harrisonian dynasty, the Gordons, bringing them up to 1987. *Dividing the Estate* (1989), which analyzes the squabbles over an inheritance, is a sharply written satire, filled with topical allusions and caricatures.[14] This full-length comedy opened at the McCarter Theater in Princeton, New Jersey, on March 28, 1989. Lucy Kroll signed an agreement with the Great Lakes Theatre Festival on May 9, 1990, for a production (HFC). It opened at the Great Lakes Theatre in Cleveland, Ohio, October 11, 1990.

The time of the play is 1987; the characters are contemporary, and the social conditions current, like school integration problems. The arrival of a Vietnamese factory in Harrison gives the comedy a very up-to-date tone, as does the colloquy of well-to-do Texans adapting to the fall of cotton and oil prices.

Within the Gordon clan, several factions materialize with regard to the dispensation of the large family estate to be divided among a son, two daughters, and the surviving mother. The most sympathetic and reasonable pair is made up of Son Gordon, the young scion, and his fiancée, Lucy. This grandson manages the farms, distributes the income, and arbitrates as well as he can between the conflicting sides. He advises keeping the estate intact and paying off debts with the annual income. Most radically, because of the critical financial problems, he favors all members of the family moving into the ancestral residence in Harrison to conserve much needed resources. He announces to Mary Jo, his flighty aunt, and his desperate uncle Lewis, "I don't want anybody's share of the money. That's all I've heard all my life. Money, money, money—" (p. 144).

Son, unlike the other kin, has come to terms with the unethical methods used by his family in acquiring their wealth. His great-grandfather

was a Yankee carpetbagger who accumulated a vast estate during Reconstruction. His father, Charlie, who has just died, precipitated the need to
settle the estate. "Papa" managed the farms profitably but lived a promiscuous sexual life, fathering white and black offspring up and down the
railroad track. His wife, Stella, lost all respect and love for him. But Son
has made peace with this past and now wants to preserve the estate.

Son's wife-to-be, Lucy, will be a worthy mate to her honorable husband. She is an open-minded public school teacher, who extends an
olive branch to another member of the family by inviting Emily, the
daughter of Mary Jo, to be a member of the wedding party.

The most entertaining member of the Gordon family is Mary Jo, a
socialite from Houston who has borrowed $200,000 from the estate but
desperately needs more money. She and her good-natured husband, Bob,
have lost their house, and his real estate business is making no money.
They need funds to pay for the lavish second marriage of their daughter
Sissie. This couple arrives in Harrison, insisting that Son divide the estate to provide them money. Mary Jo has great dreams of selling an oil
lease to solve all her financial problems. When Lucy proposes that they
should all move in together like the Vietnamese, Mary Jo retorts, "I'm not
good at this communal living. I'm not Vietnamese and I'm not Korean"
(p. 170). She tells Lucille, her sister and Son's mother, who has never
worked a day in her life, that they could all "get a job at Whataburger"
(p. 172). She visualizes: "I can just see the four of us: Lucille, Sissie, Emily,
and me all working at Whataburger with brother's girlfriend" (p. 172).

On cue, the girlfriend, Irene Ratliff, arrives with Brother Lewis, who
now enters the consultation. Irene comes from the lower class, for whom
Mary Jo can barely conceal her disdain. Irene recalls that her father
struck oil and filled up his front yard with Reos, Packards, and Buicks,
all parked under "the Chinaberry trees." Lucille then remembers Irene's
father, the town's night watchman, John Moon: "I hadn't thought of
him for the longest kind of time." Lewis relates a common saying: "We
had this joke—John Moon only comes out at night." All this time, Mary
Jo has been hoping against hope that the financial crisis will be solved by
an oil lease: "Praying every night for my deliverance on bended knees.
Praying for an oil lease" (p. 173). Such is the character of formerly rich
families in Harrison, Texas, 1987.

Tony Mastroianni wrote a favorable review of the Great Lakes Theatre
Festival performance for the *Beacon Journal* of Akron, Ohio (October 17,
1990). Mastroianni noted that though Foote asked rather than answered

questions in the play, he accepted change, which is necessary for life to continue. The reviewer's assessment was that Lucy was played as both "bold and naive," and that her "new ideas from the outside world make the family's conversation sound like intellectual incest." Mastroianni wrote that Foote's style was "low key and utterly clear."

Talking Pictures, the first play offered by the Signature Company of New York, was composed as a screenplay in December 1986.[15] Lucy Kroll wrote Foote on October 27, 1988, that Eldon Elder found *Talking Pictures* "absolutely charming and warm" and, with its humor, "a marked contrast to the tragic qualities" in *The Habitation of Dragons.* Elder hoped that one day someone would produce them on alternate nights, because they are in "striking contrast" (HFC). The play, directed by John Ulmer, had its premiere at the Asolo Theatre, Sarasota, Florida, in April 1990. This involved melodrama, with many resemblances to soap opera, records the economic changes of the 1920s, especially the transformation from silent films to talking pictures in Harrison, Texas, 1927. Clips from *Ben Hur* and *The Four Horsemen of the Apocalypse* were used in the performance. Charlie Chaplin's dance with a dog introduces the farcical elements of the play (HFC).

The genesis of the play derived from a friend of Foote's whose mother played the piano for silent picture shows in Harrison. "The boy and his mother moved away one day," Foote said; "now I realize they must have left because talking pictures came in, and the mother lost her job." That memory and his personal knowledge of the mother's personality inspired *Talking Pictures* (*Sarasota Herald-Tribune,* April 15, 1990).

This play confronts once more the previous subject that so intrigued Foote: the displaced person's fate in the land of golden opportunity. It thus has a bittersweet tone, exploding the myth of American success, and takes the antibusiness view of Clifford Odets. In this particular slice of life, a goodhearted piano player at the picture show, Myra Tolliver, has become "a grass widow" with a young son Pete. She has fallen for Willis, a kind bricklayer who occupies the garage apartment next to the house where Myra lives. Unfortunately, Willis's wife, Gladys, will not grant him a divorce and arrives from Houston to bargain. Gladys and Willis haggle over what he will pay to get the divorce, which finally comes to $150.

The Jackson family, with whom Myra rooms, provides additional interest. One daughter, Vesta, dislikes Mexicans; another, Katie Bell, is friendly to a young Mexican Baptist, Estaquio, and argues with her father, who also dislikes Mexicans. As a schoolboy, Foote knew an adopted

Mexican boy named Estaquio (*Memoir*, p. 103). Foote makes him a likable if naive convert to Protestantism. Claiming that Jesus was a Baptist, Estaquio wants to start a Baptist church for Mexican immigrants. The picture show installs a sound system, causing Myra to lose her job as piano player. Willis pronounces the emphatic moral, which his mother always said: "We mustn't despair" (p. 216). Nor do he and Myra. They get married.

Talking Pictures transferred from the Asolo Theatre to the Stages Repertory Theatre of Houston in May 1991. Critics recognized that its popular elements resembled those on commercial television. They raised the interesting question of Foote's tendency toward soap opera, which appears unmistakably in *The Habitation of Dragons*, *Talking Pictures*, and later plays performed at the Signature Theatre of New York, like *Laura Dennis* (1995) and even *The Young Man from Atlanta* (1995).

Talking Pictures received mixed reviews in Florida and Houston. Jay Hendelman (*Sarasota Herald Tribune*, April 24, 1990) wrote: "Like a movie still being filmed, the final take has not been shot and like the characters in the play and the actors in the movies we all have another chance to get things right." In the *Tampa Tribune* (April 24, 1990), Porter Anderson commented: "Though a friend of the playwright, Ulmer misses the essence of unfancy Foote work: believability." Anderson thought that "the genius of Foote's scripts lies in the fact that very genuine, quirky people in small town America are experiencing trauma as severe as their comedic counterparts on the screen." But, according to Anderson, director Ulmer's production made them stage characters "as caricatured as the Valentino" shown in 1921 footage. In Houston, critic William Albright noted without approval the resemblance to sitcoms: "The frenzied Act One finale, in which the Jacksons calmly kibitz while Gladys's boyfriend waves his gun in Willis's face, is surefire if similarly sitcom-ish" (*Houston Post*, May 7, 1991).

The New York production was popular, making an auspicious beginning for Foote's retrospective of four plays in the crucial off-Broadway venue. The Signature Company performance received two very flattering write-ups in the *New York Times*. David Richards (September 27, 1994) wrote that despite its "dusty provincialism," the play dealt originally with "broken homes, heartbreak, [and] looming unemployment" in a way that only seemed old-fashioned. Vincent Canby (October 2, 1994) thought that Foote's best work discovers an America not unlike Edward Hopper's paintings. Foote's people profess Christian beliefs, yet they are threatened "by the temptation to surrender to despair," Canby noted. "They can't go on, they won't go on, they go on—sometimes raffishly, like Gladys, sometimes in quiet triumph, like Myra Tolliver." With the transfer of *Talking Pictures* to off-Broadway, Foote showed that he had always kept his eye on New York.

As Foote reached the end of his career, new readings appeared, showing that his plays had a continuing vitality. A group of critics applied current theory to his works in general and to particular plays. They proved that the last word had not been said on this playwright.

Writing about Foote's plays in general, Tim Wright discussed them in an essay entitled "More Real Than Realism: Horton Foote's Impressionism." Despite Foote's reputation for familiar scenes, Wright said, his work goes beyond "flat realism." In Foote's dramatic impressionism the "process becomes the focal point," Wright noted; "the plot is not a means to an end, but an end in itself." One critic, Ronald L. Davis, added that it was not the plot but the "details that grab me." [16]

Continuing the concept of impressionism in "To Be Quiet and Listen: *The Orphans' Home Cycle* and the Music of Charles Ives," Crystal Bryan noted that Foote had worked with "dancers and composers." Listening to the music of Ives while composing the *Cycle,* Foote was not passive but continually questioning "why the quote from a hymn, from a march?" In fact, many such "quotes" occur in *1918*. According to Bryan, Foote believes that music is one way of defining a place. [17]

In "Squeezing the Drama out of Melodrama: Plot and Counterplot in *Laura Dennis,*" Dean Mendell says that "you can't go home again, but one can if one learns how to make the journey." Dean notes that the character Laura remembers "a youthful time when life stopped seeming simple and delightful." [18] His reading in 1998 offers a fresh view of the play.

CHAPTER

16

AMAZING CLIMAX

THE YOUNG MAN FROM ATLANTA

FOOTE'S travels to theatres across the Hudson led propitiously to
Manhattan and finally Broadway itself. His reappearance in the city
was a triumph of his long career in the theatre. Fortunately, an enterprising off-Broadway company, the Signature Theater in the East Village, was
at this juncture featuring complete seasons of important playwrights.
Founded by James Houghton, this company staged seasons of four American playwrights. The first three were Romulus Linney (1991–1992), Lee
Blessing (1992–1993), and Edward Albee, with a run of his Pulitzer Prize–
winning *Three Tall Women* (1991), during the 1993–1994 season. The
1994–1995 season offered four new plays by Horton Foote: *Talking Pictures* (September 1994), *Night Seasons* (October 1994), *The Young Man
from Atlanta* (January 1995), and *Laura Dennis* (March 1995). Clearly
Foote was making a bold attempt to succeed in the national theatrical
center again, as he had many years ago with *The Trip to Bountiful* (1953)
and *The Traveling Lady* (1954). The four full-length plays by Foote were
highly praised. *The Young Man from Atlanta,* the standout of the series,
went on to successful runs in Chicago and ultimately Broadway (1997),
where this superior play won the acclaim of audiences and critics and
continued its life on the stage.

The sequential form of production enabled critics to assess Foote's total output and recognize his main themes and thought. They saw him in
depth and analyzed his plays, relating previous ones to the current. The
critics emphasized the value of the ensemble's cooperation. In the *New
York Times* there were accompanying articles about the playwright himself and about his daughter Hallie Foote, who starred in three of the four
plays presented. The critics noted Foote's career and gave knowledgeable

reviews. Vincent Canby reported on the series, as did Ben Brantley, both of the *New York Times.* The series started auspiciously with *Talking Pictures,* and in this sequence, one play, *The Young Man from Atlanta,* won the Pulitzer Prize in April 1995. That was the proper selection for the prize, since that play stands out in the series.

Efforts to stage *Night Seasons* began in the middle 1970s but did not reach fruition until 1993, four years after *Dividing the Estate.*[1] Lucy Kroll was working industriously in 1976 to get it produced. On June 14, 1976, she informed Foote that Alan Schneider had read *Night Seasons* and called it "a lovely play which grows on you." He asked if it had been submitted to the Arena Theatre in Washington, D.C.; it had been. Kroll sent the play on July 7, 1976, to Glenn Jordan of Santa Monica, who was editing the screenplay of "The Displaced Person"; she informed Foote on July 21, 1976, that *Night Seasons* had been mailed to many theatres, like the Alley and the Ford. It was turned down by the Mark Taper and the New York Shakespeare theatres (HFC).

On September 9, 1976, Kroll enclosed letters to Foote about *Night Seasons* from several theatres, saying that it was still at the Hartford Stage and the Alley, where Nina Vance was seriously interested. *Night Seasons* was like "a lament, a strong, moving play," Vance wrote on September 10, 1976, "It was poetic, poignant, and producible." Vance was giving it serious consideration for the season (HFC).

According to Kroll on September 9, 1976, Arthur Penn was also looking at it, and Alan Pakula had given his "wonderful and supportive comments." On September 17, 1976, the prestigious Circle Repertory Theatre in New York expressed interest in *Night Seasons.* On May 6, 1977, Kroll reported that Herbert Berghof, the first producer of the *Orphans' Home Cycle,* wanted to do a reading of *Night Seasons* in the fall at his studio and would call Foote directly. Despite these many signs of interest, *Night Seasons* had to wait till February 23, 1993, for its professional opening, with Foote directing, Hallie Foote taking the lead of Laura Lee, and Jean Stapleton playing the mother Josie. It was acted by the American Stage Company in Teaneck, New Jersey. Later it was produced by the Signature Company of New York, in September 1994.

Night Seasons returns to the same theme of many of Foote's one-acts of the 1980s: the lack of a home. Leaning toward tragedy, it experiments with flashbacks, starting in 1917 and reaching to 1963. The time moves back and forth between the present, 1963, when Laura Lee Weems dies, and the past, when she was courted by two suitors, neither of whom she married. The pathetic heroine comes from the Victorian era, having been born at the turn of the century, and she shows many of its qualities. She is intimidated by her parents, most especially the domineering mother, Josie, who stands in the way of her marriage. Going first with Mr. Chestnut, Laura Lee shows him a house plan she admires. He implores her to marry him, but the family objects because he is a lowly baker; they send him off to Houston to be trained as a banker, but he soon finds a more willing wife in the big city and prospers. Mr. Chestnut was not good enough for the Weems daughter; Laura admits that she was "scared" they could not live on his income in Houston (p. 109). She also had another beau with a beautiful voice, but no financial prospects. Mr. Barsoty left town, only sending back a card. When he returns, Laura is thirty-nine years old and desperate. She offers him a loan for his trucking business, but he is engaged to be married and leaves without the money.

Laura established no identity. In her scrapbook there is not one picture of her. The laughingstock of the town because she could never make a decision when shopping, Laura dies intestate. She developed no life of her own and could never make a decision to get married. Her indecisive life makes this play a tragedy full of sad crises, or "night seasons."

The title of *Night Seasons,* a double entendre, such as is often used by Foote, suggests periods of the night, when the most revealing experiences occur: the evening, middle of the night, and early in the morning while it is still dark. The characters suffer from sleeplessness. The tormented brother Lawrence shouts "I need money!" on the square during the night (p. 88).

After two failures to get married, Laura Lee plays bridge constantly and goes to the picture show in the evening. Symptomatically, she tells her younger brother: "I haven't been sleeping so well lately." She has trouble falling asleep, and when she does fall asleep, she wakes up: "I have a hard time getting back to sleep," she reports. In fact, she says, "I just don't sleep much nights" (p. 90). Laura tries pitifully to make a home of her own. Once again the family opposes her. Laura wants to move from their hotel apartment, but before she can start her own house, her father dies, and then all plans are off. Next, she wants to buy the small cottage of Mrs. Reeves, mother of Bubber Reeves in *The Chase,* but her brother Thurman says the price of $4,000 is too high, whereupon his bank obtains it for $1,000 less. Finally when Laura is sixty in 1963, she is laying plans to build her own house, even though she will have to share it with her despised mother. Too late, Laura collapses before her mother, is confined to a wheelchair, and dies before she can even write a $500 check long promised for Doris, the practical nurse, to repair her dilapidated house. Josie, the meddling mother, survives her daughter, Laura. At age ninety-three, she has been told by her son that she should live three more years to escape any estate taxes. She proclaims bitterly: "Living is to be my punishment" (p. 113). This mother shows the consequence of foolish greed and manipulation. The father, who resembles Mr. Vaughn, also stands in the way of Laura's getting married and establishing a home of her own.

Night Seasons, as performed by the Signature Company, received three appreciative reviews. Ben Brantley, in the *New York Times* (November 7, 1994) called the play "a lucid anatomy of a subject that has always obsessed the author: the elusiveness of the idea of home." Like *The Little Foxes,* Brantley wrote, the play follows a "mercenary" family over decades "of greed and the urge to dominate," adding that it slides "with only occasional signs of structural strain into a series of retrospective scenes." Vincent Canby, in a succeeding review in the *New York Times* (November 13, 1994), classified *Night* Seasons as "a big family play" with a thirteen-member cast. In "Two Footes Forward/Horton and Hallie: Signature Events" (*Commonweal,* January 13, 1995), Marian Burkhart commented on the experimental technique, saying, "The more realistic past is revealed through flashbacks, some clearly Josie's memories." She noted that the scenes involve characters' younger selves, singing the old-fashioned songs that should mean "community." Burkhart praised Hallie Foote for being a collaborator as well as a star.

Laura Dennis is the fourth and last play presented by the Signature Company.[2] It was performed in March 1995, with Hallie Foote playing the part of Velma, a dissipated middle-aged woman. This long one-act, which may be accurately likened to a soap opera, resembles *Talking Pictures,* except that the cast consists of relatives, unlike the more diverse cast in the earlier play. The time is 1938, the decade of *Habitation of Dragons,* and also concentrates on marital infidelity and interfamily complications. Taking place entirely in Harrison, it recalls Foote's earliest one-acts, like *Wharton Dance,* with its teenagers and their tortured relations with adults. The name "Dennis" should be noted, since this is the family that allegedly stole the Hortons' ancestral property, a name not previously used by Foote. By this time the Dennis line has fallen in social rank, though they still own much property in the country, from which they can profit by an oil lease.

This play resumes Foote's favorite topic of the nonexistent home. The principal characters all suffer from the lack of a home, which robs them of any meaningful family life. Laura has moved in with a substitute family, Lena Abernathy's family in Harrison, because her father, Roscoe Dennis, has died and her mother, Cynthia, has departed for South Dakota, where, remarried, she has two children. Lena, a seamstress, provides a residence for the half-orphan Laura, whose upkeep is funded by her uncle Edward Dennis.

This melodrama is less interesting than *Talking Pictures* because it does not examine an important social issue: technological change. Furthermore, there is no compelling character, like Myra the accompanist, to hold our attention among the falling members of the Dennis dynasty.

This play, set in the 1930s, has the soap opera quality of Foote's plays like *The Chase* and *The Habitation of Dragons,* with sexual immorality and sensational violence because of amorous conflicts and with the men escaping punishment for their homicides. Foote writes this type of play many times. It evidently transcribes the violence of small-town Texas that upsets lives but is somehow surmounted.

Laura Dennis is neither tragedy nor comedy but rather a combination of both, with a lot of melodramatic additions. The life is sordid, and the language is cruder than Foote ordinarily uses.

When Ethel sees Velma, a cousin of Laura's, drinking out of a bottle of whiskey and tries to take it from her, Velma cries, "Go to hell!" Then she sees Seymour, Ethel's boyfriend, starting out and asks, "Where are you going?"

Seymour: Away from you.
Velma: Go to hell. Everybody go to hell. (She looks at Lena.)
Velma: You know that old husband of yours was always saying you were sleeping with Laura's daddy, my cousin (p. 76).

The reviewers did the best they could in assessing *Laura Dennis*. Jan Stuart in *New York Newsday* (March 13, 1995) said that the final offering of the Signature Theater's showcase is "a bit of a comedown." Ben Brantley in the *New York Times* (March 6, 1995) wrote that this was "not the strongest" of the four productions and that Harrison was beginning to look like a "Down-home Peyton Place." Brantley added, however, that even Mr. Foote's "lesser works" provided "a visceral richness actors thrive on." Clive Barnes (*New York Post,* March 14, 1995) remarked that the more one sees, the more one appreciates in Foote's work "its rich and uniquely American tradition." He pointed out that Laura lives in a town of friends, relatives, "and quiet violence," where people mostly survive, "but at a price." He concluded that the play was written in a simple mode with "no real moral, except to say life is difficult at best, hell at worst, and survival is only a temporary blessing."

Vernon Early, which opened in May 1998 at the Shakespeare Festival Theatre in Montgomery, Alabama, presents again members of the Dennis clan in fascinating but soap-opera fashion. Nevertheless, Foote writes about human nature as it appears today and analyzes the society, people, and individuals he knows well.

The Young Man from Atlanta takes place in 1950 in the big city of Houston.[3] It is a sequel to *Roots in a Parched Ground, Lily Dale,* and *Cousins,* plays of the *Orphans' Home Cycle.* Again the husband and wife exhibit the business drive of Will Kidder, plus the mindless garrulity of Lily Dale. In *Cousins* we learned that the couple was comfortably ensconced in a fine house of Houston; now they are moving into another luxurious residence. Most important, Will has become a fully developed character, which he was not in *Lily Dale.*

Accordingly, this play clearly stands out from the other three, since it features Will Kidder, the tragic father who loses his son to suicide, as well as losing his job at the age of sixty-four. He gives this play focus. The play contains humor in the subplot of the Disappointment Clubs and a nine-person cast with some other entertaining parts, including Lily Dale's.

Will believes that he lives in the best city and country in the world, but the main event presented is the loss of his son, Bill, from drowning. Although it brings to mind the deaths of Leonard's two little boys in *The Habitation of Dragons,* the tragedy of Will's son is more complex. We learn that Bill, not knowing how to swim, walked into a Florida pond at noon. The son of the real Will and Lily, who worked for a Georgia electronics company, actually died in this way (*Memoir,* p. 119). Like many writers, Foote started with a truthful event but altered it for dramatic purposes. Eventually Will acknowledges that his son committed suicide. The cause, it also becomes clear, was a homosexual liaison that he formed with Randy Carter, his roommate in Atlanta. Randy, whose allegorical name (a favorite device of Foote's) suggests sexual aggression, blackmailed Bill into paying him "a hundred thousand dollars" (p. 109), some of which his father had openly given him and some his mother had given him sur-reptitiously. Randy lied that he needed the money to care for his sister's nonexistent children.

As the play advances, Will reveals to himself and the audience how he lost his son. Like Leonard Tolliver, Will was a workaholic who spent little time with his son. What was worse, he wanted his son to be "like me" (p. 105), trying without success to make a baseball player out of him. In the psychological climax of the play, Will undergoes self-discovery. He wanted his son to be like him but never tried "to understand what he was like." He relates a typical conversation: "How was your day? Fine, son, how was yours?" In other words, he wished to mold him according to his own liking, not Bill's. The consequence was, Will admits, "I was never close to him" (p. 105). As Rebecca Briley cogently argues, the central theme in Foote's plays is the indispensability of a loving father-son rela-tionship, evident also in *Tender Mercies* and the adaptations *Tomorrow* and *To Kill a Mockingbird*.[4]

Also, Foote makes a striking addition to the riddle of homosexuality as treated by O'Neill and Williams, who similarly emphasize the influ-ence of the Oedipus complex by highlighting the mother's impact on the son's sexuality. In this play, Foote attributes the son's sexual orientation to the father. Foote is innovative in seeing the father's role as more influential. This theory makes Will Kidder a more interesting personage. Appropriately he assumes responsibility for the tragic end of his son: "I failed him, Lily Dale. Some way I failed him." Now he can only cry out, "I want my son back, Lily Dale. I want him back" (p. 105).

The question of Bill's sexuality and particularly Foote's analysis of it are central to an understanding of this play, first performed in 1995, when homosexuality was a major subject of American life as well as the theatre.[5] What is the context? It was treated earlier in American drama by Edward Albee in *The Zoo Story* (1959), where Jerry's homosexuality is clearly implied, though "the love that does not speak its name" is not named. Neither the words "homosexual" nor "gay" are openly spoken in Albee's play, as they are not in this play. The subject arises in *Cat on a Hot Tin Roof* (1955), where the leading male, Brick, tries to come to grips with his latent homosexuality. In *Suddenly Last Summer* (1957), Tennessee Williams, by now openly gay, presents a very unflattering portrayal of the predatory Sebastian Venable, who is literally devoured for his homosex-ual acts. By 1978, in Harvey Fierstein's *Torch Song Trilogy,* the homosexual is identified as such, and sympathy is extended to him.

The Young Man from Atlanta, like other plays by Foote, echoes themes from previous plays. Bill Kidder, the son of Will and Lily Dale, is another displaced person, having moved, probably for sexual reasons, from Houston to Atlanta, where he holds an unknown job and lives the anonymous life of a boardinghouse occupant. We learn that he became a close friend of Randy Carter's. Randy received large sums, for which Will discovered the cancelled checks in Bill's safety deposit box, "all made out to his friend" (p. 109). Since the purposes were kept clandestine, one concludes they were blackmail payments to conceal the two men's homosexual bond.

The ignorance of Bill's homosexuality also shows the apparent calm of American life. All seems happy in the affluent Kidder household, which in reality harbors deception between husband and wife. Lily Dale, who has refused to face reality in her previous appearances, does so most subversively here, since she calls her son's drowning an accident.

Though Foote does not make an attack on the gay lifestyle, there is an indictment of one individual's impact on the lives of others. Foote has shown his compassion for the pathetic homosexual before, in Mr. Billy Edgar's son of *Valentine's Day,* who is whipped unmercifully for cross-dressing. Here Foote honestly shows the upheaval of homosexual life and the pain it can cause. It leads to a man's rejection of himself, loss of his family, and finally death. Foote's compassion, which he never abandons, goes out not only to the parents but also to Bill Kidder himself. He tried to be a good son and loved his parents, but when the secret became too painful, he took his life.

Besides the tantalizing plot line, this play features a powerful character, Will Kidder, constituting in effect another plot. As Foote has observed, Will Kidder and his wife, Lily Dale, both reemerge after Lily Dale was seen in three plays of the *Orphans' Home Cycle,* and Will in two (p. x). The latter has become a rounded character, which sets this play apart from the others.

Will was a salesman for a wholesale supplier, but he surmounts his obsession with bigness and accepts a much lesser position. Lily Dale is still a neurotic, superficial person. She has become a religious fanatic, dwells on her illusion about Mrs. Roosevelt, and gives money to her son's friend.

The faithful companion of Will in this domestic tragedy, Lily Dale, is essential to our full understanding of the family triangle. The real Lily Dale was based on Lily Dale Coffee, Foote's aunt. She was the only person that Hallie Foote disliked, according to Hallie's son. We learn from

Foote that Lily Dale and her husband, Uncle Will, dressed in expensive clothes to impress the Footes (*Memoir,* pp. 118, 280). In the play she is a familiar type, the idle southern wife whose mindless chatter makes her a comic figure, providing much needed relief. Though a type, she is a believable character and adds to our understanding of a tragic family.

Lily Dale's previous relationship with Bill is not recounted at length but can be inferred from her character and newfound attachment to a substitute son, Randy. Soon after Bill's death, Randy began to influence Lily Dale in much the same way that Bill had. A weak person, she felt sorry for Randy's misfortunes and indulged him. This was also her mistake with Bill. She spoiled her son, while her husband neglected him. Hearing from Randy falsely that Bill has become religious and prays loudly all the time in the boardinghouse, she takes this as a reason for becoming religious herself.

Adding to the portrayal of Lily Dale is her unwillingness to recognize lies and admit the truth. In the most humorous passages of the play, she recalls the Disappointment Clubs, allegedly organized by the South's worst enemy, Eleanor Roosevelt, who persuaded the black cooks of Houston not to report for work. There were in fact warnings in the South that black women were forming "Eleanor Clubs," whose slogan was "to put a white woman in every kitchen by 1943."[6] It is clear, however, that this possibility is considered erroneous by Foote. Even after Lily Dale's present cook, Clara, and former employee, Etta Doris, have both confirmed that they never heard of or supported such clubs, Lily Dale retains her unshakable conviction. The refusal to face truth takes on a more serious tone as Lily Dale continues to believe that Bill's drowning was an accident, thus preventing realistic adjustment to a fact. When Will finally says that Bill killed himself, she can only answer reproachfully, "What a terrible thing to say about your son" (p. 104).

Lily Dale did not tell Will that she gave Randy the large sums her husband now needs to start his own business, causing him to suffer a heart attack. Feeling guilty because of her deception, she admits concealing the truth from him another time. She and Mary Thornton invited two men home when Will was out of town, implying her loneliness, but did not tell him. Conveniently, she forgets the deception she has been practicing on her husband by giving money to Bill's friend. Along with her indulgence of Bill, her inability to face the truth about her substitute son confirms this mother's complicity in the tragedy of her son's life.

Lily Dale's religious sentimentality, seen earlier in reliance on fortune-tellers in *Cousins,* points to her weak Christian faith. When she describes Bill's death to Clara, saying she has become "a nervous wreck," this maid and confidant asks where her Christian faith is and tells her that God is "going to take care of you" as "He takes care of me" (p. 52).

Lily Dale, while not a villainess, causes some real anguish, like her husband's loss of his savings. But Lily Dale and Will, cohorts of the 1890s, will preserve their marriage, picking up the pieces and going ahead with their lives. Lily Dale will even resume piano teaching, though there is no sign of her forgetting the Disappointment Clubs.

Foote settles the question of how people live with a harsh truth: they avoid it. Will ends the play, offering the assurance that "everything is going to be all right" (p. 110). Lily Dale and he choose ambiguity with regard to their son and his friend. They will make an acceptable future for themselves and not return to the disturbing question of their son's life. In this case, Foote does not choose the stance of his old mentor Ibsen, which is to face the truth whatever it may be. The young man from Atlanta takes money from Bill till the end. If Foote ever pictured an Iago, it is Randy Carter.

In *The Young Man from Atlanta* we get the final and most thorough portrayal of Lily Dale. Now it comes out that she has lied over and over to Will, saying that she has not been seeing Bill's friend and has not been near him before Bill's suicide, when in fact she gave more and more money to Randy, which originally came from Will.

Truth versus lying is another way of putting the truth-versus-illusion theme. After learning what Carson (another Atlantan and the nephew of Lily Dale's stepfather, Pete) has said about Randy—that Randy has lied about his mother's death and about Bill's praying—Randy labels Carson's words lies to the credulous Lily Dale, whose acceptance of falsehoods has increased by this time. When Lily Dale speaks of Bill's praying to Randy, she says, "Pete's nephew said you made that up." According to her, Randy, whom we never see, retorted, "He is a liar," adding, "Ask anybody back at the boardinghouse who tells lies and who tells the truth" (pp. 100–101). Here Randy reaches the apex of his lying, appealing to absent witnesses, an old device.

Finally Lily Dale reports this exchange to Will, whose reaction confirms Randy's untruthfulness. Randy claims to have given money to his sister and her three small children. Will says, "All lies, as we know now"

(p. 103). Lily Dale repeats what Randy said, "Carson was the liar." Randy was jealous of Carson because of his friendship with Bill (p. 105). She persists, asking Will who they are to believe: Carson or Randy? Randy asks to see Will again and tells Will that he, Randy, is not a liar, "that every word he has said is the truth," that Bill was very religious and prayed out loud so that everyone in the boardinghouse could hear him. Lily Dale "cried" as Randy was telling her this and adds, "I feel so sorry for him" (p. 106). Will refuses to speak to Randy. After her last telephone call, Lily Dale says Randy is "a sweet boy" (p. 110).

Lily Dale, with the poetic name, is as familiar as a magnolia blossom in the southern garden. She is a sister of Blanche Dubois with her manipulations, of Regina Giddens with her selfish treachery, and of Mrs. Compson, a selfish mother who destroyed her family in *The Sound and the Fury*. Graceful as the coquettish Scarlett O'Hara, she is an unconscious product of her society that admires saccharine language and a pretty face. A product of feminine southern society, she is therefore not wholly responsible, nor guilty of deliberate sin. She is ambiguous but undeniably destructive.

Foote's last and climactic manifestation of the truth-versus-illusion theme dominates this play, a theme that comes to light no less than fifty years after its appearance in *The Glass Menagerie*. Foote is blunt and explicit. Lily Dale believes Randy's falsehood that Bill died a believer. Randy enables Lily Dale to exist in a world of illusion where wishful thinking rules. She makes her adjustment to Bill's suicide by denying it and finding comfort in the soothing stories of Bill's happy existence in Atlanta.

There can be no doubt about Randy's place on the truth-illusion continuum. He is untruthful, one of Foote's bald liars, like Brother in *1918*. He is a calculating young man, who happens to be gay, though there is no condemnation of homosexuality as such. The question of Randy's lying, however, is answered forthrightly. Will says that he found canceled checks amounting to $100,000 all made out to Bill's friend, allegedly for his sick mother and sister. Will doesn't believe the checks were for them but says, "whatever the reasons I don't want to know" (p. 104).

Besides Randy, the other enigmatic young man is Carson. He arrives from Atlanta and tells his story; he wins the support of his uncle Pete, Lily Dale's stepfather, who will underwrite his education at the University of Georgia. Foote finds redeeming qualities in the most unlikely persons, such as the formerly mean-spirited Pete. Most noticeably, Carson accuses Randy of being a liar and in turn is called a liar by Randy. In this drama of charges and countercharges, who are we to believe? Carson admires Bill but denies that Bill is religious, as the credulous Lily Dale believes. Pete considers Carson "a fine boy" (p. 76). Carson comments that Bill's portrait, the centerpiece of the set, is not accurate; Bill was actually thin and "stoop-shouldered" (p. 81). It is my conclusion that Carson is truthful; Randy is patently a liar.

The Young Man from Atlanta ran twenty-six performances at the tiny off-Broadway Signature Theatre and won the 1995 Pulitzer Prize for Drama. In this production, Carlin Glynn played Lily Dale, Ralph Waite played Will, and Pete Masterson, Foote's cousin, directed. Plans were soon laid for a Broadway premiere, but that event, to the dismay of reviewers like Frank Rich, was postponed. It eventually was given a tryout in Chicago and soon after was presented on Broadway, a stunning success for Foote, given that no play of his had played there since *The Traveling Lady* in 1954.

This excellent work ran from January 20 through March 1, 1997, at the Goodman Theatre of Chicago. There it was directed by Robert Falls and attracted two big names for the leading roles: Rip Torn as Will Kidder and Shirley McKnight as Lily Dale. It was thought that for this major production bigger names were needed than had appeared in the off-Broadway performance.

The response in Chicago was mixed. There was much high praise for a play that was of Pulitzer Prize caliber, though there were also dismissive judgments such as the view that the play was "old-fashioned." This play provoked a large number of feature stories on radio and television, which showed the growing fame of Horton Foote. There was praise for McKnight's interpretation, with less for Rip Torn's. Uncertainty was evident as to how the work would fare in New York. Reviers felt that the subject of homosexuality was not clarified. The theme of loss was recognized, however. This was a recurring topic for Foote, who handled it knowingly, having recently lost his wife. Several critics disliked the lack of an intermission, and one was inserted between scenes 3 and 4 in the New York performance.

Though evaluations by truly perceptive critics are hard to discover among the reviewers in Chicago, two of those reviewers made valuable observations. Andrew Patner of the *Chicago Sun-Times* (January 28, 1997) commented on the often mentioned subject of homosexuality. He believed that the couple's denial of the "son's homosexuality" was done with "an indirection" that makes Tennessee Williams' treatment fifty years before seem "positively explicit." Richard Christiansen (*Chicago Tribune,* January 29, 1997) recognized convincingly that the wife had the best and most interesting part. He wrote that Torn brought too much of his television situation comedy to the role, but McKnight "unperturbed by such baggage is perfect in every nuance, right down to her neatly polished fingernails." He added, "This is Lily Dale's play and McKnight makes it a memorable one." I would add that it is essential, as with Jessie Mae, to have an actress with a talent for comedy in this role.

After a promising run in Chicago, Foote's engrossing domestic drama, with perceptive commentary on contemporary American life, opened in New York at the Longacre Theatre on March 27, 1997. There was widespread commentary by reviewers in newspapers, television, and radio shows. The best reviews were written by two experienced critics of the theatre. Clive Barnes (*New York Post,* March 28) extolled, "This is that rare thing, a living play about living—and it brings luster to Broadway." Ben Brantley (*New York Times,* March 28) said the actors conveyed "the sense of an internal furnace of pain and anxiety. . . . The effect is that of a short story with the soul of tragedy." Brantley noted that the house was again dominant. Here "the plaid-curtained, shiny surfaced living room set" was "a monument to period consumerism" of the affluent American family in postwar America.

Despite the praise, many of the reviews were negative. Linda Winder in *Newsday* (March 28) felt that the son's homosexuality, though never mentioned, hung over the play like "a shameful, toxic shroud." With some justice, she observed that "the mystery of the son's death is never made current enough for today."

Some critics found Carson ambiguous, despite convincing evidence that the character is truthful. Clive Barnes called him Pete's "probably unscrupulous nephew" (*New York Post,* March 28). Linda Winder said that Bill was "a sharp cookie" who had "a possible mirror image in Carson" (*Newsday,* March 28). Al Boswell, reviewing the performance in Chicago, wrote that Carson "appears youthfully entrapping" (*Gary Info,* January 30, 1997). These critics failed to see that Carson tells the truth in diametric contrast to Randy, whom Will, but not the credulous Lily Dale, recognizes as a liar.

As the play continued its run, an advertisement in the *New York Times* for May 11, 1997, announced that it had received three Tony Award nominations, including the nomination for Best Play. *USA Today* on March 31, 1997, declared that Shirley McKnight was "Tony Award material." However, this prediction did not prove true. The glittering Tony Award, which abruptly ended the run of *The Young Man from Atlanta,* went in 1997 to Alfred Uhry's popular *The Last Night of Ballyhoo* (*New York Times,* May 11, 1997).

Produced at the end of his career when Foote was seventy-nine, this play was beautifully crafted. Foote gave *The Young Man from Atlanta* a novel twist with its absent villain. This play considers the sociological issue of the obsessed businessman, as Marian Burkhardt noted in citing Will's dream of having the best and the biggest.[7] Vincent Canby in the *New York Times* (January 30, 1995) called the play one of Foote's most "serious and scathing works," and after the Pulitzer Prize was awarded to the play, Frank Rich (*New York Times,* April 23, 1995) pointed out its portrayal of the "psychic fissures" just below the surface of middle-class American life.

This play is Foote's last as a masterful playwright, utilizing all his imaginative and dramaturgical powers. Conceptualized three times, Lily Dale takes her rightful place as one of Foote's best creations.

During the 1980s, Horton Foote began to look back at his long career. In 1985, Penelope Niven McJunkin, his first bibliographer, printed "The Horton Foote Collection," subtitled "McJunkin Inventory, Title Index." She stated that "learning about real people tells us how a creative writer transforms real people into imaginary ones in creative work." McJunkin included a valuable list of letters from Foote's most significant correspondents: Herbert Berghof, Robert Duvall, Lillian Gish, Tennessee Williams, Agnes de Mille, Helen Hayes, Fred Coe, Elia Kazan, and Cornel Wilde. Lucy Kroll wrote Foote that she was happy his papers were being organized (HFC, June 18, 1985). This collection was acquired by DeGolyer Library at Southern Methodist University and is currently under the direction of curator Kay Bost.

In the 1980s, invitations to Foote rose, and they continued to increase in the 1990s. In 1984 he was honored in his hometown: the mayor of Wharton proclaimed May 30, 1984, as Horton Foote Day. Foote received an award at the Lone Star Celebration, January 22, 1986, and was playwright in residence at the Kentucky Playwrights Festival, March 23, 1987. On April 21, 1987, he lectured at Goucher College. Southern Methodist University invited him to a campus seminar on November 11 and 12, 1987.

By the late 1980s, Foote's reputation had expanded so greatly that he became more in demand as a speaker. He appeared on *The Today Show* and *Good Morning, America;* articles on him were published in *People, Ultra,* and *Texas Monthly.* On May 12, 1988, poet Fred Chappell thanked Foote, whom he called "the best southern dramatist," for accepting membership in the Fellowship of Southern Writers. On November 16, 1988, Foote lectured at the University of Texas at Austin. In 1989 he received the Lifetime Achievement Award at the annual William Inge Theatre Festival, where a performance of *The Land of the Astronauts* was given.

Alone, an original teleplay based on Foote's life after his wife's death, was presented on Showtime in 1997. It starred Hume Cronyn, James Earl Jones, and Piper Laurie.

Foote has received still more attention in the 1990s and 2000s. Although he has not had a hit in that time, the bulk of his work and the length of his career have reached a critical mass. He is now better known, and some works like *Tender Mercies* and *The Young Man from Atlanta* have drawn much interest. There is a clearly defined audience for "a Foote play"—educated, connected to a small town, and seeking entertainment that is not radical, nor filled with four-letter words and immoral persons, drugs, and sex without love. Furthermore Foote is receiving more attention from academics in books and articles, which has led to further scholarly interest. He has attracted both popular and academic audiences.

On March 12, 1994, my wife and I visited Wharton, two days before Horton Foote's birthday. Hallie Foote arrived from Los Angeles, and Foote's second daughter, Daisy, was also there. Foote stays part of the year at his Wharton residence on North Houston Street. At other times he resides in the East Village of New York City, which is his favorite city outside Texas. In Wharton there is a Horton Foote Drive, and two streets named Brooks and Dennis. Hamburgers can be ordered in a Whataburger restaurant. At the former site of Sycamore Grove, no grand mansion remains. On the grounds there is only a small family cemetery, marked with the name "Dennis." Foote said that when the house was torn down by the owner, "the whole town was in an uproar."

Foote directed *When They Speak of Rita,* by his daughter Daisy Foote, at Primary Stages in New York in May–July 2000, and Hallie Foote took the part of Rita (*New York Times,* May 14, 2000). Horton Foote's play *The Day Emily Married* was performed July 21–30, 2000, at the Robinson Theatre, Whittier College, in Whittier, California. This work was written in the early 1960s and is set in the mid-1950s, when oil was replacing cotton (articles in the *Los Angeles Times,* July 2000).

AMAZING CLIMAX: *THE YOUNG MAN FROM ATLANTA*

Kelly Kline, Foote's secretary in Wharton, says that Foote has some close kindred still living there. Kline keeps up with his children. Hallie is living and acting in Los Angeles. The other three children reside in New York City, where Daisy is a playwright. Hallie and Daisy continue the theatrical tradition initiated by their father.[8]

CONCLUSION

THE ACHIEVEMENT OF HORTON FOOTE

FOOTE'S work in film will keep his reputation alive. Most audiences will know him through television and movies, not through his stage plays. His best works on film are *The Trip to Bountiful, Tomorrow, Courtship,* and *Tender Mercies* and can be seen on videotape and television. The first stands out because of its three leading characters and haunting theme. Among legitimate plays, it is the best he has composed.

Too many previous discussions of Foote's plays are not knowledgeable. They often appear in journalistic interviews. For that reason, I have felt that a larger study was needed to provide fuller analyses. In the present book, I have tried to see Foote as a whole and explain his main themes. I show that he belongs to the new explorations of southern cultures, which include Texas. Foote knows and portrays southern personalities like the never surrendering Confederates (Soll Gautier of *Convicts*) as well as the social climbers of Houston (Mary Jo of *Dividing the Estate*).

In a final assessment of Foote, we should enumerate his unique assets and accomplishments. To start, he is preeminently the observer of Texas and the reporter of its life. With his plays, we acquire a more nuanced understanding of small-town Texas. Since this state, previously a nation, is enormous, we as Americans need a better grasp of its "ancient time" (anything before 1963), as Don Graham argues in *Texas: A Literary Portrait*.[1] Texas writers, even Katherine Anne Porter, have not given a thorough, broad analysis equal to what Foote has supplied. Of course there is some disadvantage in learning of a place in disparate plays written over a period of fifty years. But that difficulty can be surmounted. We must always keep in mind Foote's mythical town of Harrison. Foote lets us know the good qualities of friendliness, support for the stranger, and kindness, as shown in *The Traveling Lady,* for example. He makes clear the close connection of Southeast Texas with the larger South. We recognize the Texas variation of the Confederate heritage, the agricultural economy, and the centrality of religion, especially the Baptist dominance. Texas was behind other southern states in supplanting agriculture and Victorian customs, like the patriarchy and teetotalism. It preserved the dominance of Protestant religion through its many Baptists and Methodists. The southern connection must always be taken into account. In modern times, Texas has become like the rest of America, but more quickly than the rest of the South. The boom of big cities, like Houston and Dallas, and the breakdown of family solidarity have proceeded faster and more ominously, as seen in *The Road to the Graveyard.*

The writers with whom Foote has most in common derive from the South. The decline of the landed aristocracy, its clash with technology, and the inhumanity of business transcribe this change in Texas terms, which resemble those in Mississippi. But Faulkner's heroes are more preoccupied with the sin of slavery. The Texans must cope with oil fever; the new rich of *Dividing the Estate* show modern ugliness without the signs of grace in Faulkner's South.

Like Faulkner, Foote is a comprehensive writer who covers a long period of time and a great variety of characters. The former surveys the time from antebellum days to the late 1940s with *Intruder in the Dust.* Foote covers the Civil War days and afterward, with great emphasis on Victorian times during the turn of the century, but he goes further into modern times with urban post–World War II life than does Faulkner. Both attempt to survey and appraise a long historical period.

Tennessee Williams, a fellow southerner, makes a natural pair with Foote, though the former concentrates on the singular, unconventional southerner, whereas Foote specializes in the average, conventional one. By division of labor, the two join to describe those two sides of the southern character. As for likeness, their insights into southern women are most arresting. Williams is at his best when depicting high-strung, neurotic women like Blanche and Amanda. Foote runs him a close second in capturing the idle, gabby wife like Jessie Mae and Lily Dale. The self-centeredness and tendency to hysteria appear strongly in all of these women, who reflect the psychological neuroses and often hilarious talkativeness of southern women.

What are Foote's contributions to dramatic writing? He has been a leader in standing for artistic freedom—an urgent need in America and an important force toward that end. Foote liked early television because producers did not interfere with him, freeing him to write some of the best television plays. He later turned his back on commercial movies.

In the 1970s, Foote wrote the monumental *Orphans' Home Cycle* of nine plays—an ambitious venture with little hope of popular success. But he had a plan and stuck to it. He pioneered in independent filmmaking with artistic films from this cycle of plays and produced others that eventually showed on television. Leading the way to independent filmmaking, he produced landmark works with *Tender Mercies* and *The Trip to Bountiful*. He is one of the leading playwrights to turn his original conceptions into films that are faithful to the originals. *Bountiful* is true to his picture of a troubled old woman, desolate in an urban hell. It retains essentially the realism, social comment, and exploration of the central subject of re-turning home that was expounded in the play.

Foote should be praised for his longtime cultivation of one-acts. Along with black dramatists, such as Amiri Baraka and Douglas Turner Ward, Foote adds first-rate examples, like *Land of the Astronauts* and *The Oil Well*. He has composed some of the best television plays, like *A Young Lady of Property*, whose performance record proves its merit. Despite the dis-paraging remarks of Gerald Weales in *American Drama since World War II* (1962), Foote is not just one of "The Video Boys," an ill-chosen term used by that critic.[2] Nor is Foote a social activist in the long run; he chooses to study people, not to advocate political changes. Instead he is "a social writer," in the sense that he records impartially the mores and sentiments of a distinct society—small-town Texas. Following Porter, Foote strives above all for objectivity. He aims for the truth, like Ibsen, always being careful not to tip the scales, as he narrates the annals of his family, the Hortons, the Brookses, and his father especially. By recog-nizing the truth of their lives, we gain a better understanding of complex human beings, with all their faults and redeeming traits.

Although Foote has written many adaptations for the stage and movies, we must distinguish between *Tomorrow* and all the rest. He was careful after his first movie adaptations to choose only the best works, like O'Connor's short story. But none of them is the equal of *Tomorrow*. This is as much one of Foote's creations as it is Faulkner's. The dramaturgy is Foote's own. Deservedly, the teleplay and the film have become classics. It is true that Faulkner cannot be improved, but he did not write a play nor film of "Tomorrow." Foote, however, knew how to enhance that author in a play and a film with the leading characters who are Faulknerian but also in Foote's style. The characters derive from the country spirit of pride and hope that Foote added to this man and woman.

Foote is fundamentally an optimistic writer. He considers the Theatre of the Absurd to be the Theatre of Despair. The world, most of the time, is not headed to extinction. The strength of women like Elizabeth and men like Will Kidder will sustain it. Foote always retains hope.

Foote is accused of being undramatic, low-key, and noncommittal, an opinion Brooks Atkinson, despite early compliments, leveled at him. The charge has stuck with people for whom Foote is not to their taste. Reviewers like John Simon will never give him a dime. Indeed, Foote is quiet in *Bountiful,* the *Orphans' Home Cycle,* and his best plays, but he had strong convictions and would not change his tone to shrillness in order to attract a big audience. An appreciation of Foote's quiet manner and understated humor is an acquired taste. But the subtext, as in *Young Man,* is powerful and insistent. The endurance and resiliency of Leonard in *The Habitation of Dragons* are real.

At the end of his career, Foote proved he could still fashion a serious melodrama, with interesting characters and a provocative plot—that is, how a couple copes with the loss of their only son. *The Young Man from Atlanta* is a true picture of modern urban life.

Speaking of Foote's complete career, what were his goals? First, he wished to be a successful playwright on Broadway. Second, he aimed at making a hit. He tried with *The Trip to Bountiful* but fell short. The third goal was to write a moral and social history of Harrison, his mythical town of Southeast Texas. That he accomplished. His saga of Harrison, Texas, is his lasting glory—it still stands today. Foote drew on his family in creating characters, like Horace Robedaux and many others. He was always inventive and insightful in delineating them. Out of people he knew intimately, he drew imaginary characters who were at the same time true to life.

By the exemplars of courage and adjustment to change, Foote illuminates moral themes. He shows many examples of making poor choices and of harmful behavior, like that of Brother Vaughn. By bringing these characters to life, Foote develops his thinking on destructive individuals, as well as positive and courageous ones. Foote is a reliable observer of human nature and a past master of enlivening imaginary characters.

This study of Foote's career has not slighted information on his life and personality as a human being, and rightly so. His heart is as big as Texas. Many authors are remembered for their fascinating personalities, like Tennessee Williams. Horton Foote, on the other hand, has not led a sensational life. He remained married to the same woman and lives half of the year in the home of his birth.

Directors, actors, and even critics have developed admiration of Foote as a man, which has helped them appreciate his works. When serving as a presenter at the Kennedy Center Honors for the Performing Arts in 1998, Robert Duvall, who played Soll Gautier in *Convicts* and Mac Sledge in *Tender Mercies,* ad-libbed, "Let's not forget the great Horton Foote." Foote has held to his artistic convictions—the integrity of the playwright and his wonder at human endurance. By persistence in writing serious, honest plays, he has earned the respect and acclaim of many within and without the theatrical world.

Now that I have given an evaluation of Foote as a playwright, I would like to add an observation of Foote as a human being. His thoughtful consideration has touched the lives of scores of people. Among them are the great: Robert Duvall, Helen Hayes, and the critic Frank Rich. But also he has become known to many others, like the fans who have written him letters and the people of Wharton who have honored him on Horton Foote Day.

Foote has all his life been a loyal Texan. He has a great love for his home state. Foote has always followed politics, like his father who was a "yellow-dog Democrat." Foote abhors dishonesty and hypocrisy and wants to help the downtrodden in any way he can. He has been a true supporter and friend of African Americans and Mexican Americans. One need only view the film *To Kill a Mockingbird* and the play *Talking Pictures* to recognize that fact.

One also recognizes the benevolent nature of Foote. He is ambitious but never forgets obligations to his friends and family. And he has learned from bitter experience to forgive. He is deeply sensitive to the pains of others, as shown in the attempt to assist his alcoholic uncles.

Now Foote has become a vigorous elder statesman in the realm of the theatre. He reminds me of Verdi, who kept composing operas into an advanced age. He is a singular figure. If you see him, he is likely wearing his light-colored trench coat. That trademark is not pretentious, as Foote is not. When he meets fans, he smiles thoughtfully, and you know he is listening.

Seeing Horton Foote whole is no easy task, given his long and rich life. Unlike many other writers, Foote stands out for his character as well as his dramatic achievements. His qualities as a man combine with those as a playwright to make him an American original. We see him as television pioneer, sensitive recorder of Texas life, analyst of the South, prolific lecturer, famed screenwriter of *To Kill a Mockingbird,* and excellent playwright, author of a nine-play saga and that haunting work *The Trip to Bountiful.* Inextricably linked with these theatrical accomplishments, he has proved himself a kind human being, a man of artistic and moral integrity, who has fought the good fight against materialism and commercialism, and advocated love, humanity, and forgiveness of our fellows. He is a man to admire.

CHRONOLOGY

Occasional variation may be noted between dates here and in the text. Some plays had an early dramatic reading and then later had a premiere presentation. Also, the *Orphans' Home Cycle* was written over a number of years.

1916	Born March 14, 1916, Wharton, Texas
1932	Graduated from Wharton High School
1933	Studied elocution in Dallas
1933–1935	Studied acting, Pasadena Playhouse
1936–1942	Actor in New York City
1939	*Wharton Dance* (unpublished)
1940	*Texas Town* (unpublished)
1942	*Out of My House* (unpublished)
1943	*Only the Heart* (first performed in 1941)
1945	Married Lillian Vallish
1945–1949	Taught at King-Smith School, Washington, D.C.
1949–1956	Lived in New York City
1951	*Ludie Brooks* (unpublished teleplay)
1952	*The Chase* (novel, 1956)
1953	*The Rocking Chair* (unpublished teleplay)
1953	*The Trip to Bountiful* (teleplay and stage play)
1953	*Expectant Relations* (teleplay) and other one-acts in *Harrison, Texas*
1954	*The Traveling Lady*
1956	*Flight* (one-act)

1956–1966	Lived in Nyack, New York
1956	*Harrison, Texas: Eight Television Plays* (published collection, including *A Young Lady of Property, The Midnight Caller, John Turner Davis, The Oil Well, The Death of the Old Man, The Old Beginning, The Tears of My Sister,* and *The Dancers*)
1956	*Storm Fear* (movie)
1960	*Old Man* (teleplay)
1960	*Tomorrow* (teleplay; film, 1972)
1961	*The Night of the Storm* (teleplay)
1962	*To Kill a Mockingbird* (movie and Academy Award)
1965	*Baby, the Rain Must Fall* (movie)
1967	*Hurry Sundown* (movie)
1968	*The Stalking Moon* (movie)
1966–1978	Lived in New Hampshire
1974	Mother died
1975	Father died
1974–1978	The *Orphans' Home Cycle* (composed, afterward performed, including *Roots in a Parched Ground, Convicts, Lily Dale, Courtship, Valentine's Day, 1918, Cousins,* and *The Death of Papa*)
1977	*The Displaced Person* (television adaptation of O'Connor's story)
1979–1980	*In a Coffin in Egypt*
1980	*Barn Burning* (teleplay)
1982	*The Man Who Climbed the Pecan Trees* and *The Roads to Home* (including *A Nightingale, The Dearest of Friends,* and *Spring Dance*)
1982	*The Widow Claire* (fourth part of *Cycle*)
1983	*Tender Mercies* (movie)
1985	*The Road to the Graveyard* (teleplay)
1985	*The Trip to Bountiful* (movie)
1988	*The Habitation of Dragons*
1989	*Dividing the Estate*
1989	*Selected One-Act Plays of Horton Foote* (including *Blind Date, The One-Armed Man, The Prisoner's Song, The Road to the Graveyard, The Land of the Astronauts,* and other earlier one-acts)
1991	*Of Mice and Men* (adaptation of Steinbeck's novella)
1991	*Children of Pride*
1992	Wife, Lillian Vallish Foote, died
1993	*Night Seasons* (premiere presentation; given as a staged reading in 1997)
1994	*Talking Pictures*

1995	*The Young Man from Atlanta*
1995	*Laura Dennis*
1995	Pulitzer Prize
1998	*Vernon Early*
2000	*The Day Emily Married*
1980s–2000s	Lecturing and giving workshops at various colleges and universities

GENEALOGY

Albert Clinton Horton (1798–1865)

Mary Horton (1873–1908)

A. C. Horton II (1875–1909)

Carrie Horton m. Albert Foote (1869–1940) (d. 1928)

Loula Horton m. Dr. I. E. Irvin (1871–1940)

Renie Horton m. A. A. Rugely (1878–1927)

Lida Horton m. T. J. Abell (1880–1960)

Al H. Foote m. Hallie Brooks (1890–1995) (d. 1974)

Tom Brooks Foote (1921–1944)

John Speed Foote m. Betty Ellen Mcteer

Lilyan (Lily Dale) Foote m. W. B. Coffee

W. B. Coffee, Jr. (d. ?)

Horton Foote m. Lillian Vallish (1916–) (d. 1992)

Barbara Hallie Foote (1950–)

Horton Foote III (1952–)

Walter Vallish Foote (1955–)

Daisy Brooks Foote (1959–)

NOTES

AUTHOR'S NOTE: In my documentation, I use numbered endnotes for citing sources, and I use parenthetical references within the text for quotations within a particular work. For those references within the text, I first indicate in an endnote which edition I am referring to. Further, references to newspaper reviews and Foote's lectures are also given within the text itself.

Preface

1. Horton Foote, "Richmond, U.S.A.," *New York Times* (April 13, 1952): C3.
2. Dale Salwak, *The Literary Biography: Problems and Selections* (Iowa City: University of Iowa Press, 1996), p. 71.
3. In *The Relations of Literary Study,* ed. James Thorpe (New York: Modern Language Society of America, 1967), p. 67.

Chapter 1

1. Marion Castleberry, "Voices from Home: Familial Bonds in the Works of Horton Foote" (Ph.D. diss., Louisiana State University, 1993), p. 39.
2. Ibid., pp. 66–67.
3. Ibid., p. v.
4. "Wharton—Then and Now," lecture delivered at Louisiana State University, 1989, Horton Foote Collection.
5. T. R. Fehrenbach, *Lone Star* (New York: Macmillan, 1968), pp. 168, 279, 287, and 305 and Chapters 24 and 25.
6. Terry Jordan et al., *Texas: A Geography* (Boulder, Colo.: Westview Press, 1984), pp. 73–79.
7. Diane Jennings, "Horton Foote," *Dallas Morning News* (March 24, 1985).
8. Author's interview with Foote, March 12, 1994.
9. Marjorie Smeltsor, "The World's an Orphans' Home: Horton Foote's Social and Moral History," *Southern Quarterly,* 29 (Winter 1991): 8.
10. Foote, "Richmond,"p. C1.
11. Ibid., C3.
12. Information dated January 21, 1966, sent to H. H. Wilson Co. for *Mid-Century America* (a biographical volume of American authors), in Horton Foote Collection.
13. Horton Foote Collection. All further references to the collection are designated "HFC" and, where possible, are given in the text.
14. Annie Lee Williams, *A History of Wharton County* (Austin: Van Boeckmann-Jones, 1964), pp. 177–178. I have obtained most of my historical information on Wharton County from this volume and from *Wharton County Pictorial History, 1846–1946: Our First 100 Years,* vol. 1 (Austin: Eakin Press, 1993).
15. Author's interview with Foote, March 12, 1944.
16. Williams, pp. 177–178.

17. Don Hulbert, "Horton Foote's *Trip to Bountiful*," *Atlanta Journal/Constitution* (March 10, 1991): M4.
18. Williams, p. 127.
19. David G. McComb, *Texas: A Modern History* (Austin: University of Texas Press, 1989), pp. 126, 146.
20. "Wharton—Then and Now," pp. 9–10.
21. Ibid., p. 9.
22. Ibid.
23. See map at end of Faulkner, *Absalom, Absalom!* (New York: Random House, 1964).
24. Author's interview with Foote, March 12, 1994.

Chapter 2

1. Foote has retold the first sixteen years of his life in *Farewell: A Memoir of a Texas Childhood* (New York: Scribner, 1999). This autobiography includes numerous characters and incidents recognizable in his plays. The abundance of violence in the imaginary town especially in the early decades of the century is verified. It is a valuable addition to our knowledge of Foote and will be referred to frequently in this book. Page references in the text, designated *Memoir*, cite this edition.
2. Author's interview with Foote, March 12, 1994.
3. Penelope Niven McJunkin, "The Horton Foote Collection" (1985). Introductory unpaged statement in HFC.
4. Castleberry, p. 42.
5. Hulbert, p. M4; and Castleberry, pp. 23–24.
6. Castleberry, p. 22; Hulbert, p. M4; and author's interview with Foote, March 12, 1994. Material on Foote's genealogy is taken from Castleberry; Foote's lecture "Seeing and Imagining"; and the Horton family tree, deposited at the Wharton County Historical Museum, "Courtesy: Thomas H. Abell." For a grasp of Foote's thought and personality, I have also drawn on four informative biographical lectures: "Wharton—Then and Now," "Seeing and Imagining," "Learning to Write," and "Pasadena and Beyond," delivered at Louisiana State University, 1989, and deposited in HFC. Page references in the text cite these copies with short titles.
7. Author's visit to Wharton, March 12, 1994.
8. Samuel G. Freedman, "From the Heart of Texas," *New York Times Magazine* (February 9, 1986): 61.
9. Williams, pp. 368–369, 382.
10. Castleberry, p. 42.
11. Ibid., p. 16.
12. Ronald L. Davis, "Roots in a Parched Ground: An Interview with Horton Foote," *Southwest Review,* 73 (Summer 1988): 309.
13. Castleberry, p. 25.
14. *Wharton County Pictorial History,* vol. 1, p. 31.
15. Castleberry, p. 27.
16. Ibid., p. 39.
17. Freedman, p. 61.
18. Nina Darnton, "Horton Foote Celebrates a Bygone Era in *1918*," *New York Times* (April 21, 1985): sec. 2, p. 22.

19. Castleberry, p. 65.
20. Author's interview with Foote, March 12, 1994.
21. Castleberry, p. 62.
22. Ibid., pp. 70–71.
23. Ibid., p. 71.

Chapter 3

1. Undated letter (1938), HFC.
2. *Tennessee Williams' Letters to Donald Windham, 1940–1965,* ed. Donald Windham (New York: Holt, Rinehart and Winston, 1977), p. 84.
3. Father's Day, 1938, HFC.
4. Mary Hunter, Foreword, in *Only the Heart* (New York: Dramatists Play Service, 1944), p. 5.
5. Ibid.
6. Weldon B. Durham, *American Theatre Companies, 1931–1986* (Westport, Conn.: Greenwood Press, 1989), p. 61.
7. McJunkin, Title Index; Horton Foote, *Wharton Dance* (1939), typescript. Page references in the text cite this typescript.
8. Author's telephone interview with Foote, August 17, 1998.
9. Burns Mantle, *Contemporary American Playwrights* (New York: Dodd, Mead and Co., 1934), p. 79.
10. *Texas Town* (1939), typescript, HFC. Page references in the text cite this typescript.
11. *Wharton County Pictorial History,* vol. 1, p. 52; Castleberry, p. 100.
12. Davis, p. 303.
13. Edmund Choate to Lynn Riggs, June 30, 1941, on stationery of "Select Theatres Corporation," HFC.
14. *Out of My House* (1942), typescript, HFC. Page references in the text cite this typescript.
15. Terry Barr, "The Ordinary World of Horton Foote" (Ph.D. diss., University of Tennessee, 1986), p. 18.
16. Hunter, p. 6.
17. Ibid., p. 7.
18. Horton Foote, Author's Preface, in *Selected One-act Plays of Horton Foote,* ed. Gerald C. Wood (Dallas: Southern Methodist University Press, 1989), p. ix.
19. Ibid., p. xi.

Chapter 4

1. Hunter, p. 7.
2. Castleberry, p. 117.
3. *Only the Heart* (New York: Dramatists Play Service, 1944), p. 70. Page references in the text cite this edition.
4. Hunter, pp. 6–7.
5. Author's Preface, *Selected One-act Plays,* p. xi.
6. Letter, April 5, 1943, HFC.
7. Tennessee Williams, *Memoirs* (Garden City, N.Y.: Doubleday, 1975), pp. 107–108.
8. *Tennessee Williams' Letters,* p. 60.

9. Allan G. Halline, ed., *Six Modern American Plays* (New York: Modern Library, 1951), p. 273.

10. *Tennessee Williams' Letters,* p. 83.

11. Ibid., p. 55.

12. Ibid., p. 86.

13. Ibid., p. 84.

14. Ibid.

15. Lyle Leverich, *Tom: The Unknown Tennessee Williams* (New York: Crown, 1995), p. 511.

16. Ibid.

17. *Tennessee Williams' Letters,* p. 167. Letter, March 15, 1945.

18. Gerald C. Wood and Terry Barr, "'A Certain Kind of Writer': An Interview with Horton Foote," *Literature/Film Quarterly,* 14, no. 4 (1986): 226.

19. *Selected One-act Plays,* p. 226.

20. Letter to the author, May 19, 1992.

21. Ibid.

22. Leverich, p. 582.

23. Castleberry, p. 123, gives the date as June 4, 1945.

24. Laurin Porter, "An Interview with Horton Foote," *Studies in American Drama,* 2 (1991): 193.

25. Davis, pp. 303–304.

26. Author's interview with Foote, March 12, 1994.

27. Katherine Anne Porter, "'Noon Wine': The Sources," in *Understanding Fiction,* by Cleanth Brooks and Robert Penn Warren (New York: Appleton-Century-Croft, 1959), pp. 610–620.

28. Author's interview with Foote, March 12, 1994.

29. Don Graham, "A Southern Writer in Texas: Porter and the Texas Literary Tradition," in *Katherine Anne Porter and Texas: An Uneasy Relationship,* ed. Clinton Machann and William Bedford Clark (College Station: Texas A&M University Press, 1990), pp. 64, 69–70.

30. Author's interview with Foote, March 12, 1994.

Chapter 5

1. John Pilkington, *Stark Young, A Life in the Arts: Letters, 1900–1962* (Baton Rouge: Louisiana State University Press, 1975), vol. 2, p. 1363 n.

2. *New York Times* (obituary, March 19, 1997), late New York edition, HFC.

3. *The Chase* (New York: Dramatists Play Service, 1952). Page references in the text cite this edition.

4. Castleberry, p. 131.

5. Foote, "Richmond," p. C3.

6. Ibid.

7. *Wharton County Pictorial History,* vol. 1, p. 23.

8. Castleberry, p. 127.

9. George Jean Nathan, *The Theatre in the Fifties* (New York: Knopf, 1953), pp. 94–97.

10. Marian Burkhart, "Horton Foote's Many Roads Home: An American Playwright and His Characters," *Commonweal* (February 26, 1988): 111.

11. Horton Foote, *The Chase* (New York: Rinehart, 1956).
12. Gary Edgerton, "A Visit to the Imaginary Landscape of Harrison, Texas: Sketching the Film Career of Horton Foote," *Literature/Film Quarterly*, 17 (1989): 7.
13. Al Reinert, "Tender Foote," *Texas Monthly* (July 1991): 135, quoted in Castleberry, p. 214.
14. See David Thompson, *American in the Dark: Hollywood and the Gift of Unreality* (New York: William Morrow, 1977), pp. 182–183; Robin Wood, *Hollywood from Vietnam to Reagan* (New York: Columbia University Press, 1986).

Chapter 6

1. Barr, p. 62.
2. Introduction, *Selected One-act Plays*, pp. xix–xx.
3. Ibid., Introduction, p. xiii.
4. Ibid., Author's Preface, p. xi.
5. Ibid.
6. Terry Barr, "Horton Foote's TV Women: The Richest Part of a Golden Age," in *Horton Foote: A Casebook*, ed. Gerald C. Wood (New York: Garland, 1999), p. 39.
7. Because of references to the Broadway production of *The Trip to Bountiful*, this letter can be dated 1953.
8. For an informative chapter on Coe and *Philco Playhouse*, see Max Wilk, *The Golden Age of Television* (New York: Delacorte, 1976), pp. 125–138.
9. Edgerton, p. 5. For another appreciation of Coe, see Frank Sturcken, *Live Television: The Golden Age of 1946–1958 in New York* (Jefferson, N.C.: McFarland, 1990), pp. 80–82.
10. Wilk, p. 136.
11. Ibid., p. 130.
12. Ibid., p. 134.
13. Ibid., p. 129.
14. Ibid., pp. 129–130.
15. Paddy Chayefsky, *Television Plays* (New York: Simon and Schuster, 1955), p. 176.
16. Horton Foote, *Harrison, Texas: Eight Television Plays* (New York: Harcourt, Brace, 1956), pp. viii–ix. Page references in the text cite this edition.
17. All production information is taken from the Lucy Kroll file, HFC.

Chapter 7

1. Hulbert, p. M4.
2. Wilk, pp. 129–130.
3. Undated letter from Lillian Foote (1953), HFC.
4. Lillian Gish, *The Movies, Mr. Griffith, and Me* (Englewood Cliffs, N.J.: Prentice Hall, 1969), p. 363.
5. Ibid.
6. Foote, *Harrison, Texas: Eight Television Plays*, and *Horton Foote's Three Trips to Bountiful*, ed. Barbara Moore and David G. Yellin (Dallas: Southern Methodist University Press, 1993). Page references to *The Trip to Bountiful* (teleplay, stage play, and screenplay) in the text cite the latter work. The stage play has also been published by Dramatists Play Service (1954).

7. Author's interview with Foote, March 12, 1994.

8. Horton Foote, "The Trip to Paradise" (*Texas Monthly,* December 1987), p. 183. Page references in the text cite this article.

9. Robert Frost, "Directive," in *Norton Anthology of American Literature,* vol. 2 (New York: Norton and Co., 1985), p. 1032.

10. Author's Preface, *Selected One-act Plays,* p. ix.

11. Robert Drake, *Flannery O'Connor, A Critical Essay* (Grand Rapids, Mich.: William B. Eerdmans, 1966), p. 11.

12. Reginald Rose, *Six Television Plays* (New York: Simon and Schuster, 1956), pp. 157–158.

13. See Charles S. Watson, "Beyond the Commercial Media: Horton Foote's Procession of Defeated Men," *Studies in American Drama, 1945–Present,* 8 (1993): 175–187.

14. Foote, *Harrison, Texas,* p. ix.

15. Davis, p. 308.

16. *To Kill a Mockingbird, Tender Mercies, and The Trip to Bountiful: Three Screenplays by Horton Foote* (New York: Grove Press, 1989), p. 195.

17. Foote, Foreword, *Three Screenplays,* p. xvii.

Chapter 8

1. May 13, 1955, HFC.

2. *Lily Dale,* in *Four Plays from the Orphans' Home Cycle, with an Introduction by Horton Foote: Roots in a Parched Ground, Convicts, Lily Dale, The Widow Claire* (New York: Grove Press, 1988), p. 173.

3. *Ludie Brooks,* in *A Lamp Unto My Feet* television series (1951), p. 31.

4. Barr, "Ordinary World," p. 64.

5. Ibid., pp. 64–65.

6. *The Rocking Chair* (NBC, May 1953), p. 8. Page references in the text cite this copy.

7. Author's interview with Foote, March 12, 1994.

8. Author's telephone interview with Foote, August 17, 1998.

9. James M. Wall, "Home, Family, Religion: The World of Horton Foote," *Christian Century* (February 19, 1997): 179.

10. "Toward Films with Spiritual Vision," *Christian Science Sentinel* (April 27, 1987): 3–9; "Spiritual Values and Film: Letting Powerful Meaning Come Through," *Christian Science Sentinel* (April 7, 1991): 7–13. Quotes from these interviews, labeled "(1)" and "(2)," respectively, are given in the text.

11. Author's interview with Foote, March 12, 1994.

12. Kittie Burris, "Christian Science: The Law of Love," lecture given at the Tuscaloosa Public Library, February 14, 1999.

13. Wall, p. 179.

14. Wood and Barr, p. 231.

Chapter 9

1. All material is from the correspondence in the HFC. Details are given in parentheses within the text.

2. Foote, *Memoir,* p. 194.

3. Gerald C. Wood, *Horton Foote and the Theatre of Intimacy* (Baton Rouge: Louisiana State University Press, 1999), p. 30.
4. Jennings, "Horton Foote."
5. Freedman, p. xxi.
6. Irene Backalenick, "Horton Foote: A Retrospective," *Theatre Week* (January 30, 1995): 15.
7. I have not found a letter answering this query.
8. Marion Castleberry, "Remembering Wharton, Texas," in *Horton Foote: A Casebook,* ed. Wood, p. 32.
9. Ibid., p. 16.
10. Ibid., p. 17.
11. Ibid., p. 19.
12. Ibid., p. 23.
13. Ibid., p. 18.
14. *The Courage to Be* (New Haven, Conn.: 1962), p. 181, quoted in Wood, *Horton Foote and the Theatre of Intimacy,* pp. 42–43.

Chapter 10

1. Horton Foote, *The Traveling Lady* (New York: Dramatists Play Service, 1955), p. 29. Page references in the text cite this edition.
2. A copy of the television adaptation dated April 25, 1962, is held in the HFC.
3. Barr, "Ordinary World," p. 106.
4. Quoted by Murray Schumach, "Hollywood's Roving 'Lady': Horton Foote's TV and Broadway Play Is Meticulously Guided toward the Screen by Its Director and Stars" (*New York Times,* January 5, 1964): sec. 2, p. 7.
5. Horton Foote, *Baby, the Rain Must Fall* (New York: Popular Library, 1965), p. 83. This is the novel based on the film. Page references given in the text cite this edition.
6. Barr, "Ordinary World," p. 187.
7. Ibid., p. 197.
8. Ibid., pp. 187–197.
9. Quoted by Barr, "Ordinary World," p. 190 (from the movie).
10. Joseph R. Millichap, "Horton Foote," *Dictionary of Literary Biography,* 26 (1989): 103.
11. "Horton Foote," in *Current Biography* (New York: H. H. Wilson, 1986), pp. 143–147.
12. Edgerton, p. 7.
13. Ibid.
14. The script is held in the HFC.
15. *Tender Mercies,* in *Three Screenplays,* p. 142. Page references in the text cite this edition.
16. See Wood, *Horton Foote and the Theatre of Intimacy,* p. 96.
17. Stanley Kaufman, "A Carpenter, an Architect," *New Republic* (March 31, 1986): 24–25.

Chapter 11

1. See Rebecca Briley, "Adapting for a Living," Chapter 3 in *You Can Go Home Again: The Focus on Family in the Works of Horton Foote* (New York: Peter Lang, 1993), pp. 50–87, for a thorough examination of Foote's adaptations.

2. Barr, "Ordinary World," pp. 132–133.
3. Ibid., p. 270.
4. Castleberry, "Voices from Home," p. 193.
5. Barr, "Ordinary World," p. 149.
6. Edgerton, p. 6.
7. Harper Lee, *To Kill a Mockingbird* (New York: Popular Library, 1962).
8. *To Kill a Mockingbird, Tender Mercies, and The Trip to Bountiful: Three Screenplays by Horton Foote* (New York: Grove Press, 1989), p. 69. Page references in the text cite this edition.
9. Foote, Foreword, *Three Screenplays,* pp. xii–xiii.
10. *Baby, the Rain Must Fall* (1965). This motion picture was released by Columbia Pictures in 1966. The HFC does not hold a copy of the screenplay.
11. Rebecca Briley, "Southern Accents: Horton Foote's Adaptations of William Faulkner, Harper Lee, and Flannery O'Connor," in *Horton Foote: A Casebook,* ed. Wood, pp. 50–51.
12. Ibid., p. 50.
13. *Old Man,* in *Three Plays by Horton Foote* (New York: Harcourt, Brace, 1962), which includes *Tomorrow* and *Roots in a Parched Ground.*
14. *Portable Faulkner,* ed. Malcolm Cowley (New York: Viking, 1967), p. 650.
15. Briley, "Southern Accents," p. 51.
16. *Tomorrow and Tomorrow and Tomorrow,* ed. David G. Yellin and Marie Connors (Jackson: University Press of Mississippi, 1985), p. 3. Page references in the text to the three versions of *Tomorrow* cite this edition.
17. Ibid., p. 3.
18. Ibid., p. 5.
19. Davis, p. 311.
20. Yellin and Connors, p. 172.
21. Ibid., p. 166.
22. Louis D. Rubin, *The Literary South* (New York: John Wiley, 1979).
23. Barr, "Ordinary World," p. 184. For an excellent discussion of *Barn Burning,* see pp. 175–184 in this work.
24. Rubin, p. 513.
25. Barr, "Ordinary World," p. 184.
26. Flannery O'Connor, "The Displaced Person" in *A Good Man Is Hard to Find and Other Stories* (New York: Harcourt, Brace, Jovanovich, 1983). Page references in the text cite this edition.
27. Horton Foote, *Of Mice and Men,* screenplay, Metro Goldwyn Mayer, 1992.
28. The novella *Of Mice and Men* is in *The Portable Steinbeck* (New York: Viking, 1946). Page references in the text cite this edition.

Chapter 12

1. Laurin Porter, "Interview with Horton Foote," p. 182.
2. "Horton Foote," in *Current Biography,* pp. 143–147.
3. Horton Foote, "The Orphans' Home Cycle," lecture given at Texas A&M University, April 14, 1993, held in HFC. Further references are given in the text.

4. Stark Young, Foreword, in *Roots in a Parched Ground* (New York: Dramatists Play Service, 1962), p. 5.

5. Horton Foote, Introduction to *Four Plays from the Orphans' Home Cycle* (New York: Grove Press, 1988), p. ix.

6. Freedman, p. 61.

7. Ibid.

8. Young, Foreword to *Roots in a Parched Ground,* p. 5.

9. See also Virgie in *Roots in a Parched Ground,* p. 54.

10. Horton Foote, *Roots in a Parched Ground* (New York: Dramatists Play Service, 1962), p. 87. Further references in the text are to this edition.

11. Carter Martin, "Horton Foote's Southern Family in *Roots in a Parched Ground,*" *Texas Review* (Spring–Summer 1991): 76–81.

12. *Convicts,* in Horton Foote, *Four Plays from the Orphans' Home Cycle* (New York: Grove Press, 1988). Page references in the text cite this edition.

13. *Wharton County Pictorial History,* vol. 1, p. 160.

14. Author's interview with Foote, March 12, 1994; Davis, p. 316.

15. "The Bear," in *Portable Faulkner,* p. 292.

16. *New York Times* (December 3, 1989): sec. 2, pp. 15, 22.

17. *Lily Dale,* in Horton Foote, *Four Plays from the Orphans' Home Cycle* (New York: Grove Press, 1988). Page references in the text cite this edition.

18. Epigraph to *Four Plays,* p. vii.

19. *The Widow Claire,* in Horton Foote, *Four Plays from the Orphans' Home Cycle* (New York: Grove Press, 1988). Page references in the text cite this edition.

20. Barr, "Ordinary World," p. 13.

Chapter 13

1. Foote delivered a tribute to Berghof after his death in 1990. It is entitled "Herbert Berghof" in the HFC (no pagination, no date). Much information on Foote's relationship with Berghof is taken from this tribute. References to it are given henceforth in the text.

2. October 17, 1962 (Kroll Correspondence), HFC.

3. See Gerald M. Berkowitz, *American Drama of the Twentieth Century* (New York: Longman, 1992), pp. 173, 179.

4. These plays have been published in *Courtship, Valentine's Day, 1918: Three Plays from the Orphans' Home Cycle* (New York: Grove Press, 1987). Page references to the plays in the text cite this edition.

5. Stanley Coben, *Rebellion against Victorianism* (New York: Oxford University Press, 1991), p. 5. On character, see also Daniel Walter Howe, "Victorian Culture in America" in *Victorian America,* ed. Daniel Walter Howe (Philadelphia: University of Pennsylvania Press, 1976), p. 25.

6. Ellen M. Plante, *Woman at Home in Victorian America: A Social History* (New York: Facts on File, 1997), p. 112.

7. Horton Foote, *Cousins and The Death of Papa: The Final Two Plays from the Orphans' Home Cycle* (New York: Grove Press, 1989). Page references to these plays in the text cite this edition.

8. Albert Foote, in reality, disliked "an educated fool" (*Memoir,* p. 250).

Chapter 14

1. All correspondence referred to in this chapter may be found at the DeGolyer Library, Southern Methodist University, in boxes labeled "Personal Correspondence." All further references to this collection are given in the text.
2. Laurin Porter, "Interview with Horton Foote," p. 182.
3. O'Connor, "The Displaced Person."
4. See Gerald M. Berkowitz, "1945–1960: The Zenith of the Broadway Theatre," Chapter 4 in *American Drama of the Twentieth Century,* pp. 75–120.
5. For good surveys of American drama after 1965, see Berkowitz, *American Drama of the Twentieth Century,* and Matthew C. Roudané, *American Drama since 1960: A Critical History* (New York: Twayne, 1996). I use the term "off-Broadway" instead of "off-off-Broadway" for location; the latter term describes more radical political and social protest, which Foote did not write.
6. For more information on Romulus Linney, see Charles S. Watson, *The History of Southern Drama* (Lexington: University Press of Kentucky, 1997), pp. 207–210.
7. *Selected One-act Plays of Horton Foote,* ed. Gerald Wood (Dallas: Southern Methodist University Press, 1989), p. 297. All further references to plays in this chapter are to be found in this collection and are given in the text.
8. See Castleberry, "Voices from Home," pp. 270–271.
9. William Faulkner, *As I Lay Dying* (New York: Random House, 1964), p. 34.
10. Philip Wylie, Chapter 11 in *Generation of Vipers* (New York: Rinehart, 1942).

Chapter 15

1. Matthew C. Roudané, *American Drama since 1960: A Critical History* (New York: Twayne, 1995). Theatrical information presented in this chapter is based on this history.
2. Ibid., pp. 152–153.
3. Ibid., p. 153.
4. Horton Foote, *The Young Man from Atlanta* (New York: Dramatists Play Service, 1995 and 1997 editions).
5. Horton Foote, *Four New Plays: The Habitation of Dragons, Night Seasons, Dividing the Estate, Talking Pictures* (Newbury, Vt.: Smith and Krause, 1993). References to *The Habitation of Dragons* are from this edition and are given in the text.
6. Castleberry, "Voices from Home," pp. 296–297.
7. Cleanth Brooks and Robert B. Heilman, *Understanding Drama* (New York: Holt, Rinehart and Winston, 1961), Glossary, p. 33.
8. Author's Preface, *Selected One-act Plays,* p. ix.
9. Aristotle, *Poetics* (Indianapolis: Hackett, 1987), sec. 13.
10. *Laura Dennis* (Dramatists Play Service, typescript, n.d.). It was performed in March 1995 by the Signature Company.
11. Castleberry, "Voices from Home," p. 291.
12. Epigraph to *Habitation,* p. 4.
13. Castleberry, "Voices from Home," p. 297.
14. *Dividing the Estate,* in *Four New Plays.* Page references in the text cite this edition.
15. *Talking Pictures,* in *Four New Plays.* Page references in the text cite this edition.

16. Tim Wright, "More Real Than Realism: Horton Foote's Impressionism," in *Horton Foote: A Casebook,* ed. Wood, p. 69.

17. Crystal Brian, "'To Be Quiet and Listen': *The Orphans' Home Cycle* and the Music of Charles Ives," in *Horton Foote: A Casebook,* ed. Wood, p. 90.

18. Dean Mendell, "Squeezing the Drama out of Melodrama: Plot and Counterplot in *Laura Dennis,*" in *Horton Foote: A Casebook,* ed. Wood, pp. 194–195.

Chapter 16

1. *Night Seasons,* in Horton Foote, *Four New Plays* (Newbury, Vt.: Smith and Krause, 1993). All references are to this edition and are given in the text.

2. *Laura Dennis* (Dramatists Play Service, typescript). All references are to this typescript and are given in the text.

3. Horton Foote, *The Young Man from Atlanta* (New York: Plume, 1995). Page references in the text cite this edition. This play was also published by Dramatists Play Service (1995).

4. Briley, *You Can Go Home Again,* pp. 2, 56, 64, 109.

5. I disagree with Gerald Wood's de-emphasis on homosexuality. See Wood, *Horton Foote and The Theater of Intimacy,* p. 103.

6. David R. Goldfield, *Black, White, and Southern: Race Relations and Southern Culture, 1940 to the Present* (Baton Rouge: Louisiana State University Press, 1990), p. 37.

7. Marian Burkhart, back cover of the Dramatists Play Service edition of *The Young Man from Atlanta.*

8. Telephone interview with Kelly Kline, July 28, 2000.

Conclusion

1. Don Graham, *Texas: A Literary Portrait* (San Antonio: Corona Publishing Co., 1985), p. 7.

2. Gerald Weales, Chapter 4 in *American Drama since World War II* (New York: Harcourt, Brace, and World, 1962).

SELECTED BIBLIOGRAPHY

Horton Foote Collection

The extensive Horton Foote Collection is held at the DeGolyer Library, Southern Methodist University, and contains letters from 1878 to 1990, as well as numerous drafts of plays written for the stage and television. It is especially rich in its collection of letters, which I have used extensively, designated Horton Foote Collection (HFC, with date of the letter). The Lucy Kroll file, compiled by Foote's literary agent, is thorough and, filed by years, gives a virtual chronology of his career (1953–1990). I have used it generously. Penelope Niven McJunkin was the first compiler ("The Horton Foote Collection," 1985). She prepared a very useful introductory unpaged statement and "Letters and Correspondence" (6 pages), which are typescripts in the Foote Collection, DeGolyer Library. The "Horton Foote Collection Box List" of 125 boxes was prepared by Derrick Wright in the spring of 1993 and supersedes the preceding lists.

Selected Items

In a Coffin in Egypt, produced first at the Herbert Berghof Studio, 1980.
Lectures at Louisiana State University, Baton Rouge: "Seeing and Imagining," April 19, 1989; "Pasadena and Beyond," April 20, 1989; "Learning to Write," April 21, 1989.
Ludie Brooks, teleplay for *A Lamp unto My Feet, Religion in Everyday Life* series, 1951.
"The Orphans' Home Cycle," lecture given at Texas A&M University, April 14, 1993.
Out of My House, typescript, 1942. Four one-acts produced by American Actors Company, 1942.
Rocking Chair, NBC teleplay, May 1953.
Texas Town, typescript, 1939.
This Property Is Condemned, film adaptation of one-act by Tennessee Williams, 1962.
Tribute to Herbert Berghof, delivered after his death in 1990.
"Wharton: A Bicentennial Pageant," June 3, 1976.
Wharton Dance, typescript, 1939.
"Wharton—Then and Now," lecture at Louisiana State University, 1989.

Significant Correspondents (Prepared by McJunkin)

Joseph Anthony, Herbert Berghof, Uta Hagen Berghof, Barrett Clark, Fred Coe, Tamara Daykarhanova, Agnes de Mille, Vincent Donehue, Robert Duvall, Lillian Gish, Helen Hayes, Elia Kazan, Lucy Kroll, Frank Rich, Eva Marie Saint, Robert Sherwood, Sam Spiegel, Cornel Wilde, and Tennessee Williams.

Primary Sources

Foote, Horton. *Farewell: A Memoir of a Texas Childhood.* New York: Scribner, 1999.

Plays

The Chase. New York: Dramatists Play Service, 1952.

Courtship, Valentine's Day, 1918: Three Plays from the Orphans' Home Cycle. New York: Grove Press, 1987.

Cousins and The Death of Papa: The Final Two Plays from the Orphans' Home Cycle. New York: Grove Press, 1989.

Flight. In *Television Plays for Writers*, ed. A. S. Burack. Boston: The Writer, Inc., 1959 (pp. 107–147).

Four New Plays: The Habitation of Dragons, Night Seasons, Dividing the Estate, Talking Pictures. Newbury, Vt.: Smith and Krause, 1993.

Four Plays from the Orphans' Home Cycle, with an Introduction by Horton Foote: Roots in a Parched Ground, Convicts, Lily Dale, The Widow Claire. New York: Grove Press, 1988.

Harrison, Texas: Eight Television Plays. With preface by Horton Foote. New York: Harcourt, Brace, 1956. Contains all teleplays in *Selected One-act Plays of Horton Foote*, except *The Oil Well* and *The Old Beginning*.

Horton Foote's Three Trips to Bountiful. Ed. Barbara Moore and David G. Yellin. Dallas: Southern Methodist University Press, 1993.

Laura Dennis. New York: Dramatists Play Service, typescript, n.d.

The Night of the Storm. Published under the title *Roots in a Parched Ground*, by Horton Foote, with foreword by Stark Young. New York: Dramatists Play Service, 1962.

"On First Dramatizing Faulkner" and "Tomorrow: The Genesis of a Screenplay." In *Faulkner, Modernism, and Film: Faulkner and Yoknapatawpha*, ed. Evans Harrington and Ann J. Abadie. Jackson: University Press of Mississippi, 1979.

Only the Heart. With foreword by Mary Hunter. New York: Dramatists Play Service, 1944.

"Richmond, U.S.A." *New York Times* (April 13, 1952): C1, C3.

Selected One-act Plays of Horton Foote. Ed. Gerald C. Wood. Dallas: Southern Methodist University Press, 1989. Contains *The Old Beginning, A Young Lady of Property, The Oil Well, The Death of the Old Man, The Tears of My Sister, John Turner Davis, The Midnight Caller, The Dancers, The Man Who Climbed the Pecan Trees, A Nightingale, The Dearest of Friends, Spring Dance* (from *The Roads to Home*), *Blind Date, The Prisoner's Song, The One-Armed Man, The Road to the Graveyard*, and *The Land of the Astronauts*.

Three Plays by Horton Foote. New York: Harcourt, Brace, 1962. This collection includes *Old Man, Tomorrow,* and *Roots in a Parched Ground.*

To Kill a Mockingbird, Tender Mercies, and the Trip to Bountiful: Three Screenplays by Horton Foote. New York: Grove Press, 1989.

Tomorrow. Adapted from a story by William Faulkner. New York: Dramatists Play Service, 1963.

Tomorrow and Tomorrow and Tomorrow. Ed. David G. Yellin and Marie Connors. Jackson: University Press of Mississippi, 1985.

The Traveling Lady. New York: Dramatists Play Service, 1955. First performed, 1954.

Vernon Early. Alabama Shakespeare Festival, Montgomery, May 26–July 26, 1998.

The Young Man from Atlanta. New York: Plume, 1996.

Screenplays

Baby, the Rain Must Fall. Columbia Pictures, 1965.
The Chase. Horizon Pictures, 1966. Based on Foote's novel (1966).
Hurry Sundown. Paramount, 1967. Screenplay produced by Otto Preminger, 1966–1967.
Of Mice and Men. Metro Goldwyn Mayer, 1992. Adaptation of Steinbeck novel.
The Stalking Moon. National General, 1968.
Storm Fear. United Artists, 1956.
To Kill a Mockingbird. Universal, 1963. Screenplay of Harper Lee's novel.

Secondary Sources

"Casebook" refers to Gerald C. Wood's edited collection of 1998.
Barr, Terry. "Horton Foote's TV Women: The Richest Part of a Golden Age." In *Casebook*, pp. 35–47.
———. "The Ordinary World of Horton Foote." Ph.D. dissertation, University of Tennessee, 1986.
Berkowitz, Gerald M. *American Drama of the Twentieth Century.* New York: Longman, 1992.
Bradbury, John M. *Renaissance in the South: A Critical History of the Literature, 1920–1960.* Chapel Hill: University of North Carolina Press, 1963.
Brian, Crystal. "'To Be Quiet and Listen': *The Orphans' Home Cycle* and the Music of Charles Ives." In *Casebook*, pp. 89–107.
Briley, Rebecca. "Southern Accents: Horton Foote's Adaptations of William Faulkner, Harper Lee, and Flannery O'Connor." In *Casebook*, pp. 49–65.
———. *You Can Go Home Again: The Focus on Family in the Works of Horton Foote.* New York: Peter Lang, 1993.
Brown, Norman D. *Hood, Bonnet, and Little Brown Jug: Texas Politics, 1921–1928.* College Station: Texas A&M University Press, 1984.
Bryant, J. A. *Twentieth-Century Southern Literature.* Lexington: University Press of Kentucky, 1997.
Buenger, Walter L., and Robert A. Calvert, eds. *Texas through Time: Evolving Interpretations.* College Station: Texas A&M University Press, 1991.
Burkhart, Marian. "Horton Foote's Many Roads Home: An American Playwright and His Characters." *Commonweal* (February 26, 1988): 111.
Bywater, Tim, and Thomas Sohrchack. *Introduction to Film Criticism: Major Critical Approaches to Narrative Film.* New York: Longman, 1989.
Castleberry, Marion. "Remembering Wharton, Texas." In *Casebook*, pp. 13–33.
———. "Voices from Home: Familial Bonds in the Works of Horton Foote." Ph.D. dissertation, Louisiana State University, 1993.
Chum, John M. *Paddy Chayefsky.* New York: Twayne, 1976.
Clurman, Harold. *The Fervent Years.* New York: Hill and Wang, 1957.
Copelin, David. "Horton Foote." In *Contemporary Dramatists,* ed. D. L. Kirkpatrick. Chicago: St. James Press, 1988.
Darnton, Nina. "Horton Foote Celebrates a Bygone Era in *1918*." *New York Times* (April 21, 1985): sec. 2, p. 22.

Davis, Ronald L. "Roots in a Parched Ground: An Interview with Horton Foote." *Southwest Review,* 73 (Summer 1988): 298–318.

Durham, Weldon B. *American Theatre Companies, 1931–1986.* Westport, Conn.: Greenwood Press, 1989.

Eddy, Mary Baker. *Science and Health with Key to the Scriptures.* Boston: Christian Science Publishing Society, 1934.

Edgerton, Gary. "A Visit to the Imaginary Landscape of Harrison, Texas: Sketching the Career of Horton Foote." *Literature/Film Quarterly,* 17 (1989): 3–12.

Fehrenbach, T. R. *Lone Star.* New York: Macmillan, 1968 (Chapters 24 and 25).

Foote, Horton. "Spiritual Values and Film: Letting Powerful Meaning Come Through." *Christian Science Sentinel* (April 7, 1991): 7–13.

———. "Toward Films with Spiritual Vision." *Christian Science Sentinel* (April 27, 1987): 3–9.

———. "The Trip to Paradise." *Texas Monthly* (December 1987): 140–149, 182–183.

Freedman, Samuel G. "From the Heart of Texas." *New York Times* (February 9, 1986): 61. Also published as Introduction to *Cousins and The Death of Papa* (New York: Grove Press, 1989).

Gallagher, Michael. "Horton Foote: Defying Heracitus in Texas." *Southern Literary Journal,* 32, no. 1 (Fall 1999): 77–86.

Gassner, John, ed. *Twenty-five Best Plays of the Modern American Theatre.* New York: Crown, 1949.

Graham, Don. "A Southern Writer in Texas: Porter and the Texas Literary Tradition." In *Katherine Anne Porter and Texas: An Uneasy Relationship,* ed. Clinton Machann and William Bedford Clark. College Station: Texas A&M University Press, 1990 (pp. 64, 69–70).

———. *Texas: A Literary Portrait.* San Antonio: Corona Publishing Co., 1985.

"Horton Foote." In *Current Biography.* New York: H. H. Wilson, 1986 (pp. 143–147).

Hulbert, Don. "Horton Foote's Trip to Bountiful." *Atlanta Journal/Constitution* (March 10, 1991): M4.

Jennings, Diane. "Horton Foote." *Dallas Morning News* (March 24, 1985).

Jordan, Terry, et al. *Texas: A Geography.* Boulder, Colo.: Westview Press, 1984 (pp. 73–79).

King, Kimball. "Performing *The Death of Papa:* A Review." In *Casebook,* pp. 131–135.

Levy, Emanuel. *Small-Town America in Film: The Decline and Fall of Community.* New York: Frederick Ungar, 1990.

Mantle, Burns. *Contemporary American Playwrights.* New York: Dodd, Mead and Co., 1934.

Manvell, Roger. *Theater and Film: A Comparative Study of the Two Forms of Dramatic Art, and of the Problems of Adaptation of Stage Plays into Films.* Cranberry, N.J.: Associated University Presses, 1979.

Martin, Walter L., and Robert A. Colbert, eds. *Texas through Time: Evolving Interpretations.* College Station: Texas A&M University Press, 1991.

Martin, William B., ed. *Texas Plays.* Dallas: Southern Methodist University Press, 1990. Contains *The Trip to Bountiful.*

McComb, David G. *Texas: A Modern History*. Austin: University of Texas Press, 1989.

McDowell, S. Dixon. "Horton Foote's Film Aesthetic." In *Casebook*, pp. 137–149.

Mendell, Dean. "Squeezing the Drama out of Melodrama: Plot and Counterplot in *Laura Dennis*." In *Casebook*, pp. 189–201.

Miller, Gabriel. *Clifford Odets*. New York: Frederick Ungar, 1989.

Millichap, Joseph R. "Horton Foote." *Dictionary of Literary Biography*, 26 (1989): 103.

Porter, Katherine Anne. *The Collected Stories*. New York: Harcourt, Brace, and World, 1965.

Porter, Laurin. "Subtext as Text: Language and Culture in Horton Foote's Texas Cycle." In *Casebook*, pp. 109–129.

Reinert, Al. "Tender Foote." *Texas Monthly* (July 1991): 135.

Rice, Lawrence D. *The Negro in Texas*. Baton Rouge: Louisiana State University Press, 1971.

Richardson, Rupert N., et al. *Texas: The Lone Star State*. Englewood Cliffs, N.J.: Prentice Hall, 1988.

Roudané, Matthew C. *American Drama since 1960: A Critical History*. New York: Twayne, 1996.

Salwak, Dale. *The Literary Biography: Problems and Selections*. Iowa City: University of Iowa Press, 1996.

Scaggs, Calvin. *The American Short Story*. New York: Dell, 1977.

Shulman, Arthur, and Roger Youman. *How Sweet It Was: Television: A Pictorial Commentary*. New York: Shorecrest, 1966.

Smeltsor, Marjorie. "The World's an Orphans' Home: Horton Foote's Social and Moral History." *Southern Quarterly*, 29 (Winter 1991): 7–16.

Sturcken, Frank. *Live Television: The Golden Age of 1946–1958 in New York*. Jefferson, N.C.: McFarland, 1990.

Tanner, James T. F. *The Texas Legacy of Katherine Porter*. Denton: University of North Texas Press, 1991.

Thompson, David. *America in the Dark: Hollywood and the Gift of Unreality*. New York: William Morrow, 1977.

Underwood, Sarah. "Singing in the Face of Devastation: Texture in Horton Foote's *Talking Pictures*." In *Casebook*, pp. 151–162.

Watson, Charles S. "Beyond the Commercial Media: Horton Foote's Procession of Defeated Men." *Studies in American Drama, 1945–Present*, 8 (1993): 175–187.

———. *The History of Southern Drama*. Lexington: University Press of Kentucky, 1997.

Weales, Gerald. *American Drama since World War II*. New York: Harcourt, Brace, and World, 1962.

Wharton County Pictorial History, 1846–1946: Our First 100 Years. Vol. 1. Austin: Eakin Press, 1993.

Wilk, Max. *The Golden Age of Television*. New York: Delacorte, 1976.

Williams, Annie Lee. *A History of Wharton County*. Austin: Van Boeckmann-Jones, 1964.

Wood, Gerald C. "Boundaries, The Female Will and Individuation in *Night Seasons*." In *Casebook*, pp. 163–177.

———. *Horton Foote and the Theater of Intimacy*. Baton Rouge: Louisiana State University Press, 1999.

———. "Horton Foote's Politics of Intimacy." *Journal of American Drama and Theatre* (Spring 1997): 44–57.

———. "The Nature of Mystery in *The Young Man from Atlanta*." In *Casebook*, pp. 179–187.

———, ed. *Horton Foote: A Casebook*. New York: Garland, 1998.

Wood, Gerald C., and Terry Barr. "'A Certain Kind of Writer': An Interview with Horton Foote." *Literature/Film Quarterly*, 14, no. 4 (1986): 226–237.

Wood, Robin. *Hollywood from Vietnam to Reagan*. New York: Columbia University Press, 1986.

Wright, Tim. "More Real Than Realism: Horton Foote's Impressionism." In *Casebook*, pp. 67–87.

Yelvington, Ramsey. *The Drama of the Alamo: A Cloud of Witnesses*. Austin: University of Texas Press, 1959.

Prohibition movement, 10
Psalm 91, 89, 104
Public TV Reviews, 181
Pulitzer Prize, 227

Railroads, 4–5
Rascoe, Burton, 50
Regional theatres, 210
Relatives as models for characters, 3,
 9–10, 12, 14–15, 45, 107–109, 116,
 118, 134, 156–162, 165, 168–169,
 172, 177, 182, 189, 192, 197, 202,
 205, 229, 231, 233–234
Religion in Everyday Life, 98, 136
Remick, Lee, 130
Return, The, 60
Rice, Elmer, 125
Rice Players, Martha's Vineyard, 26
Rich, Frank, 172, 201, 205, 237, 239,
 246
Richards, David, 224
"Richmond USA," 62
Ringwald, Molly, 169
Roads to Home, The, 40, 197–198, 200–
 201, 208
Road to the Graveyard, The, 176, 204, 208–
 209, 212, 243
Robbins, Jerome, 31
Robinson Theatre, Whittier College, CA,
 240
Rocking Chair, The, 49
Roots in a Parched Ground, 159–161
Rose, Reginald, 73

Schneider, Ann, 227
School for the Stage, 30
Science and Health with Key to the Scriptures,
 96, 104
Scott, Tony, 170, 220–221
Seagall, Bernard, 59
Selected One Acts of Horton Foote, 80
Shakespeare Festival Theatre, Mont-
 gomery, AL, 231
Sheppard, Sam, 170, 211
Sherwood, Robert, 124
Signature Company, The, 112, 224, 226–
 227, 229

Simon, John, 201
Smith, W. J., 67
Soloviosa, Vera, 30, 32
Southern Quarterly, 152
Speaker, 239–240
Spring Dance, 200
Stalking Moon, The, 133
Stanislavski Method, 27–30, 69
Stanley, Kim, 61, 77, 113, 125, 129–130,
 148–149, 188
Stapleton, Jean, 170, 201, 213, 220, 227
Steinbeck, John, 152–153
Stevens, Gavin, 151
Storm Fear, 142
Story of a Marriage, The, 173, 181–182,
 184, 188, 213
Strasberg, Lee, 39
Stuart, Jan, 202, 230
Summer of the Hot Five, The, 212
Sycamore Grove, 13

Talking Pictures, 157, 212, 223, 226, 229–
 230, 234, 246
Tears of My Sister, The, 79–80
Tender Mercies, 68, 103, 108–109, 116,
 124–125, 134–136, 138–140, 152,
 156, 186, 188, 192, 232, 240, 242, 244,
 246
Texas Town, 36–39, 43–45, 48, 69,
 117
Themes in Foote's work
 —Condemnation of materialism,
  102
 —Courage and adjustment to change,
  117, 156–157, 245
 —Family: disintegration of, 211; need
  of, 115
 —Home, 182; lack of, 227, 230; loss
  of, 204; returning home, 220; under
  siege, 206
 —Marital infidelity, 199, 210, 212,
  215–216, 229
 —Ordinary events of life, 72
 —Positive outlook, 103
 —Refutation of violence, 62
 —Sense of humor, 48
 —Small town mores, 44